# Scattered Pieces

**Flora Season**

Order this book online at www.trafford.com
or email orders@trafford.com

Most Trafford titles are also available at major online book retailers.

Printed in Victoria, BC, Canada.

ISBN: 978-1-4269-2073-8 (soft)
ISBN: 978-1-4269-2074-5 (hard)

Library of Congress Control Number: 2009939673

*Our mission is to efficiently provide the world's finest, most comprehensive book publishing
service, enabling every author to experience success. To find out how to publish your
book, your way, and have it available worldwide, visit us online at www.trafford.com*

*Trafford rev. 11/24/2009*

 www.trafford.com

**North America & international**
toll-free: 1 888 232 4444 (USA & Canada)
phone: 250 383 6864 ♦ fax: 812 355 4082

*To all young people who dare to dream…*

*Dare to live differently…*

*And dare to define themselves by themselves.…*

*My story is yours.*


*Sheranetta, Sherwood III, Sherwanda, and*
*Shariff—dare to defy the odds while always*
*remembering nothing is impossible for God.*

# *Acknowledgments*

Today, I am able to recognize the many blessings of my life that are underscored by the people in it. I am blessed to have such a richly diverse family whose ties are stronger than blood lines. I am blessed to have sorority sisters who love me and accept me for being the crazy, temperamental woman I am. I am blessed to have four best friends—Sharonda, Kara, Hyacinth, and Lauren— who allow our relationship to transcend state lines. I am blessed to have a mother who is willing to be there during the birth of my children and any time that I call no matter how I may treat her. I am blessed to have a relationship with my siblings in spite of the one lacking with our father. I am blessed to have grandfathers who share with me the wisdom of their years and a grandmother who is one of my dearest friends. I am blessed with two beautiful children, Shaniah and Trey, who will live life in abundance. I am blessed with a loving, supportive, and devoted husband with whom I will grow old. And, most importantly, I am blessed to have a savior who sacrificed His own life for those whom He loves—now that's true love. Through the help of medical professionals accompanied by the workings of prayer, I have been able to bring together the scattered pieces of my life in order to see, love, and appreciate myself as being one of God's masterpieces.

As it pertains to the completion of this work, I cannot go forward without properly acknowledging those who made an effort to read and critique my memoir—my husband, who put all else to the side to listen to me read aloud chapters from my manuscript and who also helped me to develop chapter titles; Kara, my "Sistah Friend", who perused my sketchbook over brunch in Santa Monica, thank you for giving me the confidence to go forward with my story; my former co-workers Genevieve, Twanna, and Colleen; Sharonda, who only read the part that featured her (smile); my mother, who inspired much of this narrative; and my editor for his brutal honesty. I thank everyone who believed in me, and I will always reserve a special regard for those who didn't.

*"There are things of which I may not speak;*
*There are dreams that cannot die;*
*There are thoughts that make the strong heart weak,*
*And bring a pallor into the cheek,*
*And a mist before the eye.*
*And the words of that fatal song*
*Come over me like a chill:"*

*-Henry Wadsworth Longfellow (from "My Lost Youth")*

# INTRODUCTION

*"Flora. Come give daddy a hug."*
     *"No!"* I replied.
*"Flora. Come give me a hug."*
     *"Ha. Ha. Ha."* I giggled. *"No, daddy!"*

I n the Logan section of Philadelphia, on Warnock Street, in our one-bedroom duplex, I continued hiding behind the living room sofa when I noticed my mother entering the room from the short hallway which connected to the kitchen. She could have been the poster model for Adina Howard's hit single, "Tee Shirt and Panties," for that was all she was wearing, aside from her radiant, wide smile for which she was commonly known.   She was smiling and appeared to be happy to bring her man the food that she had taken great pride in preparing. With extended arms, she attempted to give her then-boyfriend, my father, the brown wooden serving tray. His observable appreciation reeked as he looked up at her with a dark grimace which I had not previously witnessed in my four years.  Never had I foreseen the consequence of my innocent, childish play.

Never did I anticipate that I would have been the cause for my father's unconscionable brutality against my mother. Never did I image that a single memory could be held so vividly, so far above all others for the rest of my days. As he slapped the tray from my mother's grasp, her smile disappeared. She inhaled quickly and audibly as she prepared for what was worse to come. He leaped from his wicker rocking chair and struck her in her face with his closed fist.

—Everything went black.

—Everything fell silent.

My brain tried to shut down. My mind tried to block out the image that it had seen too many times before. This wasn't new, but this was different. My mental concentration was broken by the sound of my father's voice and my mother's conquered visage— on her knees facing me, her chin erect to the ceiling. While his hands, filled with her long, brown, curly hair, were positioned at the crown of her head, he spoke to me: "You didn't want to give your daddy a hug. Look at what I'm doing to your mommy." At that very moment, he victimized me alongside my mother. He placed the guilt of his senseless deed upon my shoulders. At that moment, he made me responsible for my mother's pain. I begged, pleaded even, to give him a hug. I wasn't a child who was afraid of The Boogie Man, for I was unknowingly prepared to embrace a living, breathing monster. My shrill voice was unheard; my request was not granted, and the savage beating of my mother continued before my eyes. When she attempted to crawl out of the doorway leading to the foyer of the terrace level, he swiftly picked up a single weight from the floor. I do not recall having a weight bench, but I remember the metal disc; it was larger than five or even ten pounds.

Once he turned to face the rear of her—

Once he began taking steps towards her—

Once he raised the circular, black, weighted object above his head—

I saw too much. I could not stomach anymore. Feeling helpless, I sought refuge and sprinted from my hiding place behind the sofa into my parents' bedroom. I knelt down, and I prayed. Even as a child, I knew that God heard my cries. Once again—blackness. Silence. Then, sleep.

\* \* \* \* \*

My most vivid childhood memory was of a living nightmare. It made me aware of the physical abuse my mother was tolerating. Seeing her light complexioned face that the sun kissed just enough to confirm her ethnicity, accompanied with a black and blue eye or two, never meant much to me before that day. Afterwards, I attentively watched my mother's physical torment, mentally taking in every blow. I recall sitting underneath our kitchen table gazing at my father stomping my mother in the corner of our kitchen, right beside our stove. When he dragged her from the kitchen into their bedroom by her hair, my eyes followed their every move, watching my mother claw at his hands while she kicked and screamed.

An immediate change in my behavior transpired following that event, even though war constantly knocked at the 4900 block of North Warnock. Every time I prepared to cross the threshold of that duplex, a knot tied in my stomach. Nervousness overcame me. I never knew what to expect. Many days, the three of us would be in there happy, or at least I thought anyway. We'd be dancing (I loved watching him do the Hand-Bone) and singing and listening to my father tell stories about his youth. We would have his eldest daughter, my sister Keke, come visit us or his nephews, my first cousins Peanut and Andre. But when things were bad, they were the worst. I tried to console my mother when she cried and asked her questions about their fights later. Once, after my parents fought, I found my mother sobbing. I held her, stroked her hair then advised her, in my first grade jargon, to kick him in his D-I-C-K! I said it just the way Shonda and Takesha said it in the hallway at Rhoads Elementary. I slowly rolled my eyes while I simultaneously rolled my skinny neck and exclaimed "kick him in his D-I-C-K!" I had no more of a clue what a D-I-C-K was than Shonda and Takesha did, but my mother lovingly chuckled, wide-eyed with surprise at my advice and then inquired if I knew the meaning of what I spelled out. When I said, as she suspected, "no," she did not hesitate in enlightening me on the pronunciation of the forbidden word and then admonished that I not allow my father to hear that come from my mouth.

Although I was ignorant of what I was saying, I knew my intent well. I wanted her to fight and not necessarily physically. I wanted her—*needed her* to protect both me and herself. Before my horrific experience, I would willingly leave my mother to stay with my grandparents, but afterwards, I fought and even cussed when someone tried to separate me from her. One time, my grandparents grew fed up. They drove from their home in Brookhaven to remove me from the volatile situation. I pleaded with my mother not to let me go. My grandmother tried to make me understand that being with her and my grandfather was in my best interest because my parents did not have any food at their house for us to eat. But I didn't care. I looked into my mother's eyes and told her, "I don't need nothing to eat. I'll eat bread and water, but Mommy I want to stay with you." My grandmother tried to interject by pulling me away from my mother in order to reason with me, but her interposition caused me to act out of frustration. I perched my little booty in the air and told her boldly to "kiss my ass!" As my grandfather restrained her from kicking mine, I ran over to my mother and embraced her.

Normally, I stayed amongst three residences: my parents in Logan, my grandparents in Brookhaven, and my great-grandmother in West Philadelphia. Wherever I stayed, I did not bring any garments with me, for each residence came equipped with its own clothing and lifestyle. since When I was with my grandparents, I had any- and everything my heart desired—fine dining, adult interaction, toys beyond belief When I was with my great-grandmother, I had neighborhood friends to play with. But, despite the normalcy of my atypical housing dilemma, I needed to be there this time to support my mother and to comfort her. *She* was who I needed.

Strangely enough, the abuse of my mother did not put an end to the love that I felt for my father (his abandonment, lack of financial support, and deficiency in exhibiting a desire for a father-daughter relationship did that). It did, however, cause me to desire less of his presence. I unconsciously knew that he probably recognized that his presence stifled my development. My relationships and maturation were undoubtedly adversely affected by the few years that I lived in a violent home. Every event of my life, every action or decision I've ever made, I now attribute to this experience. Witnessing vicious happenings first-hand caused me to live in a constant state of anxiety. Episodes such as my father pouring gasoline on a car in the middle of the night and setting it ablaze while I and my mother watched in our vehicle had undesirable effects. I recollect watching with my parents the local news report the incident later that evening. Seeing the conflagration on television and the look of pleasure upon my father's face disturbed me so much that I immediately ran to my room and attempted to booby-trap it. I was frightened that the men to whom the car or the items within the car belonged would try to retaliate. As my father entered my room, greeted by my contraption, he found my tears and worry amusing. His response was to turn on my television to cartoons, place me in the bed, and leave me alone with my fears in the dark.

My father leaving me in the car while he visited other women and bagging up his narcotics in front of me for distribution and personal consumption showed me my level of importance. His saying that I was not as pretty as his older daughter when I lost my first tooth imbedded in me low self-esteem. His constant beating and cheating on my mother exemplified that it was necessary for me to be on my guard around men. And, since he was in and out of my life for the six years that I lived with him and because of the instability that resulted from my parent's separation, I learned not to become too attached to people.

For years, I suffered from faulty, irrational thinking that turned the people whom I loved into enemies in my mind. I nurtured violence and used it as a means to resolving issues I was unable to work out through reason or logic. Even today, whenever tribulations occur, I instinctively desire to resort to physical force and intimidation although I am small in frame. This is how I was taught to handle my problems. I am truly ashamed. I am quick tempered and break out into uncontrollable fits when enraged; nevertheless, through time, I was able to pin-point the source for my previously inexplicable actions, and that introspective quest for understanding is where my story begins.

The House on Warnock Street

# PART ONE

*An oxymoron is often humorous and so contradictory that it becomes almost inexplicable, for instance "icy hot" or "jumbo shrimp" and even "virgin hoe"—just to name a few.*

# CHAPTER ONE
## *INTROSPECTION*

I n the midst of a heated telephone debate while I was on a ten minute break from class, my sorority sister mentioned that there were some members of my line who were developing "reputations" around campus. Frustrated with the anonymous accusations, I insisted that she notify the accused directly as opposed to continually making general references about their conduct. There would be many evenings when my line sisters and I would try to speculate the identity of the nameless "hoes." Each time, we met a dead end. Most of us had boyfriends or were dealing with the same people with whom we dealt prior to crossing over in the spring. Was this just some twisted mental game played on us neophytes by some of the more mature sorors on campus? If so, enough was enough. It was time for our prophyte to confront the mystery persons once and for all. The entire subject exasperated me, and she could sense it in my tone. To honor my request, my soror candidly informed me that *I* was one of the labeled campus hoes—translation: easy, a whore, a harlot, a slut, a tramp, a smut puppy—ME!!!! How could a little picture produce such a response from someone who is supposed to be my sister? The news came like a ball being pitched ninety miles per hour. Her words struck me hard. Frozen momentarily with disbelief, I lacked a coherent response. I should have known that if I was not ready for the truth, then I shouldn't have asked

3

that particular big sister. She was a sister willing to tell it how it is. That type of earnestness is to be admired.

"Oh!" was all I was able to exclaim before using my class as an excuse to rapidly end our conversation. I returned to the classroom stunned. For the remainder of that hour, which felt like an eternity, and for the rest of that week, the conclusion of our conversation was all I pondered. Previously, I had seen myself as one widely popular student who made excellent grades, but I was ignorant of my obvious public lack of decorum. After all, I must have done something to send off that promiscuous vibe, for it wasn't the first time I heard it. I expected those who did not know me to form their ill-shaped opinions, for it goes hand-in-hand with popularity. If I had not formed any friendships with the gossips, their opinions of me were irrelevant. But, it was something about hearing that information spoken with such plausibility by someone who was supposed to be my sister that cut like a knife through my heart. To know that she and others in my chapter chose to believe the rumors enough to address their concerns was bothersome. It was now my position to figure out what that *something* actually was. My reputation became my sole reflection. Perception is reality, or in my circumstance *pre*conceptions were my reality. Things that I had put out of my mind began to return, and, slowly, it was all beginning to make sense. The soror with whom I held the conversation had no idea of the level of deliberation our tête-à-tête inspired.

Not many months following the disturbing conversation, I had an epiphany: I possess a strong generational trait of promiscuity. The pieces of the puzzle were connecting, and I was about to be formally introduced to myself. Generational cycles are powerful; often, they show strong patterns of emulation by the successors of generations past—even down to their very mistakes. One can learn a lot about him- or herself just by tracing the behavioral history of their natal family. At the age of sixteen, my maternal grandmother married the man who is on my mother's birth certificate. It's not surprising that she was "expecting" a gift at the time of her nuptials. She and her first husband were both young, and he, like my father to my mother, was abusive. Not only did he beat her, he had a continuous affair with her cousin. See a pattern? Noticing the physical and mental abuse, as well as emotional neglect, his best friend pitied my grandmother. His pity shortly developed into fondness as he began "consoling" her. Sometime during the consolation, my grandmother conceived her second child, my mother. Until this day, my grandmother professes that the man on my mother's certificate of birth is my mother's biological father, despite his family's skepticism of his paternity and my mother's uncertainty of her father's identity. While growing up, I referenced several men as "my grandfather," and this often brought tears to my mother's eyes when she tried to make sense of it to my brother and me as children.

Early in my mother's youth until her years as a young adult, my mother witnessed her step-father, my grandmother's second husband, abuse her mother. While watching domestic violence in her parents' household, she observed that, although her step-father abused her mother, he provided financial security to his family, and her mother did not leave. Their marriage of over forty years weathered many storms, and his spiritual salvation ended his infliction of physical harm upon my grandmother which gave my mother a ray of hope for her own dismal union.

My paternal grandmother was not without blemish, and her story is as equally intriguing. She birthed nine children; the youngest of her clan is my father. Her eldest child has a last name different from his siblings and his mother. Meanwhile, her following four children share a common surname, and her youngest four children have still another family name: Three men (allegedly), nine children, and one woman (the common denominator). Bear with me because it gets better, and what I mean by better is more confusing. My father shares the same last name as three of his older siblings, in ascending order. The only problem lies in the fact that the man who is documented as my grandfather was deceased at the time of my father's conception.

Ironically, my father's first name is identical to the name of his elder brother's best friend; therefore, my uncle's b.f.f. is believed by many members of his family to have fathered my father. If this was an episode of *The Jerry Springer Show,* the episode title would read: "My Son's Best Friend is My Baby's Daddy." I had the pleasure of speaking with the man who is believed to be my grandfather in his home. I pulled him into a secluded room, away from the ears of his wife, to ask him the previously unspoken question…if he was my grandfather. I told him about the family rumors springing from my father's side and how I found it more than coincidental that each of his sons bears a strong resemblance to my father and his son, my brother. The married minister of over forty years started to speak very highly of my deceased grandmother. He said she was a very beautiful woman. He began to speak of his gang involvement as a teenager and his former friendship with my uncle. I sensed he was evading my question, but I was adamant about retrieving my answer. I looked him in his eyes and asked him again, "Are you my grandfather. Are you my father's father?" His lips trembled, and he wept as he answered, "No." Despite the word he spoke, his tears gave me the confirmation I needed for our family secret.

The law of attraction amongst new thought spiritual thinkers asserts that people's unconscious and conscious thoughts determine the reality of their lives. It is my personal belief that akin spirits attract one another. Thinking in this mode, the motif of my life is more than coincidental considering my parents' biological background, their meeting, their attraction, the conception of me, and the physical abuse endured by my mother *and* her mother. Unfortunately, some of the dysfunctional energy of my ancestors transferred into my being, and I had not given it a single thought until my conversation with my soror. This was my great awakening that caused me to reflect on the events of my childhood.

As early as age five, I felt a certain inexplicable comfort and fascination with sexuality. I was intrigued by the structure and function of the penis. I became allured to the sensations that watching my cousin's pornography or late night cable television brought. My curiosity did not go unnoticed. My mother purchased me a graphic and descriptive book that was intended to answer all of my questions, but it made my curiosity grow all the more. These feelings seemed for a while illogical because I was not formally molested or sexually abused. Although my sexual childhood urges were physically repressed, I still put forth an energy that others, like the hairdresser, relatives, and members of the congregation, were interpreting as, "She's too fast; she's gonna be pregnant before she's a teenager" or "I know Flora ain't no virgin." If only these critics had some inkling, they might have hesitated in their attempt to mar the reputation of a young woman by labeling her without justification. It never ceases to amaze me how folk seem to know more about a particular female's vagina than her own gynecologist.

*The innocence of childhood it is a marvelous thing*
*And all children are untainted in their life's early Spring*
*But by the time they've reached their teens their innocence they've lost*
*And the experience that we gain from age always comes at a cost.*

*When children lose their innocence they lose their gift of joy*
*The joy that comes from innocence in every young girl and boy*
*Compared to us young children see life quite differently*
*Of the guilt of corruption they are completely free.*

*-Francis Duggan (from "When Children Lose Their Innocence")*

# CHAPTER TWO
## *KICK, STAND*

Large cities typically are not lacking in the area of exposure; therefore, their children often mature at a faster rate than those living in suburbia. A vast majority of suburban children sing William Blake's *Songs of Innocence* while they bask gleefully in their world of privilege and/or ignorance. Meanwhile, urban children are consistently and untimely forced to sing from his *Songs of Experience*.

Here is my song.

Learning how to ride a bike is one of the biggest triumphs in the life of a child. Removing a child's training wheels becomes almost a spiritual rite of passage. It signifies an advancement of fine motor skills, and the personal achievement imparts a great sense of pride in a child. But let's face it. Learning how to ride a bike can be as painful as it is agitating--you fall, you get up and try again; and often, you'll receive a scar as a souvenir for the momentous occasion.  But the lesson that can be taken away from the experience is that determination is more powerful than pain.  And, in life, even the most beautiful, fulfilling experiences frequently involve some degree of pain, like learning how to ride a bike without training wheels—learning how to steady oneself without any protection from falling.  That's part of the urban experience.

It was one summer evening in 1989 on a street in West Philadelphia, 48th and Parrish to be exact, when my training wheels were removed.  My bicycle was blue with a banana-shaped seat and U-shaped handle bars. My side of the block was crowded. All of my neighbors were outside sitting on their stoops, sitting on their railings, or simply standing on the cement. I was the focus of the evening—my training wheels were removed, and I was learning how to ride my bicycle.  Everyone was outside, and I do mean everyone…even my crush, Mike.  Mike was an older boy—a fifth grader.  He was slim with fair skin and wavy hair.  I thought he was handsome.  My other neighborhood friends who were getting ready for the first grade like me thought that he was UG-LY!  They couldn't see past how his eyes always seemed to cross whenever he removed his coke bottle glasses or the chip and stain on his front tooth, but I could.  Rumor amongst us kids was that Mike was adopted, and that he was capital B-A-D.

Mike was outside on his skateboard when I finally got the hang of it.  I was riding on my own.  My neighbor Alvin—Al for short—was teaching me.  He instructed me to ride around the block and come back.  As I was riding, Mike was skateboarding aside me.  He mentioned that he heard I liked him.  The butterflies in my stomach were doing somersaults.  And, my wide grin could not have been wiped away.  Before I knew it, we were on to the next block, Hoopes Street.  This block was quiet.  There was no action here this evening.  No neighbors to be seen, and the street lights appeared dim. Lost in conversation, I did not notice the alley on my left until I was pushed off my bike and forced into it. The alley way was narrow, and it reeked of urine. Stunned, I asked Mike what was he doing, and I demanded that he let me go. He informed me that I was going to have sex with him. I said, "Oh, no I ain't!" before being thrust onto the murky, mossy, cold stone wall; my arms were accosted and my wrists bound together by one of his hands, and, with his free hand, he banged my head against the stone. I realized that this was not a game when he unzipped his jeans and motioned to free his stubbly pink willy. Convincing myself to remain calm and think quickly, distinctly unchild-like instincts kicked in and controlled my unprecedented actions. The nature of my previously quiescent inner beast was released. Nonchalantly, I told him "Let me see it." To depict the expression of his face as shocked would be an unjust description. His reluctance diminished and his confidence increased when I flashed him my rising first-grader version of a dirty smile. Having his full attention, I took complete advantage of the situation. I laid upon Mike an unsuspecting blow that was so strong he was forced to his knees. I had followed the advice of Shonda and Takesha. Stumbling and falling, I scurried out of there. Without thinking, I grabbed his skateboard and pushed it down into an open drain in the street. Then, I jumped on my bike and proceeded to pedal back around the corner to my block. OUCH! Suddenly I felt a sharp pain in my knee. I looked down and noticed a red, raw area on my leg. I was bleeding; nevertheless, I continued to pedal. Finally safe again with my family and neighbors, my heart still beating uncontrollably, I tried to convince myself that the event never occurred and tried to block out the memory. Like the abuse that I witnessed my mother undergo, I said nothing to no one. Like the abuse that I witnessed my mother undergo, I tried to forget it. The blood on my knee clotted and scabbed, and the scab eventually came off; however, a scar was permanently left.

What did I ever do to warrant the attempted rape of my innocence? Unfortunately, what Mike sought to do would not be the last time. In fact, I had several sexual encounters before I was deemed of age to have "the talk" with my mother, all before I was out of the first grade.

*Energy can neither be created nor destroyed.*
*It can only change forms.*

*-First Law of Thermodynamics*

# CHAPTER THREE
# *THERMODYNAMICS*

—Spring 1990

We were moving from our home, a home that my great-grandmother gave to us. My brother had recently turned two, and I was the tender age of seven. The weather was beautiful, a blue sky with minimal clouds. A refreshing breeze was blowing, and a bright sun was smiling, but I could sense tension in the air. Sitting in the back seat of my mother's gold-colored Hyundai along with my brother, I felt uneasy. I stopped gazing at the sky momentarily to look at my parents. Yup, they were still arguing. They were the only people that I could see standing outside on our quiet little West Philadelphia block, Popular Street. I heard my father tell my mother that we were moving back into his duplex on Warnock Street. The worry was evident on my mother's face. I stopped watching them and decided to bask in God's glory for a little while longer. I rested my head upon my folded arms that was lying on the window's cavity and resumed taking in the beauty nature had to offer.

My tranquility was broken when my mother entered the car and sat in the driver's seat. In what seemed like a split second, my timid mother executed amazingly quick moves that seemed fit for one who had studied the ancient skill of Kung Fu. She turned to her right and pushed down the car's lock. Spinning around and climbing partially over the front passenger seat, she locked the door behind it. Dashing across me and my brother, she locked our door before finally locking her own. In a sharp imperative tone, she instructed me to roll up the manual back windows. Simultaneously, we began cranking up the ones on the right side of the vehicle. By the time we started on the left, my little arms grew tired. My speed decreased, and I didn't understand the urgency until my father's hand appeared inside my window. I cannot fathom how my body managed to maintain all of the blood that my heart was pumping at that moment. His lips were tightly sealed, and anger permeated his countenance. Beads of sweat had formed across his forehead. His fingers gripped the top of my window, and he pulled it back until it began to bow. I needed to fight. Enough was enough. This was my chance to protect my mother. I clenched my fingers together and formed a fist. I used these fists to fight off The Boogie Man, the man whose actions always seemed to invade my dreams—the time when I am asleep, and my heart is unguarded, the time in my unconscious when I am the most vulnerable to my own realities. After all, how can one block out his or her own dreams? I pounded his fingers as hard and as frequently as I could. When he let go, I was enveloped in a new sense of power. When he let go, I found the strength to finally roll up the window. When he let go, I was strong enough to yell to my mother, "GO!"

The first law of thermodynamics is "energy cannot be created or destroyed, only change forms." On that beautiful spring day, my mother decided that she had enough. The breeze comforted her while God smiled upon us, using his sun to give us hope for our future by lighting our paths. As a result from the energy that nature transmitted, the timid was made strong. She pulled out of the parking space and drove into the street. And when he, my father and her newlywed husband, daringly walked into our path, she hit him with her gold Hyundai. We sped away, never looking back.

*What matter how the night behaved?*
*What matter how the north-wind raved?*
*Blow high, blow low, not all its snow*
*Could quench our hearth-fire's ruddy glow.*
*O Time and Change!—with hair as gray*
*As was my sire's that winter day,*
*How strange it seems, with so much gone*
*Of life and love, to still live on!*

*-John Greenleaf Whittier (from "Snow-Bound")*

# CHAPTER FOUR
## *THE SHELTER*

A battered woman has limited resources which often complicates any plans for an escape. Her abusive boyfriend or spouse knows her relatives, friends, church, hair salon, favorite boutiques, and colleagues. So, where can a victim retreat when she has children and inadequate finances? To a battered women's shelter.

Women Against Abuse was the institution where my mother, brother, and I found refuge. To me, the shelter wasn't that bad. In fact, it did not feel like I lived in "a shelter" at all. I mean, how many children receive the opportunity to live with their friends? We ate all meals together, we attended school together, and we played together—this place was a kid's dream. The battered women's shelter did not resemble the homeless shelters depicted on television. It actually was like a bi-level apartment community. Each family had their own living quarters, equivalent to the size of a room in a typical dormitory. It featured a community dining facility where we would gather for our daily meals. Since a limited number of counselors and teachers were available for the younger residents, students were clustered together for school instruction according to their grade-level. For example, first through third graders may have been taught together, while fourth through sixth received the same instruction. This was where I was partially educated for the first grade. The afternoon when my mother left my father, I had to be withdrawn from my elementary school. For our safety, no one could know where we were staying, not even our family.

Miss Malayka was a counselor and teacher for Women Against Abuse. Whether she was employed by the organization or was a volunteer I am unsure; however, I do know that I bonded with her immensely. She was a middle-aged woman of a medium stature. I'm guessing she was in her late thirties to early forties at the time because she had strands of gray in her long, soft, thick, black, wavy hair. She wore glasses on occasions and had braces on her teeth, yet she was attractive. I remember her gentle spirit and soft, light chuckle. When the time finally arrived for us to leave the shelter in hopes of creating a better life, she presented me with a text book. Inside of the book was her contact information. She and I remained in contact for the remainder of my elementary school years. In fact, she was the one who taught me the Lord's Prayer. One evening, my mother permitted me to spend the night at Miss Malayka's home. There, she had her nephews and I continuously reciting the prayer until it was permanently infused not only in our memory, but inside of hearts. She was my angel at that time of displacement. She gave me a sense of normalcy.

When I think back on my shelter experience, I come to the realization that I was everything but sheltered—I was exposed. There I had to come to grips with some of the harsh realities of this world, and I wasn't alone in this reality check. Dozens of children my age were subjected to domestic violence. All of us had to live the effects of our parents' decisions. Each one of those children was there with me, but each one of us internalized his or her situation differently. All of us children shared a commonality—our mothers were battered by men. Miss Jingling Baby, as she was affectionately known for her refusal to place her massive breasts into a properly fitting brassiere, was there with her children. The mixed boy with curly brown hair celebrated his birthday there. I attended his party. His older brother gave him a surprise visit and presented him with an inexpensive electric guitar. They set up a microphone so he could perform in front of his guests. He chose to sing a re-make to Biz Markie's song, "Just a Friend." The mixed boy whose skin had a hue of red sang into the mic: "You---You got what I need---But you say it's just a rash---You need to wipe your dirty ass." All of us children were astonished. He actually said that in front of his mother! His brother swatted him upside his head. His outburst shouldn't have come to us as a surprise, for he was a troubled soul—always in trouble for something. I remember his mother, who I believed was a white woman, but, looking back at my limited understanding of the races, she could have easily been Hispanic, would often threaten him by saying, "Keep it up. I'm going to tell your brother." I guess his father did not have a respectable role in his life, either. Ol' Red Face even got me in trouble once. One evening, while my mother was attending a mandatory group meeting for the shelter, a knock came at our door. I got out of our bed to answer it, and it was him, Red Face, with two other individuals, a male and an older female. The girl with him began telling me that Red Face liked me, and, while she was talking, he snuck a quick peck on my lips. Petrified, I stood there stoic, incapable of movement until I got out of my stupor and closed the door. I climbed back in the bed and went to sleep until I was awakened by the sound of my own cry. My mother was beating me while I was asleep. Apparently, one of the onlookers who had accompanied Red Face to my room told their mother that he and I kissed. Once that rumor came to my mother's ears, she became so enraged that other women had to hold her off of me. She never asked me any questions. I was never given any chance to explain. This was the first of many events involving males where I would be judged without receiving a fair trial.

I never spoke to the Red Face, curly hair boy again. About a year after we left the shelter, my mother and I were watching the evening news and his picture appeared. Apparently, he was arrested for armed robbery of a jewelry store or the like. Like I said, everyone internalizes his or her experiences differently.

Then there was Rasheed—a fifth grader. He was my shelter crush. All I know is that his skin was a beautiful chocolate shade and his black hair was always cut low. I tried to keep my interest subtle, but I believe that he knew. Providence made it so that our mothers would attend group together, and, at the suggestion of his mother, Rasheed would be my babysitter. Never mind the fact that he was only three years older than me. Given that the room had no other furnishing, Rasheed and I watched television while lying on their bed. I was secretly happy to be there with him until he decided to climb on top of me. He was heavy, and it was becoming harder for me to breathe with his weight on top of my small body. I repeatedly requested for him to get off of me, each time to his refusal. I tried fighting him off, but I was pinned down and overpowered. Growing weary, I told him that if he did not get off of me, I was going to roll over and knock him onto the floor. He replied, "Go ahead, but you're coming with me." I thought about it momentarily before deciding to take my chances. I mustered all of my strength to push myself up and roll over in hopes of getting him off of me. The odds were in his favor because I, as he suspected, rolled off of the bed, too. Now, the both of us were on the cold, tiled floor with him still on top, his lips kissing mine. Weird, foreign, tingling sensations were happening inside of me. He instructed me to remove my clothing; without thought of right or wrong, I obeyed. I was just there—feeling new feelings. He stripped down to his tighty-whiteys. I was briefly entranced—besides my younger brother, I never seen a male in his undergarments before. Rasheed snatched my head from the clouds when he demanded that I put back on my clothing. I inquired as to why, and he responded by throwing my clothes at me. *Why was he already dressed?* I confusedly wondered. But, once again, I did what I was told … after all, he was my babysitter. I got dressed. We climbed back onto the bed and resumed watching television like nothing ever happened. That's when the door opened, and our mothers entered the room. Now, I felt a sense of wrongness because my heart was heavily racing; I could have sworn that they could hear it beating outside of my chest. If my mother wore me out over ol' Red Face, I could only imagine what she would have done if she knew about Rasheed! His mother asked a series of questions, and Rasheed did all of the answering. I was dumbfounded. Physically, I was in the room; however, mentally, my mind took a trip that left my body envious.

Today, I know that God kept me and allowed me to retain my precious feminine gift for a few additional years. After that evening, whenever Rasheed and I crossed paths inside of the shelter, we exchanged no words, only a furtive smirk. Parting from him was the most difficult part of my departure from the facility. The morning of my farewell, I slipped a note beneath his door, telling him good-bye.

After several months of living amongst dozens of other families, we finally had a Section 8 house of our own. I returned to my old school with my old classmates—none knowing what I endured. During my reintegration, I had to attend counseling twice a week at the school. Throughout my sessions, the counselor would request me to draw pictures which needed to be explained. She desired pictures of my family and events that transpired in our home. One graphic in particular alarmed her to the point of notifying my mother. I remember my mother and grandmother accompanying the counselor and me to one of our sessions, and we all sat around and discussed the picture. Can you imagine what her reaction would have been if I shared ALL of the juicy details of my first grade year? What if I revealed to her that I witnessed my father blowing up someone's car earlier that year and that my mother was his get-a-way driver (or "accessory after the fact" as she prefers) and I was a passenger. I ponder her likely reaction to knowing that as a pastime I would cut up sugar cubes and try to bag the remnants in the same fashion that my father would cut up cocaine—that was how I used my imagination. I wonder if she only knew.... Could she have helped me to overcome my deepest childhood pain of coming home from school only to learn that I could not return to the place that I called home because it was trashed by the police during a drug bust? Could she have helped me? Only if she was God.

Aside from my weekly counseling I underwent speech therapy because I stuttered profusely. Apparently, my speech impediment was a consequence to the traumatic happenings of my life. Once I knew my surroundings were safe, my stammering ceased almost miraculously.

*One need not be a Chamber — to be Haunted —*
*One need not be a House —*
*The Brain has Corridors — surpassing*
*Material Place-*

*Far safer, of a midnight meeting*
*External Ghost*
*Than its interior confronting —*
*That Cooler Host —*

*-Emily Dickinson (from "407" [670])*

# CHAPTER FIVE
## *THE TRANSITION*

4 6th Street was beautiful. The quiet inner city neighborhood had more than enough children to keep my brother and me company. Our three-bedroom row house was quaint. Outside the house featured a small gardening area surrounded by hedges and a small porch. A railing separated us from our elderly neighbor on the left, and a wrought iron black gate separated us from our vibrant Jamaican neighbors to our right. Inside there were wooden floors throughout and a faux fireplace. As cozy as the house was, trying to obtain a normal life in it became next to impossible with my everlasting paranoia. Precaution was in high order even though my family moved in hopes of a fresh start because The Boogie Man still managed to find us. My father had a friend working for a phone company who provided him with our unpublished telephone number and address. Soon, sightings of him on our block and ominous messages left by him on our

answering machine making promises to place "bullets the size of golf balls" into my mother's head were equally discomforting. Sadly enough, he actually attempted to make good on his promise. One evening we were visiting my father's older brother when my father suddenly appeared and began making a ruckus. My mother was terrified and tried to wait him out to no avail. Late at night, almost early morning, we entered our vehicle in haste, and, as soon as we pulled from my uncle's driveway, the high speed chase began. My mother was swerving across the expressway with my father hot on her tracks shooting at our car. He did not care if he struck my mother or accidently his two children who sat innocently in the automobile. With God's hedge of protection around us, we managed to escape by driving into the parking lot of a police station.

These events prompted me to begin sleeping with a kitchen knife beneath my pillow. Pulling it out in preparation to strike became my nightly ritual. As a child, I was able to connect with my primeval nature. Feeling the need to protect not only myself but my family was instinctive. I loathed my father for making me feel vulnerable. I loathed him for making my mother hurt. And, I loathed him for making my brother grow up without a dad. I vowed to be my brother's teacher, for our father had no lessons of wisdom or of love to be taught. A fervent desire to erase any memory of him or of that previous life I was forced to live enveloped me. Every picture I possessed of him I destroyed. I diminished his existence. I chose to forget. Those things never happened and if they did, I buried them deep in the corners of my mind.

* * * * *

The chapter of physical and mental abuse caused by my father ended, but a life of struggle and volatility was there to stay. My mother worked two jobs at a time just to make ends meet.

She was a laboratory technician at a hospital and embalmed bodies for a local funeral home until she was hired by the city of Philadelphia as a police officer. From the first to the fourth grade, I rarely saw my mother. To avoid doing my hair during the week, each weekend, she would braid my long, thick black hair into a single French braid and place a stocking cap on my head to preserve the style. My outfits had to be picked out for the following morning on the night before since the morning left little time for errors. Big Mom-Mom, as I affectionately called my maternal great-grandmother, graciously watched my brother and me. It was dark in the mornings when we were dropped off at her home on Parrish Street, and it was dark when she picked us up at 11 o'clock in the evening. James Rhoads Elementary School was conveniently located across the street from Big Mom-Mom's house, so I could easily walk to school before it began to get a hot or cold breakfast—depending on what was being served. When the school day ended, I sauntered back across the street to Big Mom-Mom's to complete my homework without assistance and to watch shows on my undersized black-and-white television that was to return home with me on the weekends. I watched countless hours of television—*Jeopardy, Wheel of Fortune,* and *Murder She Wrote.* And, I watched extended hours of it when there was no school—*All My Children, One Life to Live,* and *General Hospital.*

On occasions, Big Mom-Mom would permit me to play outdoors until sunset. Sometimes I wasn't allowed to leave the concrete stoop located at the front of the house; other times, I couldn't leave the block. I didn't mind very much for the most part because frequently my cousins Tony and Richard were being watched by her, too. Although Big Mom-Mom was unable to proficiently read and write, she managed to read her Bible and *Our Daily Bread* every quarter of the day like clockwork—three, six, nine, and twelve o'clock. Her fifteen-minute scriptural reading and devotional was one of the few times when her television was turned off, and, during these moments of brevity, no one in the house was permitted to speak. Tony, Richard, and I would have to sit quietly in the living room until her reading was done. This was no easy task for the menacing brothers. One of them would pick at me until I shouted out in annoyance. Big Mom-Mom, in aggravation, would instruct us to retreat upstairs and would give the eldest child cookies to evenly disperse between us younger two. Boy, was that a mistake! Once we were upstairs and out of sight, Tony would only share the cookies with his brother, Richard. When I protested the injustice and pitched my grievances to the ears of my older cousins, they responded harshly. I would angrily threaten in a quiet shout, "If you don't give me no cookies, I'ma tell Big Mom-Mom." The two tricksters shared a furtive glance before Tony's reply, "If you want a cookie, eat a boogie." Being naïve, yet obedient, I felt obliged to comply with eating the dried mucus. Without reluctance, I inserted my right index finger into the selected nostril then went to work. The boys chuckled. I proceeded to make another plea for my cookie and was greeted with the some humiliating request. This exercise continued until I ran out of boogers, and my nostrils were as dry as a well in West Texas. Angry and frustrated at my unending beguilement, I reached for the cookies that were justifiably mine. Richard always met my hand with his own and shook it uncontrollably while repeating the lyrics to the pointless song "Shake my hand; be my man; don't forget the garbage can." Each time that I released myself from his clutches, he would grab me and continue the song. Beaten, defeated, there was nothing left for me to do without any additional boogers but cry.

Stringent and strict are both two inadequate descriptors for Big Mom-Mom's stern demeanor, and, as a consequence, she and I would bump heads. Out of all of her great-grandchildren, about twenty in counting, I will boldly profess that I presented her the greatest challenge, and, boy, was she well equipped. Cream of Wheat is the only hot cereal that I can tolerate. My relatives who made this deliciously creamy dish would add flavor to the traditionally bland substance by incorporating cinnamon and sugar, milk and butter, and extracts of lemon and vanilla. They would slow cook it to avoid clumping of the grain, leaving only its smooth texture. They made this dish so good I could've slapped my mama. But Big Mom-Mom's Cream of Wheat was tasteless without apology. In fact, she would physically terrorize me at my refusal to eat it. I would more than infrequently gag with every tasteless spoonful, and she would dare me to vomit up her love-filled hearty meal. This draws me to wonder how a woman who was locally renowned for her superior sweet potato pie could create such an awful meal.

Being advanced in years with health declining did not take away from the vivacious nature of my great-grandmother. Complete with her faculties, I am convinced that she was my very first drama teacher. One day while she was watching me, she told me to bring the vacuum cleaner downstairs. She was unable to climb the stairs, so her bedroom was moved into the former dining room. At that time, only my brother and I were with her. I obediently walked up the stairs to retrieve it when I noticed that the vacuum and I stood at the same height. I, in fact, believe that it outweighed me. At least that's how it seemed at the time when I struggled bringing it down the steps. I found myself stumbling on the second or third step from the top. I looked to Big Mom-Mom for sympathy but instead was reassured with "If you drop my vacuum, I'ma beat ya ass!" She cussed at me! This was the first and only time that she ever cussed me. This eighty-year-old cussed me when I was trying to do her a favor! My own mother never cussed me, and I did not hesitate in informing her about my lack of appreciation of her choice of words. As soon as my mother came to pick me up, I ran to her telling what her grandmother had the audacity to say to me. When my protective mother looked to her for an explanation, Big Mom-Mom denied the entire ordeal. Outraged, I shouted "Mommy, SHE'S LYING!" That was all she wrote. Big Mom-Mom gave a performance certainly worthy of an Academy Award. The waterworks began, and she shook her head continuously in disbelief while verbally chastising my mother for allowing *me* to call *her* a liar. Acting out of shame, my mother turned and began giving me her reprimand. Standing there stupefied in utter astonishment, I sincerely asked my mother what was I supposed to say? So, I searched deep inside myself and found a synonym for a lie—a story. I said out loud, "Well, she's telling a story!" At my utterance, Big Mom-Mom wailed even louder. Back in the car, I began pleading my case to my mother, and to my surprise, she believed me the entire time. The lesson that she commenced to teach left me baffled. Indeed, I am without a clue as to how I'll ever be able to administer it to my own children, but it's a lesson on politeness that needs to be taught, nevertheless. She told me that it was inappropriate for a child to call any adult a liar *or* a storyteller. At that very moment, I ran out of synonyms.

# PART TWO

*There's a draught that causeth sadness,*
  *Though of mirth it seems the friend;*
*To the brain it mounts in madness,*
  *And in misery hath its end.*

*To the household hearth it creepeth*
  *And the fire in winter dies;*
*There a lonely woman weepeth,*
  *While the famished infant cries.*

*-Lydia Howard Huntley Sigourney (from "The Two Draughts")*

# CHAPTER SIX
## *YEAR OF DELTA*

C ompleting the fifth grade is a major deal for most young students. Graduating from Blankenburg Elementary made me no exception. I delivered our commencement address with confidence and excitement, yet I was nervous about what middle school had in store. After all, this is the place where it all seems to begin. I wasn't too thrilled at the possibility of attending my neighborhood middle school, so I auditioned for a magnet program that specialized in music- G.A.M.P. Since I played both the clarinet and the violin, I believed that I had a pretty good shot in getting in; however, I do not believe that I was granted admittance. So, inevitably, I was scheduled to spend my junior high school years at the area junior high school— Berger. The school was huge, in my fifth grade perspective, and uninviting. It was notorious for violence, and the fact that it was located across the street from the low-income housing projects did not help matters any. I didn't want to go to the school, but I was ready to accept my fate. I mean, I was in several physical altercations in elementary school where I came out the victor, so I was ready. I had been jumped in the school yard by a gang of girls, had a boy hold a gun to my face while I cussed him without stopping for breath, and was involved in several neighborhood fights—many of which *I* initiated, so yeah, I was tough. I could handle it. But before I had the opportunity to go, I was shipped off to spend my summer with my grandparents.

Spending summers with my grandmother was always special since she afforded me the opportunity to travel. Every summer she took me out of the confines of the city. My grandparents owned a trucking company, so I would ride in the big rigs from the truck stop in South Philadelphia all the way to the great state of Maine. Annually, we took a trip to Virginia to visit my grandfather's family. The drive seemed to last forever. I loved observing the regional changes, smelling a different kind of air, and hearing the varying dialects of people across state lines. Those summer experiences made me conscious of a world outside of my own. I was able to see walls without graffiti. I could walk streets without seeing crack cocaine vials lying in the seams of the concrete. I could experience the beauty of nature without hearing loud music, a multitude of car horns, and the yelling of neighbors. I could see a color other than brown.

The summer following my fifth grade graduation was especially exceptional because my grandparents moved out of the city and built a four-bedroom home that sat apart on a hill in Newark, Delaware. They gave me my own room and allowed me to select the color of my carpet and walls. I was allowed to have a blue room in the largest house I had ever seen. The house had two and a half baths—every home I ever stayed in up to this point had only one bathroom. If my brother, mother, and I all needed to relieve ourselves at the same time, two people were out of luck, and those two people were always me and my brother. The master bathroom had a Jacuzzi tub with a detached shower large enough for two people. It even had his and her sinks! I would pee in their bathroom every chance that I could. Downstairs consisted of a living room, dining room, and family room—never had I heard of a family room before the building of their home. The kitchen was humongous. It was so big they were able to fit an ordinary dining room table in there. It actually came with a built-in table that my grandfather kept calling an island. It had cabinets upon cabinets; hell, even the food had its own closet! But, that's not nearly it. Their home had a basement! The basement was the entire length of the house. Man! This house was a ghetto kid's paradise. I could have easily gotten lost in there.

Their home was a far cry from my norm. I was accustomed to dwelling in row homes where the most pristine abode was not immune from the community pets—roaches, mice, and rats. Adjoined neighbors' unkempt living quarters affected everyone. Sometimes you could stand right outside of a person's house and smell the unwelcoming stench from within. Lord forbid if you went inside; the odor may have never escaped your garments. The walls in the homes in which I lived were unbelievably thin. We could hear our neighbors' parties or the sounds of their love-making. Our houses constantly had three bedrooms occupied, and three was always a crowd in our small kitchens. We had only a living room, a dining room and no yard at all. The city domiciles where I lived were always brick, but my grandparents' home in Delaware had beige vinyl siding with contrasting shutters.

There weren't many blacks in my grandparents' neighborhood, maybe six families in total, and there weren't any corner stores within walking distance of their home. The nearest establishments were a Clover's and a Wawa, and they were over three miles away. The public transportation system ran only once every hour on the hour. But I didn't mind. We were always traveling any way, and my stay was temporary, only for a summer . . . or so I thought.

As the season neared autumn, my grandmother alerted me that we had to hurry up and return to Philly; there had been an emergency. When we turned onto my familiar block, I saw my house, but it was not at all how I remembered it. In the front, a window missing from its frame, and, inside, the hardwood floors were beginning to warp. Everything was wet. *Everything.* My mother led my grandparents and I in our effort of sorting through our possessions to find something that could be salvaged. An electrical fire had broken out in my mother's absence. The smoke detectors caught the signal and our good neighbors, aware of her work schedule, alerted the fire department. The water used to extinguish the fire caused much of the damage we saw. One of the firemen said that if my mother would have come home and flipped a light switch, she would have been electrocuted. Pictures of my grandmother as a teenager—gone. Pictures of her wedding to my mother's deceased father—destroyed. My life, as I knew it, was about to suffer yet another unwanted change.

My mother told my brother and me that we had no place to live. As she was a city police officer, her living outside of the city's limits was not an option. She told us that we would remain in Delaware with our grandparents and attend school until she found a place for the three of us. Meanwhile, she was moving into her boyfriend's one-bedroom apartment. She promised us weekend time and assured us that this new change was temporary. My grandmother looked at us with warm, empathetic eyes the entire time my heart breaking. It was a long, quiet drive back to Delaware that evening.

The following week my grandmother enrolled us into school and, with the registration, my middle school dreams perished. Delaware is only one state over from Pennsylvania, yet the school system differs vastly. In the state, grades k through 3$^{rd}$ are elementary, 4$^{th}$ through 6$^{th}$ are intermediate, 7$^{th}$ and 8$^{th}$ are junior high, and 9$^{th}$ through 12$^{th}$ are senior high. This means I was essentially in elementary school for an additional year. My apologies, *intermediate* school. Bottom line: this royally sucked! I had to graduate all over again only to be promoted to middle school *again*. The climate of change that I had embraced as I escaped from Philadelphia for my summer retreat in the then-underdeveloped state began to sicken me.

It was too much change too fast. I had an overdose of it. I had to make this place like home—like Philly. I met the black girls in the development, and they all claimed to have moved there from Philadelphia. Great! But they spoke differently, accents were a little off. And, they seemed soft and timid—sheltered. Never mind that. Let's just play Double Dutch. THESE GIRLS COULDN'T EVEN JUMP ROPE! All Philadelphian girls jumped rope! Not being able to jump rope was like not being able to tie your shoes. The unspoken law for female city dwellers was as follows: A little girl is to learn how to walk, run, and jump Double Dutch. This law is understood; however, I had to teach them how to play the game...all of them: Challenge, Criminal Minded, Footsy Playa, etc. Not only that, but I had to show them that I was not one to be played with. I had to affirm my reputation by beating up a girl who was twice my size on more than one occasion. My daddy would have been proud.

In my section of Philadelphia, the only people that I saw who looked remotely dissimilar to me were some of my teachers. Most of them commuted everyday from New Jersey to teach us underprivileged inner city youth. Moving to Delaware obliged me to open up to new experiences and people. I did this in full force when I tried the whole integration thing. There were a few white girls in the development that seemed pretty cool. One day after playing outdoors for a while together, one of them invited me into her home. It smelled like vanilla throughout, and the interior was adorned in country living decor. When I entered the house, her parents looked at me with surprise. In a very blasé fashion, she led the way up to her room while I and the other three girls followed. Her room was dreamy—very tidy. She had shelves with horse figurines and matching bedroom furniture. She had a desk to do her homework, and her own personal computer. Shortly after our arrival to her bedroom, her parents called her downstairs. The remainder of us was in her room for just a few minutes when she returned looking unhappy. She announced, while staring at the plush bedroom carpet and fidgeting with her fingers, "My parents said that I am not allowed any more than three guests." The four of us girls turned and looked at one another to see who was going to voluntarily go back home when she stated, "Flora, you have to leave. Sorry." I said, "okay" and walked out of the room hoping that they would all decide to simply go back outside to continue playing. That never happened. Her bedroom door closed as I walked down the stairs, and a roar of laughter from children enjoying themselves came from inside. I walked out of the front door with tears swelling up in my eyes, and I cried the entire way to my grandparents' home. I opened the door, advanced to my room, and leaped onto my bed. I sobbed heavily into my pillow and bellowed out, "I just want to go home!"

Wherever that was.

Once school began, things were slightly better. I could no longer walk to school because it was located in another city. So, I had to wake up an hour early to be bused for one hour to Wilmington. In class there was a girl with dirty-blonde hair and blue eyes named Amanda. She and I hit it off rather well. We sat next to each other at lunch, on the bus, and talked on the phone after school. Amanda decided to get off at my bus stop and come over to my house some days, so we could spend more time together; she had her parents' permission, of course. One day, I suggested that we go over to her house instead; she agreed. We walked about a quarter of a mile from my house to hers. When we arrived, I noticed that Amanda's home wasn't nearly as nice as mine. Her house was small and surrounded by dirt. I didn't mind. She was my friend. As we approached the path, her father came to the door wearing a white sleeveless tee shirt and called out to her. She told me that she'd be right back and went running towards her father. They spoke for a while, and I waited on the path. Whilst her father watched, she ran back to me. I smiled ear to ear, happy to see my friend. Panting and breathless, she told me that she wasn't allowed to play with me anymore because I was black. With that said, she turned to her left, ran back towards her house, went inside, and her father closed the door. I guess Amanda shared limited information about me when she requested permission to spend time at my home. I don't really know. What I do know is the walk back was long and lonely.

The more time spent in Delaware, the more depressed I became. I gained weight like it was nobody's business—five feet tall and 125 pounds—in the sixth grade. At first arrival, I was less than 100 pounds. I gravitated to a new style of dress—all black. Slowly, I began to withdraw from people. I missed the bus intentionally to avoid attending school and started wetting the bed in hopes that my grandmother would get fed up with changing my sheets and send me back to live with my mother. Making friends turned fruitless; I was just too different. Living in a home with my truck driving grandfather as a consistent male figure did not matter much to me at this stage of my life; it was hopeless. And, as always, whenever I begin adjusting to a new situation, BAM! I'm hit by change.

My brother had retained his own set of problems, and he never mentioned his feelings. Perhaps it's because he is five years my junior and viewed me as another mother figure as opposed to a big sister. I know for certain that he, too, was not widely accepted. Men always felt like they could do or say whatever they wanted to him because he didn't have our father in his life. He whined a lot and would often cry because of the mistreatment. I was too self-absorbed to give a care. What I knew was I didn't want him around me. I didn't want anyone around me for that matter. On one instance, he persisted on entering a room that I repeatedly told him to get out of. While I was styling my younger cousin's hair, he sneaked in undetected. She and I were talking and watching television when he unexpectedly comes running out of the bedroom closet waving his arms in fright. I jumped up, yelled at him at the top of my lungs, and all he could manage to say as he ran away was "FIRE!" I paid him no mind, but I was curious to know what he was messing around with in the closet since he had a habit of meddling. He better not had bothered any of my clothes. Casually, I walked over to the closet and opened the door—WHOOM! Flames shot up in my face. My heart raced. My breath stopped. This couldn't be what I was seeing. Petrified yet unharmed and unable to form a sound in my dry throat, I looked over at my younger cousin and howled "Run!" I ran right outside to alert my grandfather who was watering the yard. About twenty minutes late, the volunteer fire department arrived. Smoke and water damage once more. All of our clothing destroyed. Once again, we were displaced.

While the home was getting repaired, we spent about a week inside of an extended stay inn before we moved directly next door to our house into the home of my great uncle. During our stay, my maternal uncle's two children came to reside with us as well. I grew strongly attached to the children because I could see my hurts and pains in their eyes. In the early seeds of their years before life's bloom, they were already subjected to time's harsh winters. His little girl's scalp exuded raw flesh and only contained patches of dark, kinky hair; she was the tender age of five. His three-year-old son, who was abnormally pigeon-toed as a result of his mother's drug abuse and pre-natal negligence, was withdrawn and refused to speak to anyone. These children were clearly abused and uncared for. My grandmother told me they would be settling in permanently. I resolved to make myself their missionary. Daily, I washed my little cousin's hair with medicated shampoo and nursed her scalp back to health. I talked to the boy alone and showered him with endless affection. I read to him, played with him, and continued to communicate with him until he eventually spoke back. Out of all of the people he encountered daily, out of all of the social workers who managed his case, he felt safe enough to trust me and impart the pleasure of his sweet-sounding, innocent voice to me to enjoy. These children filled me with joy, and I delighted myself in their progress.

When we moved back into my grandparents' home, my uncle then brought his infant son to my grandparents' care. Initially, they did not have a crib for the baby, so he slept with me on the sofa bed. The four bedrooms in their home quickly were filled, and the four of us increased to eight when my uncle brought yet another child in addition to his previous three to live with his parents. I willingly gave up my blue room for his children's comfort. I found myself playing mommy in the sixth grade with four children under my care. I woke up in the middle of the night to prepare the bottle for the crying infant. When I went to the mall unaccompanied with my neighborhood friends, I pushed his youngest daughter in a stroller. I was sacrificing my childhood, and I didn't even care. Those children needed me. They needed someone.

Over time, the domestic demands placed upon me by my grandmother became too much unbearable. I didn't quite mind the children, but I refused to become another Cinderella before her prince. My uncle's home next door to ours started to grow in number as well when his son moved his girlfriend in with their four children. Suddenly, my grandmother started cooking every night to feed both households. Each evening, the two homes would gather together to eat in my grandmother's kitchen, on the island, on the table, and in the family room—sixteen people, four dogs, and a cat. And every night, my grandmother would tell people to leave their plates where they were; *she* would take care of them. No one lifted a finger to scrape a plate or wash a dish. Once the house cleared out, my grandmother departed for bed leaving the kitchen to my care. Every night the kitchen was filled with pots and pans where she did not clean up as she went along. Every night there were too many dishes for her double sinks to contain at once. *Every night.* There was no homework exemptions, no she takes care of the children excuses. Nothing. Nada. Zilch. The house next door had a girl two years older than myself and one two years younger; still I had no assistance, unless there was an evening where my grandfather did not have to make a run on his truck; he would take pity on me and lend a hand. Those nights were few and far between.

I cried my eyes out and would call my mother in a fit of fury. She would say, "Baby girl, just hang in there for a little while longer. Mommy's working on it." My brother and I lived there for a full year before we could return to live with my mother, ending the tradition of summer vacations with grandma. However, leaving those children felt like pieces of my heart were being painfully torn away from my bosom. My mother kept trying to convince me that they were not my children and not my responsibility; I was only a child myself. She didn't understand. They *were* mine. Each of them had some trait of me, and I poured the best of myself into each one of them. We had something in common.

*"Home is not where you live but where they understand you."*

-*Christian Morgenstern*

# CHAPTER SEVEN
## *REINTEGRATION*

Pool. Ping-Pong. The latest game systems These were the entertainments that kept the neighborhood kids craving to visit our modestly furnished West Oak Lane home. To be more factual, these pastimes kept the *boys* visiting. Moving back with my mother to a different section of Philadelphia made me accept that I am not a girl's girl. I could click with one, maybe two, that's it. I made attempts to speak to female neighbors, classmates, and youth at my home church—all ending with the same result But it was okay. because I had a lot of male acquaintances who considered me to be their "little sister," and this had its perks. Distinctly I recall a young lady from the next street over visiting our home on an early autumnal afternoon. While she and I were chatting in my living room and watching music videos on *The Box,* a fine young man on whom she had a crush came walking upstairs from my basement. He and three other hunks visited my home weekly to play pool in our basement. When he entered the living room to walk out the front door, she was unable to mask her surprise--her mouth flew open and her cheeks began to blush. He noticed and graciously shot her a little smile before telling us good-bye and leaving. After he was gone, the speechless girl found her voice and immediately asked why he was in my home. I told her, in a very carefree tone, that he was like my big brother and frequently visits. Yeah, not being widely accepted by females really wasn't all that bad.

At some stage in my pre-teens, I entered into what I call "an awkward phase." I just did not fit in anywhere or at least not within any particular group. Even though I was confident in my ability to depend myself, I did not consider it a license to pick random fights, especially with people who I felt even more confident in beating, so I did not fit in with the trouble makers. I would talk to them and sometimes eat with them, but I was not a part of them. I did my homework regularly because it was easy, and it gave me something to do, and I cared somewhat about my grades. Also, I wasn't the type of kid to goof off in school. I maintained the philosophy of that's what recess, lunch, or afterschool was reserved for; so I didn't fit in with the lazy group or the group of class clowns.

A few days a week I was withdrawn from my regular classes to assemble with a small select group of students. These students and I would travel to other schools to participate in debate. We did not receive regular coursework—we would stare at obscure images on note cards and discuss what we individually saw. This was the Mentally Gifted program for exceptionally bright students who received high test scores. I hated it. I hated being clustered with "the nerds." I hated being singled out from my classmates to attend special programs, even if I grasped the content quicker. I never wanted to appear "smart." But, I couldn't stand it when the teacher asked a question—which for me was a no-brainer—and no one raised a hand. Not a single person. *That* was torture—having to limit the appearance of one's intelligence for social acceptance. And, it never failed that she (my teacher) would continually call on me to provide her with what the other students should have known.

To make matters worse, the teacher made it obvious that I was her favorite student. Whenever she needed an errand, she called on Flora. Whenever she needed a question correctly answered—Flora. What did she do that for? There was nothing worse than being distinguished as a "teacher's pet." I had to try to maintain the little "rep" I acquired while being a new transfer student to Ada Lewis Middle School, and she and their "M.G." program were not helping. It was bad enough that I knew absolutely no one in that school prior to being transferred because it was out of the sections of the city that I inhabited, and all of the kids on my new block attended private school. My peers looked at me funny when I had to introduce myself and tell that I had transferred from Delaware. *Delaware!* I would hear, "Where's that?" or "Are there any black people in Delaware?" Most of those children had never left the state, let alone the city. Nevertheless, I did not socially belong with those "M.G." kids; I was cooler than them—my clothes were decent, and I was generally accepted by all. Generally.

There was an incident in my wood shop class when the popular female students let me know exactly where I stood in their social circle when a popular boy grabbed my rear end, and I retaliated by grabbing his penis. Perhaps "grabbing" it is an understatement. It was important for me to make an example out of him so the other boys would know that I was not one of those fast girls who found it cute when a boy grabbed, slapped, or pinched her booty. I probably wouldn't have responded as severely had I not seen his smirk when I looked to him for some sort of a rationale for the misplacement of his hands. Well, I could be as equally audacious. No one was going to put his hands on me in any manner that I disapproved of without suffering dire consequences. I walked up to the smiling, handsome male and gave him a lesson on the importance of keeping his hands to himself by firmly clenching onto his penis until my clenched fist began to shake. He quickly dropped to his knees but was unable to shake my unrelenting grip. I could see his eyes slowly begin to roll behind his head when some anonymous figure grabbed me from behind and forced me to release him. Although I could see his response, I had no clear idea of what I was doing or of the severity of my actions. I mean, I definitely intended to do *something*, but not that. It did not click until after the fact that I had his reproductive organ in my hands. I was just reacting. This was my first blackout in a fit of rage. I wonder if this is how my father felt when he divvied out his vicious attacks.

My conduct did not please my female classmates, and they showed this by conspiring to jump me after school. Thankfully, the injured boy, in an apparent effort to rectify his wrong, warned me. I would be lying if I said I wasn't afraid of being jumped, for my fifth grade attack was still all too fresh in my mind, but I wasn't about to back down or run the three miles home or call my mom to come pick me up. Those definitely were not options. I didn't back down in the fifth grade, and I wasn't going to back down now. If these girls were going to learn anything about me, they were going to discover that I was no one's punk. Acting without thinking, I walked right up to the conspirators after school and asked them directly about their plot while I simultaneously dropped my book bag, indicating my readiness to square off. The girls looked at each other and then at me and professed that they had no intentions of fighting me. The news should have eased my mind, but it did not. My adrenaline was too high; I had already prepared myself for the attack. They, like most predators, preferred to strike an unsuspecting victim. I walked home that day contemplating what could have been. More importantly, I walked home that day after school and all of the days following unscathed, and I praise God for protecting me even when I acted foolishly—jeopardizing my safety for the sake of pride and wrath.

*"A sister can be seen as someone who is both ourselves and very much not ourselves—a special kind of double."*

*-Toni Morrison*

# CHAPTER EIGHT
## *LOST AND FOUND*

I transferred to Greenfield, in South Philadelphia, for the completion of my eighth grade year. Nonetheless, it was like déjà vu. During the first week of school, I had girls planning on jumping me until an informant gave me the 4-1-1. Once again, I prepared myself to fight. Once again, nothing happened. I was in general education classes until the school discovered my test scores. Here I go again... back with the brainiacs in what this school called Gamma House. This time, I remained with the "gifted" students for the remainder of the school year, and, to my amazement, I enjoyed it. Being in a class where everyone was bright or at least on the same level academically made being intelligent delightful. I didn't have any problems out of anyone while I was with them. But, I find it peculiar how I experienced a sudden change in behavior by becoming the problem through bullying some of the nerdy kids. I did not become embarrassed by my behavior until my eighth grade class trip to Orlando, Florida. I contacted my relatives in Orlando to let them know that I was coming. I had not seen them in several years. They were excited about my visit and agreed to meet me at Universal Studios (an attraction that my class was touring). When they spotted me, I ran over to them, and we exchanged hugs and kisses. Just as we were posing for a picture, my aunt called out "Aaron?" She recognized him and even worse, he recognized her. Aaron was the nerd that I badgered the worst, and my aunt insisted that I take a picture with him. I pleaded with her, but she would not have it any other way. My classmates all stood there giggling, well aware of my behavior towards this kid. It was absolutely humiliating. I never picked on Aaron's high waters, geeky glasses, or screechy voice again. I still didn't talk to him, but at least I didn't pick on him. Later that summer, my aunt came up to Philly and forced me to go over to his house with her. She was really going to make *me* socialize with *him*. It's ironic that Aaron's father was best-friends with my late grandfather. I ascertained that piece of information while I was dining at Aaron's elegant South Philadelphia home. He and I both were uncomfortable the entire afternoon. But I left his house having learned that there was really a nice kid buried inside of that geeky exterior. Never did I tease anyone else after that event. Needless to say that it is a small world, and the occurrence with Aaron doesn't even begin to prove exactly how small it really is.

My attacks on Aaron weren't really about him and his nerdiness. It was about my mother. During this time she was involved in a violent fight on her job as a police officer. During her tussle with an intoxicated female, she sustained serious injuries that resulted in two cervical spine surgeries (one when I was in the eighth grade and another while I was in the ninth) and the removal of two disks from her vertebrae. After school, I would go home and cook for my brother, who cried over being forced to eat burned meals and take him to visit her in the hospital via public transportation. It was my responsibility to make sure that all of her bills were paid on time and act as if I was our mother whenever the school called our home requesting to speak with her. In the eighth grade, and some of the ninth, I had to become the woman of our home. I did not talk to the school about it, and I was not going to put my burden on my recovering mother. Acting out was my sole outlet. At home, I beat my younger brother into submission, and, at school, Aaron was the subject of my release.

*****

Death and serious injury have tremendous effects on people and often help them to find religion. My mother's spiritual reckoning occurred during her hospitalization. When she was released from the hospital, her habits drastically changed. Our church attendance increased. She only listened to gospel music. And, she began to speak to me more candidly about her abuse—sometimes sharing more information than a child my age really needed to know. But I understood why she did it; she talked to me because I lived it with her. I was the closest person to her who could actually understand what she endured. She told me things about my father and his treatment of her that I never physically witnessed, like the fact that he was a womanizer and had so little respect for her that he slept with two of her cousins. His womanizing is indeed a fact and not mere speculation or hearsay, for he has five children *that he claims*, all with different mothers (for the exception of me and my brother), and my mother is the only woman that he has ever married. She never talked about the mother of his oldest daughter, but she did mention the relationship that he had with the mother of my older sister, Mercedes.

Ever since I could remember, I would hear stories about this unknown sister from both of my parents, and I always hoped to meet her. While on an eighth grade field trip, I remembered a couple occasions when my mother mentioned where Mercedes's mother was employed, and it suddenly dawned on me that I was taking a trip to my sister's mom's job. I instantly felt closer to my sister just by being there. I *was* closer to my sister by just being there. The crazy thing is I had visited this science center at least a dozen times while being educated in the Philadelphia Public

Schools and never had it dawned on me until this trip that my sister's mother works here. I resolved right then to make an effort to find my sister. But how exactly? I found a security guard sitting at his post and casually asked if he knew my sister's mom, and HE DID! He said she was on her lunch break. My teacher announced it was time for us to move on, so I had to act fast. I asked him if he could deliver a note to her when she returned, and he agreed. He handed me a slip of paper and a pencil, and I wrote her a small note stating that I wanted to get in touch with my sister, Mercedes, and asked her to provide my sister with my contact information.

I went home and told my mother what I had done, unsure of her reaction. She wondered if the message would even reach Mercedes because of the bad history that she had with Mercedes's mother. But, the Lord willed it that I received a phone call from my sister days later. She and I spoke on the phone for well over an hour before arranging a meeting. I'll never forget when I first saw her on 69th street—she was beautiful, fair skin, petite, stylish, and classy. She looked nothing like me but held a strong resemblance to my brother. Their mouths form contortions identical to our father. I looked up to her and wanted to be just like her. Every slang word she used, I incorporated into my vocabulary. I found my sister after 14 years of not knowing who she was. Before our meeting, I could have sat next to her on a bus and had no idea of our close kinship. During our conversation, I learned that I was attending the very same school that she graduated from. My eighth grades friends knew my sister; in fact my eighth grade teacher was also her teacher. The hallways that I walked five days a week, my older sister walked before me. Finding my sister Mercedes was more than a mere coincidence; it was a work of divine providence.

When I lived in West Philadelphia, I would often spend weekends with my sister Keke, but, in the process of incessant moving, we lost touch. Hooking up with Mercedes reconnected me with Keke because the two of them were in contact. The three of us managed to have a relationship in spite of our father; still, he did present an issue. My oldest sister is our father's first child, so the two of them share a special bond. She is our daddy's little girl, and, out of all of his children, she walks the most in his footsteps. Once the three of us reconnected, talks transpired about arranging a meeting with our father and me bringing along our little brother. I had not seen that man in seven years and, until this school year, had not thought about him since the second grade. I truly believed in my heart that if I saw him I would make an attempt on his life. My body quivered at the sheer thought of seeing him, and my mind flashed with ideas about how I could inflict bodily harm. How could I make him feel the hurt that my mother felt? How could I make him feel the pains that I could not express? How could I let him know that I saw and remembered everything down to minute details without crying, going back to that place in my mind, and attacking him with murderous venom? I had forgotten. I convinced myself that I had actually forgotten, and they just took me back. To that place. To the 4900 block of Warnock Street. No! I wouldn't do it. I couldn't do it. I had too much of him inside of me. I knew I would have regrets. "No" flat out I told them, "I'm not ready." Logically, our getting together would naturally spark some conversation about contacting him—our father, my Boogie Man, but I wasn't thinking logically. I was at the early stages of being a young romantic. I hoped to meet my sisters; I hoped for us to build a relationship; and I hoped to never, ever see *him* again. Period. Why couldn't we just talk about the years that we've missed together and our different experiences without any mention of *him*? Why couldn't *he* be our unsung commonality? Why couldn't life just be that simple? Granted, he beat on all of our mothers; however, I was the only child who physically lived with him. My experience with *Daddy* was totally different from theirs; it was even different from my brother's who was too young to remember all that occurred—who was too young to learn the truth behind his conception. Keke had the relationship, Mercedes desired it, and I didn't want it. And, I for sure wasn't about to introduce him to our brother—*my* brother.

*Therefore, if anyone is in Christ, he is a new creation;*
*The old has gone, the new has come!*

*-2 Corinthians 5: 17*

# CHAPTER NINE
## *CHOICES*

Hanging out with my older sisters helped me to discern my inherent self. I noticed commonalities in our personalities: the three of us are quick tempered, and we each have difficulty with trusting others. Mercedes and my brother, A.J., were both sheltered, so the two of them are more alike. Keke and Mercedes were both brought up as their mothers' only children, so they have that in common. However, my sister Keke and I have many similarities. Both of us are cunning, and we are both hustlers. Our difference lies in the means of our hustle. Both of us are fighters, although she is hands-down more about it than I am. We are both formally educated, we care about having a relationship with our half-siblings, and we are seriously pensive. Mercedes and I have comparable temperaments. We are not easily attached to people; without a second thought, she and I can write a person off quicker than we can write a check; we can even write off each other.

Even though I did not live the majority of my years with my father, I always felt his presence—all of us did. His blood runs thick through our veins. My actions do not favor those of my mother, and I have so much in common with two women with whom I never shared a residence. Knowing this and all that I was capable of, I had to make certain choices, and those choices began in high school.

My oldest sister frequently tells me that I cannot escape who I am—a ghetto girl from West Philly, the daughter of a monster. This is true. It matters not the number of degrees that I acquire, my eloquence of speech, or the amount of success I achieve. My DNA cannot change; however, I can dare to be different. And I DARE. I dare to reject and alter parts of myself that are not representative of who I aspire to be—who I really am. This is almost a daily fight between contrary natures. It isn't easy. One part of me craves illegality, malice, deception, and materialism. The other part seeks peace, joy, happiness, patience, kindness, goodness, gentleness, faithfulness, and self-control.

Choosing my secular nature would have been all too easy. I could have easily took the woe is me cop out and blamed who I have come to be on my absent father or inattentive mother. It would have been as equally effortless to blame my poor choices on me being a product of my impoverished environment. But, I will not enable anything enough to take away my innate right and power to choose—who I am, what I do, and who I am to become. Choosing the latter takes effort and work and diligence in a world that makes depravity and immorality permissible and excusable. Are certain behavioral patterns genetic? Yes—alcoholism, drug addiction, etc. Aren't behaviors learned? Absolutely. Exhibit A—my narrative up to this point. So, when a person is educated enough to know what he or she is up against, he or she becomes empowered with the ability to avoid certain behaviors. For example, if your father died from alcoholism, your grandfather, and your great-grandfather, you know it is in your best interest to stay away from the booze—to not even tempt yourself by tasting it. God has granted us enough common sense to do that much.

In high school, I learned that, in order to keep my dual natures in check, it was imperative for me to surround myself with positivity. I needed positive people in my life to bring balance. I needed friends who were warriors-- friends who were willing to check my negative behavior; friends who had delightful spirits that would counter my negative one. I learned early on that I could be easily influenced by negative people because there was a part of my spirit that craved it, desired it, and fed on it. I had to make a choice. I had to establish what I wanted to do in life (go to college, become a teacher, and have a family), and the type of person that I wanted to become (a Proverbs 31 woman); therefore, it was vital for me to yoke myself to like-minded individuals. And, once I made these choices, I was faced with a series of tests that shaped me into the strong, interdependent woman that I am today—clothed in fortitude. As you will see, in some of the challenges, I frankly did not make the grade, but I did, however, walk away with a lesson well learned from each and every one. Sometimes the lesson instantaneously came; other times, its manifestation took a little more time. Because of my lessons learned, I have no regrets. There are things that I have done that I am not remotely proud of, but I do not regret them, for they were integral components of my personal and spiritual growth.

Although it may not appear this way in the pages to come, 1997, my ninth grade year, was the year I started my personal walk with God. And, on my journey through HIS Word, HE brought me across a few scriptures that were applicable to my life. HE spoke to me through HIS Word. Just as I felt the presence of my absent father, the presence of my Heavenly Father burned even the more. HE made it known that HE was with me, and HE kept me through all of the tribulations of my life—the jumping, the gun in my face, the attempted rapes, the shooting by my father. HE let me know that I found favor in HIS eyes, and, at that time, I requested the wisdom of Solomon. HE brought me to the following passages of scripture to let me know that HE understood my personal endeavors:

Trust in the LORD with all thine heart; and lean
not unto thine own understanding.

In all thy ways acknowledge him, and he shall
direct thy paths.
(Proverbs 3:5-6 KJV)

I can do all *things* through Christ which
strengtheneth me.
(Philippians 4:13)

Equipped for the trials, I made my expedition through the
most unstable, unpredictable, incomprehensible, and trying four
years of my life—high school.

# PART THREE

# CHAPTER TEN
## *MISCONCEPTION*

Now, readers, you should know by now my feelings about nerds. So, when I agreed to accompany my best friend on a campus tour to Central High School, a magnet school, *the* second best public school (at the time academically) in the city of Philadelphia, I had no intentions of attending until I saw our campus tour guide, Blaine. He wore gray sweat pants, a baseball cap, and a swagger that I found oh-so-appealing. I told my friend from Greenfield right there on the spot, "I'm coming to this school, and he's going to be mine." She laughed me off and called me crazy, but I was sincere. I remembered nothing that he and his fellow sophomore companion, Nick, told us about the school, but I remembered their names, their class, and that was all I needed for my mind to be set. Once I was granted admission, I showed up on the first day of school ready for my hunt.

The girls at C.H.S. did not play in the wardrobe department, and I really had to step up my game. By this time, my grandmother was helping only infrequently with our clothes, so my mother started doing the shopping. One day she came home with some outfits from the seven dollar store—THE SEVEN DOLLAR STORE!—orange pants and a shirt set with huge yellow sunflowers and a matching blue one with white sunflowers. I was livid. How was I ever going to get Blaine wearing that crap? When I said that I wasn't wearing those costumes and followed that statement by clearly outlining the acceptable designers that fit my newly acquired C.H.S. taste—Donna Karan, Versace, and Iceberg—she told me "If that's what you want, you need to get a job because I ain't buying that. I don't have that kinda money."

That was okay. by me. I did one better; I found two jobs. One job I got paid minimum wage—a whopping $4.75 per hour, and the other I received commission and tips. But, that mother of mine was not about to make things easy. She refused to drive me to work, so I had to walk four miles in all sorts of weather. When I requested a ride home during the end of my twilight shift, she often said, "Can't you find anybody to give you a ride?" When I gleefully brought home my first pay check and showed my mother, she insisted that I pay a bill, pay her rent, tithe, purchase my own bus tokens for transportation to and from school, buy my own lunch, and, of course, purchase my own clothes. Damn! This sure taught me the value of a dollar. But, I still managed to save my money and buy nice clothes. It wasn't the designers that I had proposed, but it was a lot better than the outfits at the seven dollar store.

By making me assume some adult financial responsibility and by having more withholdings than the State of Pennsylvania and Federal Government combined, my mother indirectly taught me that if there was something I wanted, I was going to have to work hard for it. Nothing was going to be given to me—not even by her. For the rest of my teenage years until the present, I did not and do not feel my mother owed me anything. In fact, whenever I asked for even the most trivial material possession, she'd say, "Flora, I don't have it" or "I'm broke." I didn't bother to question how she could afford to get her hair done or how she was able to attend every church conference that our church hosted. I just understood and learned to have no expectations—not for my mother, not for anyone.

Basketball games at C.H.S. always drew a crowd—the cheerleaders cheered, the pep squad stepped, and the crowd was energetic. The first basketball game I attended at C.H.S. drew ... you guessed it ... Blaine. This was my opportunity to walk over and reintroduce myself. And, to my surprise, he remembered me. He smiled at me, talked to me, and appeared to be interested in me until Nick, the other tour guide, came blocking. Nick's intentions were clear and, like a good friend, Blaine conceded leaving me to be Nick's conquest. He walked away. Blaine walked away. Damn it! Nick was still talking. Damn it! I was so close. Initially, I was annoyed by Nick's antics and then I caught wind of what he had to say—what he had been saying all along during each of our previous encounters. Nick told me things I never heard before, and he made it all sound so good. He began every greeting with "Hello beautiful" even though he was fully aware of my name. No male ever told me I was beautiful before. Maybe I wouldn't have been so taken back by his flattery and sweet nothings if my father would have told me first. The more persistent Nick was after the game, the more I started being attracted to him. He would go out of his way to say things that made me feel special.

I received an invitation to skip school to attend a cut party. Now, this was before I understood the connotation of the slang, *cut*. Later, songs like "Some Cut," by groups like Trillville, made it more apparent with lyrics like: "what it is hoe what's up/ Can a nigga get in them guts/ Cut you up like you ain't been cut/"; however, I considered a *cut* party to encompass a group of truant students who cut (meaning skipped in this context) school to literally party i.e., listen to music and dance, something similar to the hit 90s movie, *House Party*.

With this understanding, I was all too eager to attend because, at this point, I was cutting class and school regularly. Gracing a class with my presence was seldom. My sole purpose for school attendance was socialization. To prove it, some days I would spend all seven periods in the school's cafeteria playing dominoes. I made it pretty clear that I was an "A-B" student prior to Central High, but this school made me face new challenges with the rigorous courses and scholastic competition with diverse students who were just as smart and cool. Here I was nothing or no one special. With this being said, yeah, I was all for not going to school, and I brought my best girlfriend along for the ride.

She and I took the subway and the "El" across various sections of the city to our party destination—Nick's house. As the ninth and tenth guests to arrive, we immediately recognized everyone present which invited a level of comfort until the game began... the ultimate teenage game—Truth or Dare. The first round consisted of all truths. Someone posed the question, "Flora, do you like Nick?" With a pounding heart and what felt like a thousand burning eyes peering into my soul, I replied, "Yes." Next round—Dare. What was my dare? —To go upstairs with Nick. He held my hand while leading the way up his stairs to his bedroom, but his touch could not soothe my nerves; it only increased my nervousness. We arrived to his already occupied room. Nick gave the occupants a quick apology before guiding me to a new location—his parent's bedroom. We sat in a chair across from the bed with me upon his lap and began kissing passionately. While our lips locked, our tongues exploring each other's mouth, his hands began to travel across the ravines and peaks of my body. My breasts enjoyed their first attention, and I took pleasure in the sensation, yet I shuddered at the stimulation springing from my unexplored terrain. On no account had my imagination explored the infinite possibilities of my "first time," but this situation did not feel right. This wasn't the purpose for my visit. This was not what I wanted. I liked Nick but not enough to give him any part of me. The pressure was too intense, so I seized his hands to preclude the unbuttoning of my jeans.

"What's wrong?" he inquired with a bit of concern. "Are you on your period?"

"No," I responded honestly.

"Then there's no problem," he said assertively and went back to kissing my neck with his full lips.

I looked into his eyes and spoke the following words slightly above a whisper: "Nick, you can try all you want. I'm not going to have sex with you."

And try he did without success. He relinquished his endeavor when a knock came to the door. He jumped up and went to rejoin the party leaving me to get myself together. I reemerged a few minutes later. Back downstairs. Back to the game. For a second time someone dared me to go upstairs with Nick and before I could protest, he spoke out with an objection and a request to be hooked up with someone else. He didn't have to wait for the reselection because another girl (who had already had a baby in the ninth grade) volunteered. The two of them walked cheerfully upstairs while my friend and I walked out the door. My girlfriend wondered why he and I were upstairs for such a long time, and I told her everything. She then made clear to me that one of the male partygoers, a close friend of Nick's, was telling everyone in our absence that Nick and I had sex. I shook off the comment and reassured her that my virginity was still intact.

The following day at school, Nick was acting weird. When I spoke to him, he'd just give me a sly grin and kept moving. Our phone conversations were brief. One time his phone had a beep, so he clicked over. When he clicked back to me, he said he had to go; his mother just called and needed some cheese. SOME CHEESE!!! This wasn't the Nick I knew. I was genuinely perplexed by his complete 360 until one of my male admirers, who did not attend the party, approached me distraught. He exclaimed that he was surprised to know that I was having sex with Nick. Quickly I corrected the young brotha by telling him that Nick and I DID NOT HAVE SEX of any form. He was confounded because Nick told him and a couple of other guys the opposite. Oh, HELL NAW! This-negro-was-straight-up-lying-on-his-penis! More importantly, he was lying about me. I was still a virgin, yet I had sex. How was this even possible? . I sought vengeance. I wrote a humiliating rap about his behind that I shared with anyone and everyone who would listen. I even tried to call into the local radio station to "spit it" over the air waves, but it was always busy. Deep-seated rancor flowed through my heart for that young man. If I was fully open to it, I could have learned several lessons from this exploit.

1) I should have learned about being in the wrong place at the wrong time. If I would have kept my tail in school, none of this would have happened.

2) I should have learned a lesson on perception. If I did not want people to think that I had sex with Nick, I shouldn't have placed myself in the position. Really, what was I thinking going UPSTAIRS and to HIS PARENT'S BEDROOM? I didn't think—and here lies the problem.

3) I should have learned a lesson on how males can hold a female's reputation in the palms of their hands.

4) And, I should have learned that females often give these males the power. Prime example, I went upstairs with him and stayed for a long time, therefore, making it easy for him to lie and giving plausibility to his fabrication.

These lessons were missed opportunities for me in the ninth grade. Instead, I put up the wall common for most females who have been hurt in their past; the wall that screams "I DON'T CARE WHAT ANYONE THINKS ABOUT ME." I was content in knowing that I was still a virgin. I was satisfied with knowing the truth about that day. And, I stopped caring about how others perceived me. After all, people are going to believe what they want to believe, therefore, forming their truths.

*Tears streaming down, her heart is broken*
*Because her life is hurting, so am I*
*He wears a frown, his dreams are choking*
*And because he stands alone, his dreams will die*
*So, humbly I come to you and say*
*As I sound aloud the warfare of today*
*Hear me, I pray*

*What about the children*
*To ignore is so easy*
*So many innocent children would choose the wrong way*
*So what about the children*
*Remember when we were children*
*And if not for those who loved us and who cared enough to show us*
*Where would we be today*

*(from "What About the Children?" lyrics by Yolanda Adams)*

# CHAPTER ELEVEN
## *STORY TO TELL*

There was a point in my freshman year where I felt myself slipping and tried to pull myself back onboard the academic ship; but it didn't happen. I lost all interest in scholastics. The only classes capable of keeping me interested were Spanish and Art. The rest of them were a done deal, especially my fourth period English class. My teacher who held a doctorate degree received her PhD in Boringogomy. Her class was a serious snoozer. We read *The Lord of the Flies, Fahrenheit 451,* and *To Kill a Mockingbird*—and those were good because of the stories' plots, not because of anything that she did special. After reading the epic poem *The Odyssey*, which in my opinion is entirely too long to be considered a poem, I refused to read *The Iliad;* moreover, I refused to listen to her monotone voice do it further injustice. I rarely listened to her at all—I would write poetry and share it with my classmates during her class or sleep. But, one day in the course of my routine nap, she made an announcement about a writing competition. The focus of the essay was "Children living in domestic violence." My ears immediately perked up, and I instantaneously sat at attention. After the bell rang, I stayed behind the other students to ask her for a copy of the writing competition. She gave me one without asking a single question. That was fine because I didn't want to talk to ol' Four Eyes any way about my personal business.

I took the paper to my room at home and read over the entry requirements several times before I began writing. I didn't have much time, for the deadline was only one week away. I cared not for the prize; I just wanted to lend my voice to letting people know that these children are out there, living their lives the best they know how. I unlocked my memory momentarily for the cause and began drafting my experience onto paper. I wrote—tore it up—and wrote some more until I contrived a product worthy of my pride. I took the completed composition to my mother for her perusal. And while she read it, tears rolled down her cheeks as she said, "You remember all of that?"

I nodded my head and faintly told her "More."

More than a month passed, and that writing contest was the farthest thing from my mind. I did my same go-to-school-go-to–work-and-come-home routine when a letter came in the mail addressed to me. I opened it, and it was an invitation to come to City Hall to meet the mayor and other local dignitaries. It stated that I was a finalist in the competition and the winner would be announced at the ceremony. I was elated! I ran to share the news with my mother, and she was excited also. She was so happy that she managed to turn my celebratory event into her own.

She jabbered about how her boss, the mayor, and her former colleagues were going to know her life story and wondered what people she knew would be at the event. And, the more she spoke, my enjoyment lessened. My mother had an annoying way of sharing my happiness.

It was cold and damp outside during the night of the event. I remember my mother and me walking briskly across the dark street and entering the enchanting, historic building of City Hall. We were greeted warmly, and the place was filled with people— caterers, politicians, students, parents, and news reporters. Gloomy compositions from student contestants hung around the walls of that room in City Hall—stories written by children who lived in the city and witnessed domestic violence first hand. There were too many tales to read in one sitting. My essay received honorable mention and placed third in the contest. The winner rightfully deserved his recognition. He lost his mother to the hands of Domestic Violence. Hearing his story made me think how I could have easily have been him. My mother could have shared the same fate as his mother had she not gotten out in time. My feelings were erratic. I praised God in thankfulness and simultaneously cried for him, for his family, and for the multitude of children who shared our pain; for we were members of a special club all our own. Children who are dwelling in homes with domestic violence come in all shades; they are members of all faiths; they are both male and female, and are of various socio-economic groups. The majority of these children will become parents—some of them will abuse their children, some of them will abuse their spouse; some of them will be drug addicts and alcoholics. Some of them will go to jail for committing a violent crime. Some of them will shy away from the opposite sex because of fear. Some of the young men will have difficulties loving and respecting women, while some of the young women will find knowing her worth difficult; and some of these children will find the strength within to do great and noble things. Where did I fit in this sea of hurting children?

*2. a desire to satisfy any bodily need or craving.*
*3. a desire or inclination for something; taste.*

*(Random House Webster's College Dictionary: 2001)*

# CHAPTER TWELVE
## *APPETITE*

C yphers give lyricists a competitive arena to display their talent in unrehearsed musical rhetoric. The lyricist with the strongest "punch lines" wins the free-style challenge. It is amazing to watch gifted men and women orally construct syntax with evolving metaphorical tropes without the use of any writing materials and without reciting lyrics previously written. Blaine was the master at his lyrical craft. Typically, I would listen to his raps blare from my radio speakers at home, cheering all the while he "ate up" his competition on the station's weekly free style battles, or I'd watch him at the bus depot on Ogontz Avenue battle anyone willing. But, on this brisk autumn afternoon, I decided to watch the rapping sophomore phenomenon "battle" his opponent, a senior football player, at school. The classroom that housed the Cypher was packed to capacity. Many students of various classes remained after school to witness the highly anticipated slaughter. The football star confidently took his place on a piano's bench and used it as his platform for "spittin'" his rhymes. Blaine stood next to the black piano studying the sitting challenger, taking in his every word, until it was his turn to deliver. I loved watching him in the act—he'd scrunch up his face, curl his upper lip, and squint his eyes as the cleverly arranged words flowed effortlessly from his mouth. He'd wave one hand around like a band instructor waving his baton while his other with opened palm moved back and forth in front of his groin. It was the funniest thing to witness in his zealous presentation.

Blaine's verse struck a palpable nerve in his senior opponent: with each line that surged from Blaine's mouth, the football star began to slowly rise off of the bench with his fingers erect pointed at "The Boi B." Blaine remained cool and seemed to enjoy knowing that he was able to rouse such a powerful emotion from his senior opponent. Blaine was the winner, and his victory was apparent to everyone—even the football player.

My girlfriends and I bellowed a cry of laughter over the lyrical slaying as we walked out of the room, bent over from an aching belly, into the hallway. I took the liberty of entertaining my friends by imitating Blaine with all of his performance mannerisms and repeating one of the verses he said to the senior: "I'll rip out your esophagus and piss on your tonsils!" My girlfriends found it extra amusing seeing Blaine standing there watching unbeknownst to me. He walked over and commented on my impersonation while my girlfriends made their exit. His commentary led to longer conversations which eventually led to him asking me to be his "girl." Mission accomplished. I definitely liked him enough to be in a relationship. In fact, I liked him more than he even knew. He was one of three contenders in the running to the unlocking of my chastity belt. The ordeal with Nick awakened dormant childhood feelings implanted by the experience with Rasheed. No longer did I want them repressed; I yearned to satisfy my appetite.

I listened to the scare tactics of adult advocates for abstinence: once a boy gets what he wants sexually from a female, he loses interest in her. I wanted to experience the pleasure without being subjected to the consequence, so I developed a plan for prevention—I would tell my candidates that I held a staunch position on pre-marital sex. The gentleman who respected my wishes would be rewarded by the receipt of my special once-in-a-lifetime gift. The winner who was given the key to unlock my chastity belt was Blaine's classmate, Champ— he claimed his prize later that summer. A boy from church and Blaine were my two runners up. Blaine lost his shot when he followed up the question "Do you want to be my girl?" with "Are you having sex?" Just like that, he posed his query without a smooth transitional sentence. His subsequent question caught me off guard and soured the excitement of being his girl. I caught my breath and enlightened him to my feigned moral position. His thought-provoking reply was "What's the difference between being boyfriend and girlfriend from being regular friends if you ain't fuckin'?" Blaine was prepared to lay down the rules for females considering being his girlfriend. I definitely respected forthrightness. Most males would have agreed to date me all the while having ulterior motives, but not Blaine. Since I was without a definitive answer, I decided to bow out gracefully from the prospective relationship and make the suggestion that he and I simply remain friends. And friends we remained until the both of us transferred schools.

My final choice, the champion, was safe. He didn't pressure me; he wasn't a player; and he didn't betray my confidence. He and I remained a couple until my freshman year in college. Even though he was scrawny, he had the willingness to come to my defense to protect me against guys twice his size. Everyone knew that he loved me, and I deeply cared for him.

*"Heaven has no rage like love to hatred turned /*
*Nor hell a fury like a woman scorned."*

*(from The Mourning Bride (1697) by William Congreve)*

# CHAPTER THIRTEEN
## *JEALOUS GIRL*

A s a young adult, I was not in want of male attention, for I received more than my share of it. In high school, I perceived that I was not the prettiest girl, but I had definite sex appeal. Whenever I walked into a room, my nonverbal presence demanded attention. My body was curvaceous: a small waist coupled with a round rump, and I inherited the sashay and infectious smile of my mother. As I entered the cafeteria, neighborhood, or church, I noticed no one, but I could sense eyes targeting every inch of me—I could feel male eyes exploring my body, sizing me up in determination of whether or not they considered me to be their type. I could feel female eyes dissecting every fiber of my wardrobe while calculating how much of a threat they considered me to be. As I walked, I would put on a face of confidence and focus, but, internally, the eyes made me feel uncomfortable and the attention was unwanted.

Guys were mysteriously attracted to my sassy attitude, especially when I met their advances with rejection. The words "I have a boyfriend" were apparently Greek to the horny male pursuers. A female classmate once called me "ignorant" after I publicly and boisterously rebuked an aficionado. I wasn't being intentionally rude; I just never considered their feelings—I only considered my own. I grew tired of males approaching me and interrupting my conversations to make their interest known or commenting on my anatomy as if they've just made some great revolutionary scientific discovery all the while insulting me by sharing their detection as if I did not see it every day in the mirror. To me, *they* were the ones who were rude. I grew so tired of their backhanded compliments that I wrote the following poem on March 30, 1997 and revised it in 2005 (when it was still applicable); it's appropriately entitled *"Lines"*:

*Hey yo, shorty can I get your name?*
*How about your number?*
*You got a minute? Matter of fact, do you got a lover?*
*Is he treatin' you right? If not, hit me up.*
*And maybe we can get together and have a little fun*

*Excuse me miss. Hello, my name's Blazae.*
*I saw you across the street and said, "Damn, swing that my way!"*

*What's up, Sexy? Why you walkin' all alone?*
*The way you look somebody might grab you and take you home.*
*Damn girl! How old is you carrying all of that?*
*Shorty got some pretty legs and a fatty in the back.*

*Ya'll don't know who I am? My name is Shanita.*
*Or maybe I forgot, did I tell you my name was Keisha?*
*Or Sabrina or Tamika, what number did I give you?*
*Was it a fax, a Chinese store, or did I hang up and pretend I lost my signal?*
*Do you really expect to be taken seriously when you come at me like you do?*
*No, you weren't rude, but I heard the same line from corn ball one and number two.*
*When you approach me, I expect you to step correct.*
*Have your pants pulled up, hair brushed, and a tight rap.*
*Stimulate my mind—there's no need to talk about my body.*

*And, please think before you speak*
*Before you spoke, I could not tell that you were a dummy!*
*The best line you can spit is something genuine—from the heart.*
*Something not rehearsed and something that can produce a spark-le*
*in my eye*
*or a twitch in my lips to form a smile, of which you can never*
*forget.*
*My reply to you will be, "I've never heard anything like that."*
*Proving your distinction and giving approval of your rap.*
*And then I'll give you my birth name and even the right number*
*So later we can converse, discuss your line, and maybe go out on a*
*date…*
*or something.*

After my classmate brought my discourtesy to my attention, I practiced being nicer to gentlemen who were courageous enough to face potential rejection from a member of the opposite sex. Depending upon their approach, I figured they deserved civility at the least.

Champ satisfied my sexual appetite, but he was unable to repair the chip on my shoulder that ran deeper than any ocean. Early in our relationship, I shared that I had trust issues with males because of my father. I opened myself up to him like to no other before by telling him some of the horrific details of my childhood and entrusting my heart to his care. As time progressed, I gradually began tearing down some of the bricks that formed my Berlin wall. As I said before, Champ was safe. He was cute—a complexion of butter with wavy jet black hair and eyes that appeared light brown when hit at exactly the right angle by the sun—but he was also extra skinny, so I was confident that if he ever tried to lay a hand on me, I could wipe the floor with him. Watching my father physically abuse my mother influenced my decision early on of not selecting large or muscular guys. I wanted to know that if it ever came down to us having a physical altercation, I could stand a chance. Champ had no resemblances to my father—he was a straight edge guy who didn't smoke, or drink, or womanize; he was openly affectionate, compassionate, and generous—this made him perfect for me. People would tease me about him and say that I could do better because his teeth weren't the best, he wasn't a flashy dresser, and he wasn't the typical neighborhood boy. But those types of guys were high risk to me; the ones that every girl swooned over did not interest me in the least. Guys who flashed a lot of money and boasted about street pharmaceutical sales did not impress me. And as far as school boys go, I didn't want a jock. I wanted someone different…like me. But Champ wasn't perfect; he was still a man, or, even worse but more accurate, he was a teenage boy.

Flirtation was Champ's vice; he wouldn't cross the line, but he treaded it too close for my comfort. I was an attractive girl who could have had almost any guy that she wanted, but, after I lost my virginity, I became obsessively possessive over my nerdy boyfriend. When I saw him talking to any female that I knew he had been romantically involved with, my blood boiled with jealous rage. Where did these feelings come from? They weren't there before…or were they? There was a freshman girl who he admitted he had slept with prior to our relationship. According to him, she was a known "smut," and he could "get it" from her whenever he pleased. Well, I had him meet me in the cafeteria one day while she was present, and I walked up to her and invited myself to join her at her table. Once there, I cut straight to the point without entertaining any polite small talk. I made it crystal clear that he was my man, and she was not permitted to talk to him anymore. I was like a bitch undoubtedly marking her territory. I made him confirm my words to avoid any misunderstandings. She said, "okay" and that was that.

Later that week, I decided not to go to my seventh period Chemistry class, and I wanted to call out of work for the day while I was at it. I picked up the receiver to a pay phone in the hallway, put my quarter in the coin slot, and dialed the number to my job. Champ had no clue that I wasn't in class. While delivering my fabricated excuse to my manager, I glanced to my right only to see Champ walking in the hallway behind a girl with his arms firmly wrapped around her waist and his chin resting on her right shoulder—the same girl that I had spoken to on the week before. They must have thought that I was joking. They had to have believed that I did not mean the words that I spoke. Either that or they were blatantly taking me for a joke. I dropped the phone and sprinted as fast as I could down the hallway; I was going to beat her until I could no longer see her. The girl had some form of intelligence evidenced by her running whilst he grabbed me by the waist in an attempt to constrain me. I was a living spectacle. I kicked my legs in the air at the same time as I beat him upside his head. He carried me inside my classroom twenty minutes late, told my teacher that I belonged in there, and shut the door whilst I cussed him as loud as my voice could carry. I angrily took my seat, slouched down, and wore an expression that dared even the teacher to say one solitary word.

His ex-girlfriend was the biggest one on my list to hate. She was short, light-skinned, and cute. He had the nerve to tell me once, after he found out she was dating someone steadily and lost her virginity, that he regretted the fact that he never slept with her. Oh! Really! This was how he felt after he slept with me and took my virginity. I really, really despised her when I should have been angry with him and myself. The poor girl did absolutely nothing to me and was always sweet as pie, but the fact that he wanted her, *and I knew it*, drove me insane. I wanted to hurt her physically and tried many times to provoke her so that I could get the opportunity. I wasn't one of those girls who walked over to someone and said, "Hey, I wanna fight you." That wasn't my style. I needed to be given a reason. And, when someone wasn't giving me one on their own, I tried to provide them with a little assistance. I wrote things about her in the school's notorious *Slam Book,* a book that was passed around from person to person where you could write any and everything you wanted about a person for all eyes to see. One day she and her friend approached me about the things that I was writing and saying about her. She tapped me on the shoulder while I was talking to Champ and one of my girlfriends outside of our school's gym. I turned around, noticed her, and looked her up and down good enough to say, *WHAT!?!*

She said "I heard you got a problem with me, and my name keeps comin' out of ya mouth."

I chuckled light-heartedly and looked toward her big, ebony girlfriend who was- socially- like a flightless bird. The two of them together approaching me like they wanted to actually do something was all too comical. I ceased my laughter long enough to say "You already know I don't like you and when I talk about you I call you everything but your name."

With that said, I turned my back to her and her queer sidekick and resumed my conversation. Seeing the expression on her face was priceless. If I was her, I would have hit me, but she outclassed me by far. Since I did not get the response from her that I inspired, I decided to seek gratification by hurting her pocketbook instead. One day after school, I broke into her locker and stole all of her text books. Please keep in my mind that we had six class periods and a lunch. I strategically placed each text book in a different trash can around the school making it impossible for her to recover all of them. I knew that she would have to pay for those books before she was able to graduate, and each book cost at least fifty dollars. Seeing her stunned expression the following day when she opened her locker was invaluable, and it was a joy I had to savor alone, for I could never bring myself to share the information with Champ.

Champ and I shared lockers. We used his locker (which was directly next to his ex-girlfriend's) for our books, and my locker for our gym clothes since it was the closest to the gymnasium. Every day, he would walk me to each of my classes. Sixth period I had gym, and he had lunch, so his female friend would accompany us to my class, watch us kiss and hug, and go to the cafeteria with him for lunch. She would always say what a cute couple we were and *"awww"* after each time we smooched. Eventually, she stopped walking us to my gym class and decided to just meet him upstairs in the cafeteria which was perfectly fine by me. When she stopped accompanying us, I noticed a change in his behavior. He was short with our conversations, would peck me and rush off. One day I tried to make him stay longer, and he protested by saying that he couldn't because *she* was waiting for him. I snapped and retorted that I was his girlfriend, not her.

I asked him if he liked her and he replied "No, you're just being insecure."

I felt stupid for even asking and started questioning myself. Was I really insecure? After all, she wasn't prettier than me, in my estimation. Her bottom teeth overlapped her top, her clothing was wack, and her hair was rarely done. What was there for me to feel threatened by?

May 1999 quickly arrived, and the time was nearing for Champ and me to celebrate our one-year anniversary. He came over to my house while my mother wasn't home, and we sat on my deck chatting. I sat on his lap with my arms around his neck while I told him how much I loved him and how excited I was that we had spent almost a year together. He smiled faintly and was unusually quiet. I asked what was wrong, and he requested that I move to sit in a chair. I did. He looked at me, and then looked away. Then, he turned and looked at me again with tears in his eyes. He kept talking to himself, saying repeatedly, "I ain't shit." He was beginning to scare me. Without further hesitation, he told me that he *almost* cheated on me with Nene, his female friend that he ate lunch with! I wanted him to define "almost." He clarified by saying that he *almost* kissed her and that he had grabbed her butt. So, now he was in the booty-grabbing business of unattractive females while *not* secretly wishing that he could screw his ex-girlfriend.

How could he do this to me when I told him how I felt about men? I told him that I had trust issues. He waited for me to tear down my wall and leave my heart vulnerable for him to hurt me. Happy one year anniversary to me! I experienced heartbreak from a man other than my father for the very first time during my sophomore year of high school. He was square, he was scrawny, he was safe…but, he was a young *man*.

*My eyes grew dim, and I could no more gaze;*
  *A wave of longing through my body swept,*
*And, hungry for the old, familiar ways,*
  *I turned aside and bowed my head and wept.*

—Claude McKay (from "The Tropics in New York)

# CHAPTER FOURTEEN
## *UPROOTED*

Often, it takes losing something that you love in order to place what's truly important into perspective. It's unfortunate that people are wired that way. Tragedy, misfortune, or a loss of some sort always seems to do the trick. It took me losing the most stable environment I ever had for me to get my "ah hah" moment. My mother was not very involved with me throughout my childhood, and until the age of sixteen, I always understood. *Mommy has to work, I understand. Mommy is a single parent, I understand. Mommy doesn't have any money, I understand. Mommy makes me clean the entire house while my brother gets to play, but I understand; it's because I'm a girl and I'm going to be someone's wife one day. My mommy punishes me more than my brother, but I understand; she's easy on him because he doesn't have a father, and I'm lucky because I have her.* My mother believed in her heart that, since I was a girl, I didn't need a father—all I needed was her, my mother. This is one of the biggest misconceived notions. I needed a father's love, also. I needed a father's affirmation of my self-importance, acceptance, and love. A girl receives her first impression of how a man is supposed to love a woman, protect a woman, and provide for a woman through her father.

I was looking for a father's love in my boyfriend, and, the moment he let me down, I was crushed. Yes, I had the presence of my mother. She fed me, provided me with shelter, talked to me about her life, and took me to church twice a week (and all youth activities) to encourage my spiritual growth, but that's it. I received nothing more from her. I was alone virtually raising myself and hurting inside. I had no one, except my boyfriend, to take any interest in me or my future goals. Therefore, why did my mother act so surprised when she received my end of the year report card which documented that I had over sixty absences in my classes? She questioned me with wide bewildered eyes, and I return her look with cynicism. She wanted to know why she was finding this information out now, at the end of my sophomore year. I told her it had been no secret, my absences were marked on all of the progress reports I received. She then wanted to know why she never received them. I told her frankly, "Because you never asked. Come on Mom let's be for real. Do you really believe that this was the only report card that I received all year?"

My mother had a rough three years with two cervical spine surgeries, two hospitalizations, and bad ends to her relationships. I stuck it out through it all, but her relationship with her fiancé drew a wedge. I hated the way he treated my brother and my mother. He would speak to her as if she was mentally challenged and had problems with comprehension. Love was never discerned between them. And, there was something about his spirit that clashed with my own. I believe that if they would have remained involved, he would have tried to molest me.

A few years back, during fall of 1999, he started ranting about how our home was his house. I did not hesitate to remind him of reality. He continued his rant while my mother went into the kitchen to cook, and I tried to ignore him by playing on our computer, in our dining room. Being ignored did not suit his ego, so he walked over to me and scooted down beside me. I told him to move and leave me alone. I was beginning to feel like a volcano, suppressing my rage. My mother taught me to be respectful to adults; I admit that was a mouthy child, but I never cussed them—he wanted to be my first. He kept talking, and I kept ignoring him. He shot me a furtive smirk that I saw from my peripheral vision and acted as if he was about to get up to leave when, out of the blue, he whirled his tongue around the inside of my ear and licked my left cheek, his tongue moving from my jaw line upward towards my eye.

I had uncles who played too much, cousins who played too much, a brother who played entirely too much, but a grown man has no business placing his tongue inside a child's ear, especially a child who is supposed to be like his daughter! I cussed him. Boy, did I cuss him. I was furious. My expletives spewed out of my mouth like lava; I erupted. I was so angry that I could no longer speak when I went into the kitchen to tell my mother. I couldn't even see her because she was blurred by my tears. She told me to sit down at the kitchen table and calm down. He walked into our kitchen grinning, and, when she asked him what was wrong with me, he looked over in my direction, grabbed my mother by her ass and tongued her down right in front of me. She put up no resistance and made no objections. More venom spewed from my lips. He stopped kissing her. Looked over at me again and this time he palmed her left breast and started jiggling it in my eye view.

I yelled out, "Fuck you pussy! I hope your dick falls off!"

My mother shouted, "FLORA!!!"

I ran upstairs to my room and bawled into my pillow. Shortly after that event she severed their relationship. Not because of what he did to me, but because she realized he wasn't in it for her. Later she apologized to me for the event, but, in my mind, I had too many "what ifs."

For my sixteenth birthday, all I wanted (and I made it clear) was my driver's license. My school did not offer driver's education, so I studied the State of Pennsylvania's driving manual for months on my own. My mother knew that I could drive: I learned how at twelve while vacationing in Virginia. I could parallel park and everything. I didn't even request a car; all I wanted was for her to take me to the exam, so I could test for my license. I was even willing to pay for it.

When my sixteenth birthday came, it was special. My friends at school really outdid themselves with balloons, cards, flowers, cake, etc. I had so much stuff, that I couldn't take it all on SEPTA. I called my mom to pick me up. She did. I couldn't wait for her to take me to the Department of Motor Vehicles. The excitement was all too much. She brought me to our home, and I ran my stuff up to my room. Shortly thereafter, she entered carrying a gift-wrapped box. What was this?—a present. She didn't have to do that. I told her all that I wanted was for her to drive me to the D.M.V. This was sweet. I smiled and un-wrapped the box. It was a women's devotional Bible.

I was confused. I looked up and said, "Mommy, you bought me a Bible last year."

She said, "You can never have too many Bibles, and this one is a Women's Devotional. The other one was a student Bible."

I felt that it was necessary to inquire if we were still going to the D.M.V. She said we were not. I asked why, pleaded my case, and ensured that she would not have to pay a dime

"No."

Just like that, my sweet sixteen was ruined. Well, according to her, I was no longer "sweet" anyway because I wasn't a virgin.

A couple of weeks after the receipt of my report card, my mother dropped a bomb. She said that I was moving back to Delaware because I wasn't doing what I needed to do at Central, and she did not want me attending our neighborhood high school. She wanted me to end the relationship with my boyfriend, and, since I refused, I had to move away. The three years that I spent in West Oak Lane had brought a sense of stability, and now, she wanted to take that away from me.

I thought she was bluffing. In fact, I was convinced. I knew that I was going to spend the summer in Delaware like years past and come back home to Philly. I was cool until she started bringing home boxes and talking about how she didn't want to split up the family so all of us were moving to Delaware. This chick was really serious. Since her injury, my mother was unable to return to active duty. She was not even able to take a desk job because it would require the constant bending of her neck. The city of Philadelphia deemed her to be disabled and retired her from service; therefore, releasing her from its mandate of residing in the city. With the city's rules for residency no longer in effect, I had to start planning. There had to be a way around this. I hated living there. Without a car for a teen, Delaware felt like a teenage death trap.

The three of us and our Rottweiler, Onyx, moved into two of the four bedrooms in my grandparents' home. All of our belongings, excluding our clothing, were placed into storage. I was a miserable sixteen-year-old girl forced to share a room with my younger brother. Privacy was a luxury in lack. I placed pictures of all of my friends from Central and my West Oak Lane neighborhood on the wall adjacent my bed to give me a sense of belonging. I tried to cop deals with my grandparents. I had it all figured out: Their trucking business ran out of Philly, so they traveled to the city daily. They could simply take me with them to the city in the mornings, and I would ride the Orange line from South Philly's Oregon Avenue to Olney to get to and from school. And, in the evenings, I would accompany them back to Del-hell-where.

My grandparents slyly smiled at my proposal and agreed, but not before asserting, "Only if it's okay with your mother." Dang it! Why did everything always have to go past her? She rejected my proposition, of course. Straight shot me down. Said that we were going to head over to the local high school next week to get me registered. This was not going to happen without a fight! I overheard her discussing my schooling with my grandparents. She mentioned the registration requirements; she needed to bring my shot records, birth certificate and/or social security card. I crept out of my listening quarters—the hallway—and up the stairs into her room to embark on my search. Without these records, she was powerless. There was no way she could place me in that school. I searched…and searched until I finally found my birth certificate and social security card. *VICTORY,* my heart sang. *Let me see her register me now,* I thought. *She'll have no choice but to send me back to Central.*

The time for registration came, and she could not find my records. I told her that I had them and that I was not going to that school. She sternly demanded that I give them back. I said that I couldn't because I destroyed them (I lied). She was beyond the point of frustration, and I was in high spirits. Now, she could see how I felt. But, I have to give it to her. My mother was smart. Either that, or she associated herself with some really bright people—people who were intelligent enough to outsmart me. She went to have a little talk with the school and brought me along as an additional punishment. She explained our entire situation to the registrar without sparing any details about my behavior. The glorified receptionist enlightened her while keeping her eyes locked on me that they could admit me temporarily for ninety days which should give my mother more than enough time to order a duplicate certificate and card. WHAT? She could get *another* one? And after all of my troubles, I still was going to that school. My mother looked over at me and smiled good enough to say, *Now, who got who?* I officially fell victim to defeat.

The cyclone of depression swept me and my mother's growing concern over my well-being intensified. I refused to go anywhere, and cried enough tears to cure the Sahara of its drought. My weight plummeted. My mother was beginning to rethink her decision to make me attend school in the state. To uplift my spirits, she allowed Champ to come visit me. I stopped loving Champ the moment he told me what he *almost* did with his "friend." He broke my trust, and I was not about to give him another opportunity to hurt me. Nevertheless, neither he nor my mother had any idea that I no longer wanted to be in a relationship with him. I only continued to date him because I felt stuck. I felt like since I took it upon myself to disobey God and willingly give myself to this man before marriage, I had to marry him. My rationale was the biblical account about Tamar who was raped by her brother. The law stated that if a woman was raped, her assailant had to marry her. I wasn't raped, but I kept the same mode of thinking. I was willing to remain miserable in the relationship because I did not want to dishonor God any further. Man, was I confused. Although my intention was to honor God by sacrificing my happiness and marrying Champ, I was not willing to cease fornicating.

Seeing my boyfriend did not alleviate my depression; it only magnified it. My mother caught us having sex on my grandparents' living room sofa, and, in those brief moments, any hopes that I had of returning to Philadelphia fled faster than a crack head running from the cops. I wouldn't even dare to mention returning to school in Pennsylvania unless I was prepared to relive the experience of her thrashing my head into the garage door. Besides, in the height of her anger over witnessing me in "the act," she disclosed that I couldn't return to Central because I had been disinvited. She said that the school sent her a letter stating that I could not return because of my poor academic performance. All this time, she had used my ignorance to protect me from the pain of learning the consequences of my actions. She willingly moved our family because she did not want me to attend our neighborhood school. She knew all of this while undergoing my relentless attacks and accusations. But now, her sympathy diminished and she was more adamant than ever about her decision to relocate. She suggested that I find a job to take my mind off of my unchangeable situation.

In July, one month before school began, I took a job at a local grocery store. Working was the medicine that I needed. The antidote assuaged me by keeping me occupied and away from home, leaving no free time for my wandering mind. Working presented me an opportunity to escape my desolate situation and to create goals for my earned wages.

Pretty women wonder where my secret lies
I'm not cute or built to suit a fashion model's size
But when I start to tell them
They think I'm telling lies.
I say,
It's in the reach of my arms
The span of my hips,
The stride of my step,
The curl of my lips.
I'm a woman
Phenomenally.
Phenomenal woman,
That's me.
I walk into a room
Just as cool as you please,
And to a man,
The fellows stand or
Fall down on their knees.
Then they swarm around me,
A hive of honey bees.
I say,
It's the fire in my eyes
And the flash of my teeth,
The swing of my waist,
And the joy in my feet.
I'm a woman
Phenomenally.
Phenomenal woman,
That's me.

*Men themselves have wondered*
*What they see in me.*
*They try so much*
*But they can't touch*
*My inner mystery.*
*When I try to show them,*
*They say they still can't see.*
*I say*
*It's in the arch of my back,*
*The sun of my smile,*
*The ride of my breasts,*
*The grace of my style.*
*I'm a woman*
*Phenomenally.*
*Phenomenal woman,*
*That's me.*
*Now you understand*
*Just why my head's not bowed.*
*I don't shout or jump about*
*Or have to talk real loud.*
*When you see me passing*
*It ought to make you proud.*
*I say,*
*It's in the click of my heels,*
*The bend of my hair,*
*The palm of my hand,*
*The need of my care,*
*'Cause I'm a woman*
*Phenomenally.*
*Phenomenal woman,*
*That's me.*

*—Maya Angelou ("Phenomenal Woman")*

# CHAPTER FIFTEEN
## *G-HIGH*

"**G**-High." That school was on serious lock-down. At the time, it reminded me of a maximum security prison without the cavity searches and metal detectors. All of the class and school cutting that I was accustomed to doing at Central was not going down here. These students had zero freedoms. At Central, I was permitted to leave campus to patronize a local store for lunch and had the liberty of eating outside on the school's lawn if I so desired, but, at G-High, the school lunch served in the cafeteria or a brown bag lunch from home were my only dining options. The school was small in contrast to Central High, and the students were not made of the same stock. I often found myself sitting in the classroom bored—not because I preferred to be somewhere else socializing or because I was unmotivated or even because the teacher did not have an interesting delivery of the content, but I was bored to tears because the curriculum lacked rigor; it was unchallenging, and yet many of my classmates still could not grasp the very simple concepts. Attending that school made me appreciate all that I had taken for granted with my education.

At the end of the marking period, I brought home my first report card, and my family was elated because I achieved straight "As." They'd say, "What's wrong Flora? Honey, this report card is beautiful. We're proud of you." Their pride meant absolutely nothing to me because I wasn't proud of myself.

I was very forthcoming when I replied, "I had to attend a stupid school in order to get all "As." Not even a perfect report card, something that I had not previously received in high school, could elevate my spirit.

Being a social butterfly as opposed to a scholar was my downfall at Central High. I did not have to worry about making the same mistake twice at my new school. It did not take long for the Wilmington girls at G.H.S. to zero in on me, and the school cafeteria gave them a stage for their shenanigans. My school attire consisted of heels, dress slacks or nice jeans, and a blouse. If I so desired, I could leave school and go straight to a job interview without changing my clothes. My country club casual style from my previous high school was not well received here. The Wilmington River Side, East Side, and West Side girls liked to wear white tee shirts, jeans that weren't properly fitted, sneakers, or improperly laced Timberland boots. Their hair weaves were horrendous, and they were obscenely loud. Often times one could hear them yelling out their sections of the small city: "I'm from Riverside" or "I'm from Westside." This always struck me as peculiar because it seemed as if each respective side was only a block away from the other. I always said that I lived around the corner from the housing projects in West Philly and even I was not nearly as "ghetto" in my public conduct. I found these girls to be repulsive in every way, and I had no yearning to be associated with what I perceived to be gutter trash. Their unladylike mannerisms put a bad taste in my mouth for their entire city. The group of female thugs obviously picked up on my air of superiority and took it upon themselves to bring me down a peg or two by reminding me of exactly where I was at—G-High…in Delaware.

A girl from my grandparents' development attended the school, and she introduced me to her boyfriend while we were standing in the cafeteria line. When I politely said, "What's Up?"(as is the customary greeting for youth), he picked up on my foreign accent and inquired where I was from. I professed that I was from Philly, and he immediately commenced to loudly mock our city vernacular.

"Yo, Philly is WACK! Ya'll keep saying that old shit, 'corny.' That's so corny."

"Philly is wack?," I replied as my neck jerked back and my face scrunched up in playful disbelief. "But ya'll still say 'wack' and that played out wit Kris Kross... 'Cause inside out is whiggida whiggida whiggida wack!'"

I playfully quoted a Kris Kross lyric with my tone equaling his as I poked fun at their regional dialect in defense of my own, and it seemed that everyone was having a good time. There was a hefty, dark-skinned female standing behind me in line and even she was laughing at my jokes. At the ringing of the bell, I got up to leave the lunch room and walked down the first flight of stairs to get to my next class when someone tapped me on my shoulder. I turned around and there stood before me a frail girl wearing a god-awful stingy side ponytail that looked more like an unbrushed pigtail. The young lady asked me if I was getting smart with her brother in the lunch line.

I asked, "Who is your brother?" and she told me Beazer. Beazer? Who in the world was Beazer? That wasn't the name that my acquaintance used when she introduced me to her boyfriend. But, I hadn't spoken to any other guy, so it had to be him. Maybe it was his nickname or something. I kindly let her know that I was only joking with him. She started talking about how he didn't take it as a joke and some of the girls wanted her to come over to fight me.

Fight. Did she say FIGHT? Even though I was from a different state "Fight" was a language that I spoke rather fluently.

"Oh!" I said as I removed my earring from my left ear.

"Oh, naw, I ain't goin' fight you," said she with a startled expression on her face. You could tell that this wasn't the response that she was expecting. "I just wanted to let you know," she explained. I told her that if she wasn't trying to fight then she should never touch me again or bother me with any dumb shit.

I continued to my destination leaving the young lady standing there in a stupor. The same classmate at Central that called me ignorant in my conduct to male admirers also told me that I was "bourge-ghetto" meaning that I had an uppity demeanor all the while being ready to fight or cuss someone out at the drop of a dime. These girls were about to be formally acquainted with my other side.

The following day I retrieved my lunch, a sub sandwich which was a poor excuse for an Italian hoagie, and, as I was walking to my table, a group of female hecklers yelled out, "Ill! Why does she walk like that?" and "Ha. Ha. Ha. Look at how that bitch walks!"

I was confused. Were they addressing me? They couldn't have been. Sure I had my personal convictions about the school and its location and even many of its attendants, but I kept those thoughts to myself. I didn't go around running my mouth or trash talking. I purposefully kept myself secluded to avoid the drama. So, on what grounds could they have to single me out? None I was convinced, so I looked around to see who exactly it was that they were talking to, and, sure enough, I was the only person walking. No one else was even standing up, and I sensed every eye in the cafeteria staring in my direction waiting to see my next move. I decided to take the high road by ignoring them and continuing on to my seat. WHAM!!! Something hit me in the side of my head. I stopped in my tracks and looked down at the ground, and, on the floor near my left black shoe boot, was a lonely tater tot. No, someone did *not* just throw a damn miniature potato at my head.

I glanced over at the table that seated a number of those classless Wilmington heifers, and all of them were slapping five and bending over shouting in laughter. I just stood there for a moment dumbstruck contemplating retribution. Sizing up my opposition, I figured that I was clearly outnumbered, and it would be in my best interest to brush it off, so I proceeded to my seat. My neighbor and her friends decided to make an already uncomfortable situation worse by saying,

"Flora, you just gonna take that?" and the infamous egg-on phrase, "If that was me, I wouldn't take it."

I said, "What else am I supposed to do? If I fight all of them are any of you going to jump in to help me?"

Unanimously, the table said just what I already knew "No." The things some people will do and say to see a fight is beyond amazement. This group of ugly, cowardly, tatter-tot throwing females had a reputation for 'banking' people, as the Wilmingtonians liked to call a gang of people simultaneously fighting one single individual. I was no fool—at least not while I was thinking clearly; I studied these girls long enough to see how they operated, and they fought dirty. A fair fight was beyond their comprehension. I knew I was alone in that school, and I wasn't about to allow myself to get jumped by a group of oversized females. I started relaying messages through people to the pusillanimous group that they could come and step to me one–on–one whenever they were ready. I'd show them exactly how "prissy" I really was.

While they were together in a group, they didn't get a rise out of me, but, on the few occasions I caught some of them by themselves in the restroom and approached them when they weren't supplied an audience, they'd chuckle and exclaim that they didn't have a problem with me.

The heckling persisted for about a week, and my neighbor told me that the hefty sistah who stood behind me in the lunch line laughing along with us while I was joking around with "Beazer" started the whole fiasco. Rumors spread around the school that I wanted their men. When I rejected all advances and the populace noticed my boyfriend driving up from Philly to pick me up from school every Friday, the immature girls supposed that I thought that I was too good for their men. If I wasn't previously motivated about graduating from high school, I was motivated at that time. I wanted to complete my last two years and get as far away from that school as possible. But, for the moment, Champ was my lifeline to the outside world, so I started to look forward to his visits. He'd pick me up and take me back to Central to socialize with my old classmates. He took me to his proms. He took me back to where I really wanted to be—Philly. The harassment helped me to stay to myself and remain focused on what I came to school for: an education. I reset my sights on college and became determined that nothing was going to distract me from my goal.

Attending the school turned out to be a blessing in disguise because it afforded me an opportunity to take advantage of things that weren't at my disposal prior to my attendance. It offered a driver's education class of which I took full advantage. The class gave me an avenue where I no longer needed my mother to obtain my license; any adult in my house could sign for me. I then took on a new goal. I was going to buy a car. I was able to save two thousand dollars from my part-time job at the supermarket, and I had a comparable amount in my joint account with my great-grandmother. A car would get me a couple of steps closer to my exit from Delaware.

G-High also allowed me the opportunity to discover my passion for cheerleading. Central had a cheerleading squad; however, when I attended, it was unspoken, yet understood that cheerleading belonged to the white female students and Pep Squad belonged to the black. There were always one or two token black females (who could have easily passed for white) on the squad. At G-High, the cheerleading squad was diverse: there were males and females, blacks and whites, plump girls and skinny girls. The squad was dynamic and had a renowned competition team known for winning regional cheerleading championships. These young ladies and men used football and basketball games as additional practices for their competitions.

I tried out for the squad without any expectation of actually making it, but, to my surprise, I did. I made junior varsity. It seemed like most of the squad members, j.v. and varsity alike, craved competition cheerleading. The criterion was that, if a squad member competed, he or she had to also cheer for basketball, football, or both. I tried competition cheerleading initially, but I was not competitively driven. I just wanted to cheer for fun, not sport. So, I elected to cheer only for the basketball games. This was odd because most of the cheerleaders preferred football. I couldn't see any fun in cheering in the freezing cold. Yes, you could do more stunts and tumble across the track, but that did not take away from enduring the harsh northern winters in the process.

Basketball presented an entirely different energy. Since the sport is played indoors, one is able to fully feel the crowd. You can hear their deafening yells echo around the gym and see their excitement. And, as a basketball cheerleader, all eyeballs can be glued on you. I absolutely loved it. I didn't need narcotics or alcohol because cheerleading supplied me with the rush. It was the only time that I enjoyed people watching my every move. I loved performing in front of a crowd and leading them in a victory chant, and I was able to enjoy every minute of it because I took on a different persona during game time. Although I was enthusiastic about my activity, I was not enthused by my teammates. I tried to limit all communication with them by saying only what was absolutely necessary in practices. While cheering at a game, I looked happy and excited about being a student at the school, but in retrospect, I wasn't. For a while, I wanted to quit the squad because I didn't have a sense of belonging, especially at practices when squad members could be cliquish. But I was determined not to be a quitter like I was on the C.H.S Pep Squad. I loved cheering, and there was nothing that anyone could say or do to make me remove myself from my passion. After all, I wasn't cheering for my teammates or to make friends or to even become popular; I was doing it because I loved the high I felt at the games.

Towards the end of my junior year our girls' basketball team played in a championship game against a private high school. The feeling was indescribable. I had gas during the entire game, especially when it was time for us to present our half-time performance. Every bleacher in the sporting complex was occupied. The moment we ran onto center court, we were surrounded by people in the stands meeting our smiles, kicks, and spirit chants with a roar of boos. Looking into the audience for a friendly home-team face that I could focus my attention on in an effort to calm my nerves, I noticed some of the students from *our* school booing us along with the fans of our rival team. Despite the warm hospitality, we cheered our hearts out with unprecedented energy.

After our show, some of us retreated to a nearby restroom to regain our composure. In the midst of my excitement, I forgot that I did not associate with my teammates, and I found myself taking part in a conversation with two of them after making use of the facility. The two girls were sophomores and seemed interested in my personal background. I briefly answered their questions, and, while trying to appear somewhat interested in getting to know them, I met a few of their questions with my own. Even though I had cheered with them for an entire season, this was the first time that I learned their names.

We walked back to take our seats with the other members of our squad and resumed cheering our team. One of the girls that I met in the restroom, named Sharonda, sat directly in front of me. She was a petite, brown-skinned girl with the prettiest straight, long, thick jet black hair I've ever seen—and, it wasn't a weave. Since we were just acquainted, and she seemed cool, I took the liberty of whispering something to her cheer related. This girl whipped around and snapped at me telling me never to touch her again and then she slowly rolled her ovular, brown eyes as she turned back around and continued her cheer. My eyes opened so wide with astonishment that they felt like they were going to pop out of my head at any moment. While all of the girls on my squad cheered and executed their motions, I sat there motionlessly staring at the back of her head. I envisioned myself grabbing hold of her hair and wrapping it several times around my hand while I beat her in her face like it was a paddle ball. Why couldn't I do it? She was sitting right there in front of me; all I had to do was just reach out and grab her. I knew that I would have had the advantage in the way that I planned on gripping the crown of her head into submission, yet I silently wept because I didn't act on my feelings. Something wouldn't allow me to do it. Exhibiting self-control instead of acting out of emotion was painful. The internal struggle inside of my soul was far worse than any blow a person could have delivered. I was actually angry for not striking. What was the problem? Was I afraid of this girl who wasn't as big as a toothpick?

I didn't have the answer. But, I praise God that HE didn't allow me to strike her; had I done so, I may have lost out on a relationship with a friend who is closer to me than my sisters.

How our relationship unfolded remains unclear. Perhaps it was on our cheerleading trips to rival schools. But one thing is certain Sharonda and I shared an unusual life parallel. She was accepted into Central prior to her parents' move to Delaware, and she also has an annoying younger brother who is five years her junior as well as an estranged sister from my father. She always wanted an older sister to fill that void, and I became one to her—giving her advice on boys, doing her makeup for her prom, and talking with her about our love for Christ. Even though I was a year older, I admired Sharonda immensely. The thing I admired most was her obedience to her parents. When she felt she was treated unjustly, she vented to me but always remained obedient. I cannot account one thing Sharonda did while in high school, outside of getting a 'C', that was against her parents' wishes. To me, she was the ideal daughter, student, and teenage girl. She was everything that I wanted to become, and it was important for me to surround myself with her for my personal and spiritual grounding.

*God grant me the serenity to accept the things I cannot change; courage to change the things I can; and wisdom to know the difference.*

*— Reinhold Niebuhr*

# CHAPTER SIXTEEN
## *SERENITY*

B eing forced to change schools is one thing, but being forced to change churches is another. The church where I was saved, baptized, and received my first kiss is the one that my mother decided that we needed to leave after an eleven-year membership. She said that she could no longer afford the weekly commute to Philadelphia. Our new church was in Wilmington—of all places. It felt like everything familiar that I loved was being taken away from me by force all at once. My attitude towards my new church matched that towards my new school (at least I was consistent); however, I was more receptive to my church peers. It's hard being mean inside of the house of God, even when some of the people inside of it act like devils.

One morning while my mother and I were sitting in her room inside of my grandparents' home, she mentioned to me that we were moving again. Our living situation with my grandparents had been less than ideal. My mother had a rocky relationship with my grandmother all throughout her teenage and adult life, and those two dwelling under the same roof was anything but healthy. I definitely was excited about the prospect of moving. I looked forward to not witnessing my mother's daily humiliation when my grandmother decided to publicly cuss out her only daughter; I looked forward to the prospect of no longer having to share a room with my pre-teenage brother who smelled funny; and I looked forward to our lives reacquiring some sense of normalcy.

I sat on her bed beaming all the while awaiting the particulars about our new location and the date for our next family adventure when my mother shifted gears and began telling me some bizarre story about how the Lord laid it upon her heart to give a family in need that attended our new church $2,500 to save their home from foreclosure, and, in return, the family agreed to let the three of us move in with them for six months. Huh? I was only a high school senior, but something didn't add up. For starters, we didn't know these people. We had been attending the church for only three weeks. Two thousand five hundred dollars seemed like enough money for us to move out of my grandparents' house and into a home of our own; why were we giving this money away? *We* were homeless. *We* needed it. I tried questioning her to uncover the logic, but she was adamant about it being what God told her to do.

The move was occurring faster than I anticipated. Later that day, my mother took my brother and me over to our new residence to meet the family. They were nice—a husband, a wife, two little girls, but, as they were showing us around, they pointed out the area where they were placing *the three of us*— a tiny room big enough to be someone's small home office. For additional storage space, we were allotted use of the basement. Their basement served as both our closet and our dresser, for all of our clothing had to remain in garbage bags down there.

Did my father knock the brains out of my mother's head or what? Why was she voluntarily doing this to us? Although the family verbally gave us free range of their home, the three of us nomadic outsiders made certain that we remained unseen. We stayed out of their house as much as possible, only returning there to rest. Neither my mother nor I felt comfortable preparing a meal in a married woman's kitchen or lounging around in our night attire in their family room. Since they believed that their children were impressionable,, they understandably did not want my boyfriend around their home. It was easy to tell that our situation was not what my mother imagined.

About three weeks into our stay, my mother came to me after school and asked if I could attend a family meeting with her at the church. I didn't have to work that day, so I agreed. At the meeting, it was she and I, a deacon (who acted as a mediator), and the married couple we were rooming with. The wife looked pissed off, and she kept her lips tight. Shortly after the start of the meeting that began in prayer, she and my mother went back and forth while I and the woman's husband just sat there trying to tune them both out. I hate the sound of women arguing in the church because they try to mix scripture up in between their *Rah Rah* noises. My mother told them that they used her for her money, and, when she quoted in front of the minister the amount of money that she actually gave to them, the wife shut her eyes tighter than her lips were pursed. She clenched her fists mid-way in the air and brought them down hard with one strong pound to her knees. Her lips parted, her mouth opened, and she finally snapped *"GET OUT! WE WANT YOU OUT OF OUR HOME!"*

Now I was listening, and so was my mother who was quiet for the first time during that meeting. The woman's husband rubbed her back in an effort to calm her down. The deacon sat silent, looking as if he was waiting on the Lord to give him some words to say. Out? They wanted us out? My mother told me that we were going to be living there for six months, and we were only there for three weeks. Where were we going to go? She just gave away our money to a random, unappreciative family who she felt needed it more than we, and this snag-a-tooth heffa is sitting here saying that her and her husband wanted us out. They wouldn't have even had a home to put us out of if it wasn't for my mother's money. I knew my mother wasn't going to take that. I knew my mother was going to rise up and whoop that lady's behind. Huh, if she thought that she was missing her bottom tooth before, wait until my mother gets through with her. I saw my mom fight women in the past, and she could definitely handle her business. And, when I saw my mother grow silent, I thought to myself *Oh, it's on now!*

The family gave us three days to vacate their home. Three days. In that time, I felt that I really needed a vehicle and an additional means for keeping my mind occupied. I found myself a second job at a bank and later discussed the idea of me getting my own vehicle with my mother. She agreed, and, before she had the opportunity to change her mind, I called to share the news with Big Mom-Mom. I told her that I was finally ready for the money that she'd been holding for me. From age three to five, Big Mom-Mom entered me into baby contests and fashion shows. She established a joint account for the monetary awards I received for my participation. Quarterly, she would show me the bank statements, so I knew exactly the amount I had in savings— enough for a down payment on a nice car. Big Mom-Mom was excited about me preparing to make my first big purchase and told me I could drive her to get her ears pierced once I got my new car. Hearing this increased my enthusiasm all the more. When she finished joking, she said that she had been very ill and my great aunt, her youngest daughter, had power of attorney over her accounts, and, since my name was listed as the beneficiary under her name, my aunt had control. She urged me to call her to get the information about how to retrieve my funds.

I hung up the phone with Big Mom-Mom and called my great aunt (who is my godmother) on her line (she conveniently lived in my great-grandmother's living room at the time). She answered the phone and put on her usual happy to hear from me. I made small talk with her before telling her about the conversation that I had just minutes before with Big Mom-Mom. In the blink of an eye, all of the sweetness evaporated from her voice leaving only these chilling words:

"That money's gone. I spent it."

"What do you mean you spent it? it was my money—money that I've been saving since I was a little girl?" I said.

"I spent it, Flora, what else do you want me to say?" she indifferently replied.

"BUT THAT WAS MY MONEY!" I shouted painfully into the phone while my voice cracked. I hung up the phone. This couldn't be happening to me. I called Big Mom-Mom back when I got myself together and repeated verbatim the words of my great aunt, my godmother. Big Mom-Mom didn't question, she only cried. She apologized to me and wished that there was something she could do. She said that my great aunt knew that the money belonged to me; she had made it a point to tell her.

Crushed. Devastated. Another dream torn away by someone I loved. This was not fair. My life was not fair. What did I ever do to my godmother to deserve such betrayal? I bawled in that tiny room, in that house where we weren't welcome, and my mother held me like I was her baby.

It was midnight when we finally got the last of our belongings out of the basement and the bedroom of that house. As my mother returned the key to the wife, she didn't hit her as I had hoped. Instead, she tried to say some kind words to her while the woman slowly closed the door THAT WE PAID FOR in my mother's face. Behind the door we heard the woman shout, *"HALLELUJAH!!!"*

We got inside my mother's car, and I looked in her face. I saw defeat. I saw embarrassment. I saw hurt. The face that I saw sitting there beside me was not the countenance of the mother that I remembered. I remembered my mother having a fighter's spirit. When I saw her before, her face had radiated strength. But, not this time. It didn't appear that any fight was left in her.

I knew about her prior injury and surgeries, so I kindly asked my mother if she wanted me to whoop the lady's ass on her behalf. "No" was her reply. I asked if she wanted to damage their car that was parked right next to ours, and she said rejected that idea as well. Letting that family get away scot-free without a single repayment, court order for repayment, or ass whoopin' for repayment just didn't seem fair. My mother looked to me and said unreassuringly, "Everything's going to be okay." She cranked up her car and repeated the phrase again, this time sounding more like she was trying to believe the words herself. She pulled out of the driveway, away from the big suburban home, and drove us back to my grandparents' house.

*****

Our new church sponsored several of the youths in their ministry to attend a youth camp for a weekend in Dallas, Texas. My mother authorized me to attend. I cannot even front; I was thrilled about the trip. I had never been to Texas before, and one constant remained in my life of consistent unpredictable change—my love for travel. So, on June fifteenth of the year two thousand, my brother and I boarded a plane with several members of our church and flew to worship the Lord in Texas.

Dallas was miserably hot and humid. Breathing was a chore. And, if I thought that the people from Wilmington, Delaware sounded funny when they spoke, I was in for a treat while worshipping with the Dallas saints. The mass of Dallas Christian youth who attended the youth camp were fired up for Jesus. They kept jumping up and down shouting, "Get Crunk for Jesus! Get Crunk for Jesus!" A girl from my new church looked over to me and asked if I knew what "crunk" meant. I told her that I was without a clue. She and I shared a mischievous smile and started jumping up and down simultaneously joining in the screams with our Dallas peers, "Get Crunk, Get Crunk!!!" Neither one of us had a notion what we were saying, but we were having a blast. The youth from our church laughed at us as they remained seated, not getting caught up in the contagious exhilaration. Finally, she asked a local seated near her what "crunk" meant, and the girl laughed hysterically. She told us that it meant hype or excited then inquired where we were from. My church companion said "Delaware." She obviously misspoke. I told the local that *she* was Delaware and *I* was from Philly. I didn't want there to be any geographical misunderstandings. Of course, as I previously experienced, the local girl had no idea where on earth Delaware was located, but she heard a lot about my hometown.

As we were conversing, a youth pastor approached the podium and silenced the young, vivacious, robust crowd. He spoke and called us into prayer and worship. He said that it was a time for forgiveness and healing. He called youth who were hurting forward into the aisles for prayer. I nodded my head and closed my eyes and began to pray for my troubled peers. A few minutes into the prayer, I felt my feet leading my body into the aisle alter bound. I found myself intertwined with the mass of hurting youth who came forward seeking deliverance. With closed eyes but an opened heart, images of my father and his brutality against my mother came into clear sight. Now, I was hurting. Now, I could remember all of the pain that I had tried to lock away for years. Why was God making me remember? A quiet voice in my spirit kept whispering, "Forgive." But, why did I need to forgive a man that I rarely thought about?

"Forgive," it persisted.

Acknowledging that the voice was not my own, I answered back through my inner voice "Lord, I hate this man. I can't forgive him."

"Forgive!" it commanded.

My spirit continued to wrestle with the Spirit until I was overtaken by His love. I felt invisible arms wrap around me letting me know that it was okay. and, although I felt alone, I wasn't alone, and I had support. The Spirit let me know that it was okay to forgive him and there was freedom to be obtained through my forgiveness.

In my heart, I said "I forgive," but that wasn't enough. The Spirit demanded that I profess it with my mouth. This was another struggle. I had to profess all the things that I forgave him for. I wept. Oh, how I wept. The pains that go along with letting go of pain were spiritually agonizing. Forgiving my father still wasn't sufficient. I had to also forgive my great aunt for stealing my money and the family that took advantage of my struggling mother. I surrendered myself into His will and wailed like I was the only one present in the sanctuary. I spoke the words that I meant in my heart, and I forgave those persons even when they never sought my forgiveness. Oh, the freedom!—The glorious, wondrous spiritual freedom that I experienced when I decided to surrender myself and my will and entrust God fully with my heart. I felt relief. I felt joy…real joy—the joy that comes only from the Lord.

In Dallas, Texas, I changed. I received a cleansed heart. Now, I had to perform my final act of forgiveness: I needed to face my father. I told the Lord that I was willing, but I just needed Him to give me a little more time to muster up the strength to do it.

June 20, 2000, two days after my return from the youth camp, my mother drove me to work and took my brother and younger cousin along with her for the ride in her fully loaded Honda Accord EX. This was my first day back to work since my trip. The four of us were laughing and joking on each other and just having a plain ol' good time. My mother stopped at a red light behind two other vehicles on a single lane highway when she decided to crack a joke. As usual, her joke was not funny. In fact, it was so corny that one had to laugh at the sincere effort. I sat in the front passenger's seat shaking my head and smirking at her unbelievable corniness then decided to turn to the right to stare out of my window—CRASH!!!!!!!!!
Sudden Darkness.
Deafness.
Pain.
As I regained my consciousness, I noticed smoke coming from the cracked dashboard. I turned to my left and noticed that my mother was trapped. She mumbled while her head was

resting against her inflated airbag that she couldn't move. I turned around farther to see my brother and cousin holding their necks and moaning in the back. Smoke! I had to get out of there and quick. I unbuckled my seat belt, opened my door, and fell out of the car in my supermarket uniform. I stood up and noticed that our car was sandwiched in between the vehicle that rear-ended us and the vehicle that we were pushed into ahead of us.

I had no voice to scream for help, but, luckily, an ambulance, fire truck, and police officer were in very close proximity and came to our rescue. The paramedics questioned us about the location of our pain and placed each one of us on stretchers and rushed us to the emergency room. The injuries sustained by brother and cousin were minor; however, due to my mother's previous medical history, hers were more severe. Thankfully, no one was hospitalized, including myself, and no one had to undergo surgery.

Later, without a vehicle, my mother told me that it was time for me to get a car. I told her how much I had saved from working at my two jobs, and she told me to use that money to pay for my insurance. She was actually buying me a real gift. We went to a lemon lot and purchased a gas-guzzling, paycheck-taking, nine-year-old, high-mileage vehicle, and I absolutely adored it because it was mine.

The money that my mother was to acquire from her totaled vehicle sparked a bitter battle between her, my grandmother, and my grandmother's sister—the thief. Since the car was registered under my great-grandmother's name, my aunt tried to claim the check for the value of the totaled vehicle. However, the insurance was under my mother's name, and she retained records that proved that she made all of the payments on the vehicle; therefore, it was rightfully hers. My grandmother also felt as if she had invested interest in the accident. All-in-all, everyone wanted a slice of the pie. The feuding in the home made it once again uninhabitable, so my mother announced another move. This time she mentioned *buying* a house in Wilmington, and, on that note, I had to speak up. I told her that I didn't leave my 'hood only to be moved into another one. We could have stayed in Philly if she wanted to move us into the most urban section of Delaware, Wilmington. She finally listened to me and rethought our locale.

House hunting was entertaining. I enjoyed driving by homes and touring the inside of them while trying to picture myself inhabiting that space. One home that we toured had ten bedrooms, an indoor pond, intercoms in every room of the home, a basketball court, volleyball court, swimming pool, and water well. I begged my mother to purchase that home. The outside of the house was quite deceiving for it was a hideous shade of green, very simple in structure, and not aesthetically appealing; however, once I crossed its threshold, I was enthralled.

My mother and her realtor brought us to a three-bedroom row home, what suburbanites refer to as a town house, which had a front and back yard and all of the accommodations that we were familiar with in Philadelphia with the exception of its multiple bathrooms and dishwasher. At last, my mother was considering moving into a house that had a dishwasher. I detested dishwashing; in previous years, my mother would wake me up 4 o'clock in the morning just to prove a point about going to bed while leaving dishes in her sink. I vowed to never wash a single dish by hand again once I moved out into a home of my own. I shared my enthusiasm with my dream-shattering mother who immediately made it plain that *I* was the dishwasher, and, even if the house came with a mechanical dishwasher, it was not to be used. She didn't have to get smart.

She was talking like the house was already ours. Wait a minute … it *was* ours! She said that we were about to make our last move because she had already bought that house. No one would tell us to "get out" again. I no longer had to share a room with my disgusting younger brother. I could invite company over to *our* home. Standing inside of the quaint residence, with its aged brick colored carpet, I understood what Dorothy meant when she said in *The Wizard of Oz* that "There's no place like home."

*There is no disguise which can hide love for long where it exists, or simulate it where it does not.*

—*Francois de L5a Rochefoucauld*

# CHAPTER SEVENTEEN
## *BOY~FRIEND*

During my initial transfer to G-High, I was required to attend New Student orientation where I met several male students in my class, one of whom ended up being in my homeroom. The boy was very attractive—tall and brown skin with a resounding masculine voice. His smile was wide and bright and reminded me of my own. But I was not overtaken by his beauty because he wasn't my type. The moment school began our junior year, it was hard to use a female restroom or sit at a lunch table filled predominately by teenage girls without hearing how "FINE" he was. He was one of those guys who was confident in his appearance and secure in the fact that he could get anyone of those females at the school—well, almost anyone. That type of male never interested me. I didn't yearn for the guy who all females swooned over. After all, who really wants to be in competition with their counterpart?

He and I spoke infrequently during our junior year, but, in our senior year, that all changed. We found ourselves developing a strong fondness for one another. He appreciated my difference and noticed how I did not make a fuss over anyone or involve myself in silly gossip. Instead, I came to school, participated in cheerleading, and went home. He liked how I didn't throw myself at him like many of the girls, and he especially liked how I carried myself in a respectable manner. I enjoyed his conversation and wit and found him to be very easy to talk to. And the fact that he exhibited no attraction to me was a plus. We developed exclusive pet names for each other in which he and I held the sole right of reference—I called him He-sh because I told him that he looked like a guy and whined like a girl, and he called me Shim because he said I *was* a dude.

Homeroom became an interim class that I looked forward to attending, for I knew that I was sure to see my friend. He and I discussed the state our relationships—he was my male confidant, and I was his female. He was impressed by the relationship that I had with Champ—how it was long distance, and how we were together for almost three years, and how he was the only person that I was intimate with, and how I was faithful to him although we lived far apart. As our friendship grew stronger, I confided in him that all was not as it seemed between Champ and me. I told him how he betrayed my trust and how I remained in our relationship out of obligation. He spoke to me in confidence about him getting his girlfriend, who he met the summer before school began, pregnant. He told me that she initiated everything from their first meeting all the way to their romantic encounter. He admitted that he had regrets but intended to do right by her and their child. I encouraged him to do so and applauded his willingness to step up to handle his responsibility. He encouraged me to find the strength to get out of my hopeless relationship. Having a male friend that I could talk to and lean on without any strings attached was comforting.

He-sh and I exchanged telephone numbers and spent many nights on the phone griping about each other's insignificant other. Eventually, those conversations that began with the purest of intentions lead to us feeling more for one another. I conveyed to him while trying to convince myself the reasons why he and I could not be together—we were both in relationships and his involved a baby. Neither of us wanted our partners to get hurt by our actions. Also, we differed in our faiths and the Bible preached about being unequally yoked. My mother would have jumped out of her skin if she knew that I was getting cozy with a Jehovah's Witness. Although I had established boundaries, I felt that the time had come for me to end my relationship with Champ. It was my thought that if I was fantasizing about being with another, it was a definite sign that we shouldn't be together.

I made the decision to no longer ride on my self-created love roller coaster by contacting Champ; however, he made breaking up with him next to impossible. He reiterated what he told me during his senior year in high school that his purpose for attending college in Delaware was to be closer to me. He followed that statement by displaying no evidence of pride while proclaiming his love and intention of making me his wife. He professed that if I decided to step outside of our relationship to become involved with someone else, he would be hurt by my infidelity; yet, it would not lessen his desire to remain with me. I thought to myself, *This guy is sick.* I apologized to him as earnestly as I could before telling him that it was over and hanging up the phone.

He called so many times that evening that I was forced to turn off my cell phone if I wanted to get any rest for school the next day. Worry free, stress free, and Champ free is how I felt as I walked through the hallways of G-High the following day. At the chime of the seventh period bell, I rushed outside to my vehicle only to notice a familiar image standing by my car—Champ. There he was standing beside it telling me that we couldn't break up; he loved me. He looked pitiful and pathetic. I was embarrassed. What was I to do? I couldn't even escape him at school. I didn't want to listen to him beg and plead any longer, and I certainly didn't want to put him through any more pain, so I agreed to stay.

The longer I remained with Champ, the stronger my feelings became for He-sh. He and I would pour out our affections in letters which we'd address and sign in our special names. In his notes, he'd confess his guilt for dreaming about me while lying in bed with his expecting girlfriend. I would tell him how I shared his admiration but protested against acting out on our feelings. He and I dared not to tell our closest friends because we both had much too much at stake. We remained very discreet and did not associate with each other outside of homeroom. But all our caution didn't matter when his live-in girlfriend came across one of my letters. When she approached him, he assumed full responsibility for the letter but refused to reveal my identity. He and everyone else in the school knew that his girlfriend was not dealing with a full deck of mental cards. She was a master in martial arts and played a small role in a film where she beat the crap out of a very muscular man. In school, she intimidated many females, and males for that matter. I, of course, knew all that I was up against when I allowed myself to fall for her baby's father. He-sh honestly felt that he handled the situation and I had nothing to worry about; boy, was he wrong.

She'd spent a number of consecutive days out of school because she was ill from her pregnancy, but upon finding the letter she returned the next day without He-sh's knowledge. This was one momma on a G.A.T.A. mission. She went around the school inquiring "Who does [he] call Shim?" Ultimately, she found her answer. I was sitting in the cafeteria laughing with my best friend, Sharonda, when his girlfriend came and sat directly in front of me. I didn't pay her any attention at first, but I could feel her eyes burning a hole in my skin. She made it her business not to talk to anybody. She just sat there—across from me— quietly, calmly staring me in my guilt-ridden face.

Growing tired of the awkwardness of the situation, I broke the ice by asking her "Do you have a problem?"

She folded her hands and moved forward on the table, resting her chest against its edge and responded, "Not anymore now that I found the girl that has been writing my man letters!"

My throat fell into my feet—I was speechless. I wasn't going to label this truth as fiction, so what could I really say? Geez, I wished He-sh would have prepared me for this. She slid her legs from beneath the table to stand up and remove her jacket while publicly disclaiming that she was about to talk to me with her fists. Damn it! Why did I wear a skirt and dress shoes today of all days? I didn't wake up this morning look in my closet and say, "You better dress for a fight today." But, damn my attire. Where I'm from, if somebody calls you out for a fight and you refuse, that makes you a punk. And, I was nobody's punk. My instinctive nature got the best of me, for I certainly didn't know any karate when I boldly accepted her challenge by stating "We can do whatever!"

With these words, our side of the cafeteria roared with excitement. This was one fight they wanted to see—the pregnant karate kid kicking the stuck-up cheerleader's butt! Sharonda turned to me and said, "You can't fight her; she's pregnant."

She's pregnant? She's pregnant. I didn't even think about that. Thank goodness for my little sister who acted as my voice of reason. One part of me thought, *Shucks. If she didn't care about her baby, then why should I?* Another part, (the more logical one) knew that it wasn't right to fight her while she was carrying his baby. Honestly, I didn't care much about her or her unborn child, but I did care about him. I asked her if we could go somewhere to talk, and she complied with my request. Once alone, she softened. I could see that she was an actual caring and feeling person when she started crying. I began to feel remorse as she spoke of the promises that He-Sh had made to her. I explained to her as best I could that it was all innocent. I tried to reassure her that neither of us crossed the line by carrying out any of our feelings. I apologized for the pain that I had caused her and gave her my telephone number in case she had any questions later on. She told me that her family and friends volunteered to jump me since she wasn't supposed to fight while carrying a child, but she declined their offers. (That wasn't something that I was expecting to hear.) She also mentioned how I was the last person who she would suspect to be after her man. She told me that she admired my willingness to fight her and that she had a lot of respect for me.

At that point, I was at a matchless low. We ended our conversation, and I walked out of the door towards my car, not caring about the school's consequences. I couldn't face the disgrace of having people know that I was going after another female's man while I had my own.

He-Sh apologized and explained everything to me. We both agreed that it would be in everyone's best interest if he and I ended our friendship. Homeroom wasn't the same seeing him every day but being unable to communicate with my friend. We made a point not to look at each other or even speak to each other. And, to put the icing on the cake, his baby's momma made it her point to walk him to homeroom each day and slob him down right in front of me. She would look at me crazy and make constant sly remarks. Now, I said I was sorry and that I would leave her man alone, but I wasn't about to take much more of her disrespect. The phone number that I gave her to call in the event that she had any questions she abused by playing on it— cussing and calling me various names. I shifted from sympathizing for the girl to despising her very existence.

*A fingerprint is unique to its owner. It contains indubitable evidence about he who it marks. There is power in the impression of a fingerprint.*

# CHAPTER EIGHTEEN
## *FINGERPRINT*

Things weren't so bright during my last few months at home. My mother knew that I longed for the day that I turned eighteen so that I could finally get out from under her roof. Everything that she forbade me to do, I did not indulge in (with the exception of sex), but my obedience was not enough for her. My mother upheld me to hypocritical standards and acted as if I did not know the person she was prior to her salvation. She forgot that I was in the car with her and her younger brother when they were smoking marijuana in the projects. She purposefully neglected the fact that I and my brother were witnesses at her wedding to our father. She ignored the numerous times that she lived in sin. Yet, she was disappointed in me for not reserving my virginity for marriage and took it upon herself to discuss my personal affairs with numerous members of the church. She would often comment on how I wasn't like the preacher's daughter or the deacon's daughter when *she* made the decision to make me the drug dealing womanizer's daughter. My parentage was now my fault? She was completely delusional. The closer I got to the day where I could declare my independence, the more spiteful she treated me. When I received college applications, she refused to pay for their submission. When I completed my documents to be awarded government financial aid, she refused to sign them and to provide me with her personal financial information. I couldn't believe her, but I was determined to leave her home one way or another.

I searched her bedroom for the location of the documents, and, when I found them, I had to wait for her leave the house so my theft and forgery could begin. When my opportunity came, I procured all of the documents that I needed, transferred the information on the form, signed her name to the document, and mailed it in so I could receive my award. The acceptance letter to Delaware State University and my Pell grant award letter were my two Emancipation Proclamation documents. I was officially on the road out with graduation only months away.

Late March, exactly two weeks away from my eighteenth birthday, I arrived in my bedroom with a desire to change my clothes. I wanted to get out of the chic garments that I wore earlier to school and into something more comfortable. I rummaged through my closet for my favorite gray oversized sweat pants. I remembered precisely where I left them, but, for some reason, I couldn't find them. After tearing my closet apart, I decided to look through my hamper, and there they were at the bottom. *How did they get dirty when I haven't worn them?* I wondered. I took them out and gave them a whiff. PEW! They smelt just like my brother. I turned them up and down and all around for further inspection and two holes in the crotch area caught my eye. I marched hurriedly into his room for the confrontation, and there he was playing video games while wearing my blue denim overalls. I verbally chastised him reminding him that I asked for the courtesy of him not wearing my clothes and scolded him for ruining my favorite sweat pants. In the middle of my vociferous speech, my mother appeared out of nowhere swinging her fists at me. WHOA! *Am I dreaming?* I thought as I ducked her swings and blocked her blows while repeatedly asking, "Mom, what's wrong? What did I do?"

Beads of sweat formed on her upper lip. Her nostrils flared. Her breaths were quick. My mother stood in her fighting stance ready to fight me, her daughter. She never verbally responded to my question; she only kept swinging. On our block in West Philly, seeing a daughter fighting her mother was common; however, I believed in honoring my mother at all costs. I needed to evade this situation before I did something regrettable. I screamed, "YOU'RE CRAZY! I'M LEAVING!" She yelled back as I ran down the stairs, "NOT IN MY CAR!" Was she referring to the car that she purchased for me as a gift? The vehicle that I placed every single paycheck into and paid all of the insurance on? I continued down the stairs with her trailing me. Out the front door I went, jumping into my car and cranking it up in haste. My rear driver's side door opened before I had the chance to press the lock button and in came my mother. I told her to get out of my car. She ignored me and continued ranting something that my ears and mind tuned out. My blood boiled, and I was starting to see red. I could feel myself being overtaken by rage. I turned to face her and looked at her in a way that I never viewed my mother. I told her brashly to "Get out of my fucking car."

She sat back in the seat wearing a stunned expression. Never had I cussed my mother. Never. Her driving me to the point of disrespecting her compelled me to wrath.

I said, "Is this what you did to my father? Now, I can see why he used to whoop your ass."

She started speaking again, and again I could not make out her words. "You don't want to get out of my car. Fine." I rammed the gear into reverse. "I'll crash this motherfucka wit you in it." After backing out of the parking space, I did a three-sixty in the middle of our small street. Gaining control of my vehicle and positioning it in the direction of a wire fence that was perpendicular to our street, I slammed onto the gas into the direction of that metal barrier without a single thought. Something had control over me. I was not the one driving that vehicle. My mind entered into another sphere prior to me being yanked back to reality. A hand grabbed me by the crown of my head which compelled my head to jerk backward against the head rest. Immediately, I slammed on the brakes. As the vehicle halted, my mother jumped out of the car and fell onto the ground. She said as she was getting off of the ground to head to her house that she was going to report the car stolen. So what? I didn't care. Besides, I had proof to the contrary. There was no need for me to counter her. I got what I wanted all along—her away from me. I reached behind my driver's chair to pull the back door closed when I saw a handful of my hair covering the seat where my mother sat.

Quiet. That's all I wanted. Peace and tranquility. I was fine during the drive to my grandparents' home. I used my keys for entrance into their house and found my two younger cousins, whom I had cared for a few years prior, inside. They were happy to see me because they were there alone. About fifteen minutes into me catching up with the happenings in their lives, someone came rapping at the front door. To my surprise, a police officer was standing on the outside steps. I knew why he was there, but I'd never guess she'd really do it.

"I believe you're looking for me," I said.

"Who are you?" The officer inquired.

"Flora Garnier. I'm glad you're here because I can show you proof that the car belongs to me." I stepped a few feet away from him to grab my wallet which contained my insurance card that listed me as the sole driver insured under my limited liability coverage. It also held the registration to the vehicle which listed both my mother and I as its owners. Assuredly, I approached the officer with the information in hand. He didn't bother to take it. Instead, he requested for me to step out of the house. I complied. He then asked me to sit inside of his patrol car.

"Why?" I asked the man who wore brown instead of the traditional blue.

"Because I would like to ask you a few questions," he nicely replied.

Reluctantly, I did what he requested. I didn't have anything to hide. I would gladly answer his questions. There was no need for resistance. I entered the back of the vehicle, and he closed the door behind me before saying what no black person wants to hear, "You're under arrest."

Under what?—ARREST! How could that be when I wasn't even handcuffed? I didn't hear my Miranda rights. Under arrest?

"For what?" I inquired. He ignored me. The kind officer who was at my grandparents' front door was replaced by a rude son of a female mammal right before my very eyes. He ignored me, picked up his radio, and started calling me in:

"Yeah, this is officer Pricalski. I have Flora Garnier in my custody. She's being picked up for domestic violence and terroristic threatening."

I had no idea what terrorist threatening meant; that charge went right over my head, but I did recognize the term "domestic violence." I lived in domestic violence. I lived in a shelter because of domestic violence. I wrote about domestic violence. I had nightmares about domestic violence. I did not inflict any domestic violence on anyone. This guy was clearly misled.

I told the officer, "If you want to charge someone for domestic violence, you need to go get my mother. She pulled my hair out. I never touched her. If you don't believe me, go look at the backseat of my car. I have a headache from her pulling out my hair. In fact…I want to file a complaint."

He didn't move; he didn't even acknowledge my words. There was evidence in the back seat of my car, and he wasn't interested in investigating.

"Sir," I called him politely, "how can you arrest me without hearing my side of the story?"

"You're a minor," he said. "Your story doesn't count in the state of Delaware." My story doesn't count! I work two jobs and pay taxes just like every other hard-working American, and my story doesn't count? The *truth* doesn't count for anything? Now, I was pissed and apparently, so were my little nine- and six-year-old cousins.

"Where are you taking my cousin?" the nine-year-old asked.

"To jail," the officer plainly stated.

"For what?" she asked defensively.

"Go in the house," he ordered while ignoring the child's concern.

"No!" said she defiantly.

"Go in the house right now!" he commanded.

The brave nine-year-old, whose maternal family had numerous negative encounters with the law, tested the law enforcement officer who obviously bit off more than he was prepared for. I bet he never suspected that when he knocked on the door to pick up a juvenile from that beautiful middle class neighborhood, he would have a nine-year-old challenge his authority so boisterously.

"What chu gonna do pig?" she retorted. "I'm a kid. What chu gonna do arrest me too, Pig? I'M A KID!" I rolled with laughter in the back seat of that patrol car. That was my baby—so much so that I didn't want her to get into any trouble on my account. I stopped laughing long enough to get serious. I instructed her to listen to the officer and take her little sister into the house. I told her that once she got inside, she needed to call our grandmother. The cop interjected while pointing his index finger in her direction that she wasn't to phone anyone. She ignored him—rolled her eyes, sucked her teeth, and asked me for our grandmother's cell number. I called the number out to her through the window as the officer mechanically rolled it up while I was talking. He was ready to get the heck up out of there. If that's how the nine-year-old little girl acted, he didn't want a run in with my grandmother. He ordered me to put on my seat belt.

"What's going to happen if I don't," I sarcastically retorted, "Are you going to lock me up?"

He abruptly turned around to face me and used his best authoritative voice. "Either you buckle it up, or I'm a comeback there and do it for ya!"

"Ooooh," I flirtatiously responded.

His face turned beet red. I got a rise out of him…good! I didn't want to complicate things any further so I said, "Alright. Alright" and did as I was told.

I stared out of the patrol car's window during the short ride to the New Castle County jail. Nothing was going through my head. Nothing. I passed familiar places and saw startling familiar faces—my grandparents. I had to concentrate at the image before my eyes. It couldn't be them. Yup, it was. They pulled up next to us at a red light and laid on their car horn. I perked right up. From the passenger's seat, my grandmother yelled out of my grandfather's driver side window, "We're gonna to meet you at the jail, Baby Girl. Don't worry. Mommy and Daddy are right here."

God! I love my grandparents. No matter what happened in my life, they were always right there to support me. And, although my grandmother's husband isn't my biological grandfather, I love that man like he was my daddy. He has been the closest thing to a father to me. When my mother took it upon herself to tell him that I was having sex, he took me for ride to give me the very uncomfortable "talk." When I got my monthly cycle, he took me to buy maxi pads. Now, when I got arrested, he drove to the jail and sat for hours with my grandmother. I acknowledge both the man on my mother's birth certificate as my grandfather and the stand-up gentleman who claims paternity over my mother today. But, the man who I've known all of my life and grew up calling dada; the man who spoils me silly; the man who my grandmother is presently married to and has been for over 45 years, that man I call my daddy and no ounce of blood could make us any closer.

My grandparents were allowed to visit me while I was being processed up until it was time for me to be placed in a holding cell. I sat there with various criminals and crazy people who talked to themselves. Some woman kept trying to make small talk (she must have taken me for the social type) by telling me about all of her problems as if I really cared. I watched the clock. It didn't look like I was getting out before my shift at the bank, so I called my manager from the payphone in the holding cell and left him a detailed message on his voicemail. Tick Tock. Tick Tock. I watched the big and small hand move around that jailhouse clock until it struck ten; that's when I heard an unfamiliar male voice call "Flora Garnier." FREE AT LAST!!! Syke. I was called into a dimly lit room and instructed to sit at a table across from two adults. They started in asking me all kinds of weird questions like "Are you suicidal?"

"No," I told them. "The moment that I've been waiting for is almost here. I'll be eighteen in two weeks and going to college. No, I don't want to kill myself."

"Then why did you try to run your car into a wall?" they legitimately asked. Hmmm…so, a fence is a wall now, huh? Forget it. There's no sense in arguing. Anyway, that was a really good question; one that was so good, I didn't have an immediate answer for it. The answer to that question was going to require some serious thought on my account. I was straight up with them when I said that at the time of the event I was angry. I really didn't intend on hurting anyone including myself.

One of the people said, "You could have been more than hurt. You could have been killed." I could have died. I could have seriously died at my own hands with my eighteenth birthday just days away. I didn't even consider the possibility of it. The effects of my temper were really starting to hit home. The compassionate individuals I was speaking to told me that I was free to go, but, in a few days, I had to stand before a judge alongside my mother at Family Court. I walked out of the doors to the jail and into the parking lot with my grandparents. I had a lot to think about. As I was heading towards their car, my mother approached me, and my grandparents laid into her. She tried to explain how after she filed the report, the officer informed her that I'd be arrested. According to her, she told him then to forget about it because that's not what she wanted. He then told her that there was nothing that she could do because the state of

Delaware was taking over the case due to my "terroristic threat." Even though from the outside, it may have looked as if I was ignoring her, but in all actuality, I was trying to digest her words: She called the police on me. She obviously lied to them and said that I attacked her because I cannot fathom how else they could produce a domestic violence charge against me. I mean, she did have bruises on her arms, but they were from her jumping out of my car and onto the paved road, not from me laying an invisible hand on her.

As I'm trying to make sense of the situation she tells me in front of my grandparents, "I was talking to a girl inside of the jail who was waiting to be processed. And, she was saying that she couldn't believe that you would behave in such a way towards your mother. And, during our conversation, I started witnessing to her. And, Flora, she cried and accepted Jesus Christ into her life."

I was thinking to myself, *Wow, with the exception of the girl talking smack about me, that's pretty awesome* until my mother looked me in my eyes with sincerity and spoke these very words:

"Flora, baby… I know why you had to go to jail tonight. This was not about you. You had to go to jail so that that girl could get saved!"

Now I officially knew my mother was off her rocker and definitely "Coo coo for cocoa puffs." I could no longer stomach her. I had to walk away. My blood was starting to boil again. I climbed into the back of my grandparents' vehicle and she just kept talking. I begged them to close the door. I was beginning to feel the feeling that I felt when I was about to crash my vehicle, an act that led to a terroristic threatening charge.

Four days before my eighteenth birthday, I had to ride in the same car as my mother to the courthouse in Wilmington. I didn't know what to expect. After we found parking, we went inside to sign in and were told to pick a number. My mother was given paper work on a clipboard to complete before we could see the judge. As she filled in her answers, I didn't want to sit anywhere near her. They say that time can heal all wounds, but not enough time had yet passed. So, I chose a different location in the waiting area to sit while we passed the time.

One of the questions on a sheet of paper was in reference to how my mother wanted to proceed, and she read the question and her response out loud, loud enough for me hear from where I was sitting: "I want to drop all charges against my daughter." I looked at her and gave her a faint smile. She motioned for me to come and sit beside her. I did. She continued to write about how the officer blew the situation out of proportion and none of this was her intent.

A couple of hours passed before our number was summoned. My moment of reckoning was here. We stepped inside of the court room and took opposite tables. A white lady with black hair wore a black robe and sat at the judge's bench. She asked us to state our names and then granted my mother the floor to speak. I stood there silent. My mother told the judge that she was a retired Philadelphia police officer and that she wanted the charges dropped. The judge sat there listening attentively. She then focused her attention on to me. She didn't extend me her floor. She didn't talk to me; she talked at me and went on and on about how having a vehicle was a privilege and how my mother was nice enough to allow me to drive her car. All the while my mother stood there shaking her head in agreement. This woman who knew absolutely nothing about me or the truth behind my situation was starting to really piss me off.

I interrupted her—cut the judge off in mid-sentence—and stated that, according to the state, the vehicle belonged to both of us since it was registered in both names. And, since my mother did not feel the need to intercede, I informed her that my innocent mother had not put one dime of her money into the car to keep it running. I was so passionate about my position that I was raising my voice at the judge.

My mother looked at me and pleaded with me to shut up. She said, "Flora, she's a judge."

I told my mother, "I don't care who she is", and proceeded telling her honor that I paid the four hundred dollar insurance on the car every month, and it was only insured in my name. That lady banged her gavel so many times that I thought it was going to break. She warned that if I spoke another word I wouldn't be placed in "juve" but into women's correctional since I was close enough to eighteen. *Huh! Women's correctional...I could care less. Is her threat supposed to scare me?* I thought.

The speech given by judge hit home with my mother; she gasped at her words and stared at me with tearful eyes. This was developing into something more serious than the retired police officer projected. The judge ordered that I attend school every day and be on time. She said that someone from the courts would be checking my attendance regularly.

She asked, "Where are you staying?"

I said, "With my grandparents."

She wanted to know how long I'd been staying there with them. And, I told her since my arrest. She faced my mother and asked her if she wanted me home.

My mother declared, "Yes, your honor."

The judge started writing on her paper. She stopped long enough to look up at me and order me to return to my mother's house.

I spoke up, again. "I don't want to live with her. How are you going to force me to live with her when I'll be eighteen in four days?"

"Flora, shut up," my mother said.

"No," I replied, "I don't want to live with you."

"SHUT YOUR MOUTH!" The bailiff instructed while pointing his finger in my direction. The judge made her order clear and told me that I was lucky that she wasn't sending me back to jail. Then, she ordered my behind out of her courtroom.

If I had to live with my mother against my wishes, I might as well have been back in jail.

We went down into the basement of the courthouse where they kept their records and ordered a copy that showed that all charges had been dropped, *Nolle Prosequi.* This legal document showed employers that, although I'd been arrested and fingerprinted, I had not been convicted of any crime. It was a good thing that we obtained that paperwork when we did because I was going to need it sooner than I anticipated.

****

"Flora."

"Ma'am, could you hold on for one moment while I finish reviewing your account?" I asked the customer on the phone whose account I was in the process of bringing up to date. I spun around in the chair at my cubicle to face my co-worker who had interrupted my call.

"Flora, Joel told me to finish up this call for you and document the account. He needs to see you in his office."

"Okay.," I said before bringing her up to speed on the customer's needs. Once she was fully knowledgeable about the account, I got up and walked into my manager's office. He hung his telephone just as I was walking in.

"Hey Joel, what's up?" I asked. "Carrie said you wanted to see me."

"Flora, you need to report to personnel immediately," he said while his face reflected concern.

"Alright. What floor is it on?" I asked. Aside from the directions to personnel, my manager provided me with no further information. I took the elevator to their office and let the receptionist know that I was there. I didn't sit long in the reception area when a personnel officer came out with my manila employee file in her hand. Without an introduction, the officer walked up to me and said that security recently ran my fingerprints, and a record indicating my arrest appeared. The personnel officer read my charges aloud. I was confused because I had always thought that a juvenile criminal record was impermissible once the child turned eighteen. The personnel officer explained to me that no employee of a financial institution could have the felony charge of "terroristic threatening" despite their age when the charge was placed. Was I being fired? I was one of the highest performers in my collection's department even though I was the youngest and the only black. I showed up to work on time, worked over-time, and exceeded all of the bank's goals. Just one month before they spoke to me about not going to college and continuing to work for them and they'd make me a manager. How could they now be firing me? Didn't all of my hard work and diligence account for anything? This charge was who I was on paper; it did not reflect who I truly was inside. They couldn't be firing me. I tried to explain everything to the personnel officer—how I was innocent, how my mother lied, how I went to court and they dropped the charges.

She said, "If the charges were dropped, where's your *Nolle Prosequi?*" My what? I didn't understand. She told me that I needed to obtain a *Nolle Prosequi* before I was able to return to work. She said that I should be able to get one from the records office of the court. Hold up…I was already there. *Nolle Pro*—I had that document already in my possession. I told her that I was going to run straight home to retrieve it and bring it back to her office.

I walked at a brisk pace through the halls of that elaborate bank and in its parking lot until I arrived to my car. I got in all ready to place my keys in the ignition, but all I could do was rest my head onto my steering wheel and sob. What had my mother done to me? Was this what I was going to have to go through for the rest of my life? Was I always going to have to prove my innocence? Was I always going to be looked at as a criminal?

I went home and asked my mother for the papers. She wanted to know why I needed them. I told her that I had to keep them in my possession and not in hers because I had to use them to provide my employers with proof of my innocence. I told her about what happened to me at work. I told her how humiliated I was and how she had ruined my life. My mother dug in her personal files and handed me the papers that I requested. She did not show me any sympathy. All she did was repeat her words to me the eve of my arrest: "I already told you that your arrest wasn't about you; it was about that girl getting saved." One month since my arrest, three weeks since our appearance in court, and still no apology from my mother. Even if she sincerely believed that her having me arrested served the greater purpose of winning a soul for Christ, she could have at least acknowledged the permanent imprint it left on my life.

Every step that I took to the personnel office of the prestigious institution was a stride of redemption. I looked the personnel officer in the face and handed her the proof that she requested. I reclaimed my job and my pride. They were not going to make me out to be one of their statistics: I told you that we shouldn't have hired her because she was black, or young, or a student who attended school full-time. I proved that, against all odds, I produced excellence. The personnel officer smiled at my proof. She explained to me that the bank uses an F.B.I. database which reflects all employee fingerprints and how they've been used, meaning if one was fingerprinted for employment purposes versus criminally. If the prints were entered for criminal reasons, only the associated charge will appear; it does not reflect any dropped charges. I understood protocol, but I never viewed that job the same again. I knew my manager viewed me differently, for his demeanor changed around me; however, I wondered how many more people around that branch heard about the crimes for which I was wrongfully charged?

*I hear and I forget. I see and I remember. I do and I understand.*

*—Confucius*

# CHAPTER NINETEEN
## *GRADUATION*

N o cake was purchased, sliced, or consumed to observe the date of my birth. There was no party or gathering of family and friends to celebrate my eighteenth year of existence, yet I could not have been any more joyous. With graduation in clear sight, it would not be long before I'd be departing from my mother's nest at last. This bird would be free to fly and fall, break a wing and heal, but nothing but death could keep me from soaring. I dreamt of paving my own path in life and treading it with God's guidance. I did not want to walk in the footsteps of my parents or grandparents, my aunts or uncles, or even my cousins; I envisioned leaving big enough footprints of my own that any willing shoe could fit. What dreams I had. What goals I set. And what plans I implemented to follow—it's a wonder that my mind and this world were both immense enough to contain them all. I, Flora Garnier, was gearing up to face the cold, harsh world with the determination of leaving my warm imprint; one that would be too intricate to be decoded. Nothing could hold me back any longer.

On my eighteenth birthday, my wings emerged, and my mother did not have to drop me out of any tree. I wasn't afraid of falling. Win or lose, rise or fall, this woman with the spirit of a mighty eagle was prepared to take flight on the eve of her high school graduation.

My thirst to embark on to the path of parental freedom did not resonate well with my mother. She knew she was being forced to relinquish her reins and thus had a difficult time coping. On graduation morning I found her sobbing in her bedroom. She was crying as if someone had died on a day when I just beginning to live. Her bedroom door creaked as I entered to discover the cause of her distress.. Traces of her mascara ran down her reddened cheeks and, despite her sniffles and wipes, her ruby nose continually dripped. She cocked her head to the right facing the doorway where I stood and motioned for me to have a seat next to her on the bed. After I sat, she took hold of me in her arms and wailed like a little child. I held her tight, stroking her hair and her back gently with my hands. I could not fathom what the problem could have possibly been, but I knew that my mother was in pain.

After several minutes, my mother finally elevated her head from my shoulder. She erected her posture but spoke to me with downcast eyes. In her words I found a warped clarity. She finally answered my previously unanswered question, *what did I do to provoke such a violent response from my mother just days before my eighteenth birthday?* The answer was nothing profound; it was simply that I grew up. I was leaving my mother and there was nothing that she could do about it, for my maturation was inevitable. The way that she and I both learned to handle a problem that we could not resolve was to resort to violence. Now it was making sense, and I was beginning to understand her again. The reason why she was unwilling to surrender her personal data for my college financial aid package was because she was afraid of me leaving her. The logic behind her trying to fight me was that if she pushed me away, it would be easier on her than me willfully leaving. Since the three of us began living apart from my father, I had made it painfully obvious to my mother that I did not want to live with her. Weeks after her first surgery, I requested to be sent to a boarding school. After she tried to beat me when I was entering the tenth grade, I even went as far as running away. Constantly, I told her I could not wait until I was eighteen, so I could move out of her house. Now the time had come when she and the courts could not regulate my residency, and my mother having to witness my happiness about moving forward only added to her distress. Even if her choices in life resulted in my tumultuous childhood, even if she caused me to have a criminal record unjustly, even if she tried to provoke me to wrath, I loved my mother, and I relayed that message fervently to her when she needed to be affirmed the most. I told her to not take my leaving as a sign that I no longer loved her because nothing could be farther from the truth. My conversation with my mother confirmed that I was really about to graduate that evening. My dreams were about to be my reality.

On the night of graduation, the terrible memories and strong negative convictions that I possessed towards my alma mater vanished. As I stood in the narrow corridor preparing to march inside the auditorium of the convention center alongside my classmates, sadness overtook me. On that evening, I saw that as much as I tried to shield myself from my peers, many of them were fond of me, nevertheless. People requested me to accompany them in pictures that they would treasure for years to come. They were willing to keep me in their memories when, just a day ago, I wanted no more than to dismiss any remembrances of attending the school from mine. I walked down the long row of fellow graduates hugging numerous people. One person whom I embraced with a heartfelt good-bye was He-sh. He and I had been through a lot together that school year. We chatted for a little while until the call had come for us to take our places. I turned to walk away when he grabbed hold of my hand and placed a small sealed envelope inside of it. I looked at it and up at him perplexed as I continued to walk to my spot. *What is this?* I thought as I marched out into a sea of screaming, clapping, and picture-taking relatives and friends who were awaiting our entrance. I was entranced. The boy whom I cared for with feelings stronger than I had for my boyfriend of the past three years, and he to whom I just said my good-byes had thrown me a curve ball. My stomach was in knots, anxiety hovered over me, and it was not because I was about to receive my diploma. The biggest day of my teenage life was happening and all I could focus on was my secret letter.

*"I can resist everything except temptation."*

—*Oscar Wilde*

# CHAPTER TWENTY
## *DREAMS FULFILLED*

The self-inflicted damage to my grade point average during my freshman and sophomore years at Central was irreversible. Despite my four beautiful semesters at G-High, I graduated with only a 2.7. To make matters worse, I bombed my S.A.T. Half way through the completion of the single most important test of my high school career, I grew tired of taking it and decided it would be a great idea to just bubble in random responses. I made cool charcoal gray patterns with my number two pencil on the test's answer document and completed the entire exam in less than forty-five minutes. My overall S.A.T. score, which colleges use to measure scholastic aptitude, was only eight hundred forty five out of a possible sixteen hundred points. On paper, I looked like a real idiot. Numerous colleges and universities sent me application packets; however, I had applied to only three; I would have applied to more had their applications been a little shorter—many of the universities that I considered until I looked at their requirements for admittance desired two or three essays, numerous letters of recommendations, and personal references. I did not want to bother myself with all of the red tape. My first choice was Drexel University; they rejected me right off the bat My second choice, The University of Delaware, accepted me for their parallel program which was an alternative program that allowed students who struggled academically to take University of

Delaware classes taught by the University of Delaware professors at the local junior college for one year to show academic merit. Once proven, the student could transfer to the main campus for residency and/or to take courses. Their acceptance letter might as well have been a memorandum for rejection, for I was truly insulted at the time. I couldn't comprehend in my teenage mind how I was good enough to give them my money but not good enough to step foot on their campus.

My last choice was the school that my boyfriend attended, Delaware State University. It was my last choice for two reasons: firstly, my boyfriend, whose love I did not reciprocate, attended it. Secondly, it is an H.B.C.U. I viewed historically black colleges and universities in a negative light because, in my mind, attending a school where the majority of the people share the same racial demographic was a negative. *The world isn't all black, so why should I attend a college that is all black? Doing so would inadequately prepare me for the real world,* I ignorantly thought. On the other hand, Ivy League schools and other private institutions that confer degrees upon only a small minority populace should have always been equally perceived as a negative in my book, but they weren't. I was as stupid as everyone else who deemed the quality of education to be subpar at an institution where the vast majority is African American.

Nevertheless, my final choice, which I applied to only as a contingency plan, accepted me with open arms in the spirit of those that the institution was founded to serve. D.S.U. not only gave me a shot at academia, but it provided me with a vehicle to fund my education—a full scholarship. Never in my wildest dreams did I imagine I would attend college at no expense to myself or my family. I prayed and asked the Lord that if going to college was His will for my life then to please make a way. I knew my mother wasn't going to pay for my education, and I refused to take out any student loans, so going to college would have to be a blessing from no one other than God. As a last resort, I was prepared to defer my dream in order to work until I could save up enough money to put myself through school. Never did I believe that this blessing would be possible. As rejection letters came in from  colleges I hoped to attend, my college ambition became obscured. Delaware State University restored my hope. It made what looked like the impossible for me possible.

D.S.U. mandated the attendance of all new students to new student orientation. Several student volunteers from student government as well as athletics spoke with us about the importance of getting involved in our campus community and give us the 4-1-1 on campus life in general. These students were kind enough to entertain any questions that we had about our new school and how to have the ultimate college experience. The reigning Miss Delaware State University solicited interested young ladies to run for the position of Miss Freshman in her royal court. She was beautiful, classy, talented, and well-spoken. I said to myself, *that's a position that I want to hold.* In order to reach her status, I had to be well known around campus for other students to give me their vote. I could definitely do that for my newly discovered long-term goal of being elected Miss Delaware State University in my junior year. And, I knew running for the title of "Miss Freshman" to be an important stepping stone to the title. The cheerleaders arrived to the event in full uniform and gave us freshman guys and gals information about their upcoming tryouts. Even though I was a cheerleader for two years in high school, I didn't think that I'd have any real chance at cheering at the collegiate level; all the same, I entered the tryout information into my "things to do" calendar and thought *It's worth a shot. And besides, what do I have to lose?* Now that I had my prospective social organizations in order, I needed to figure out what I wanted to major in. After all, scholastic achievement was why I was here. The student volunteers who spoke to us candidly and introduced us to our new campus really helped me feel comfortable with my decision to attend the university.

During the thirty-mile drive from D.S.U.'s campus to my mother's New Castle residence, future plans swirled through my head. I returned to her house dreaming only of Colombia blue and Cherry red. I walked inside the front door and headed straight to my mother who was in the kitchen busy preparing dinner. I sat down at the breakfast table and started babbling on and on about how great the school was and all of the student activities that they offered. I told her how I wanted to be Miss D.S.U. and planned on running for Miss Freshman as soon as classes began and that I was going to drive back down there next week for cheerleading try-outs—

"Good...good" she said while interrupting me and giving me an empty stare. Rarely was she excited about or took interest in any of my hobbies or interests. But I didn't care. I was and had been since elementary school self-motivated. Besides, my grandmother was my biggest cheerleader, so if I expected any enthusiasm about my endeavors I went to her.

Abruptly switching topics without presenting a shed of curiosity about my new school, she said, "I spoke with your uncle today and he told me that your father's in jail. Apparently he was involved in a big check scam where he had women in different states cashing stolen checks for him."

Despite my initial shock, I blew off the information about my father just as she blew off my information about my college. I started inquiring about my uncle. It had been a while since I had spoken with him. Aside from my sisters, he and his daughters were the only members from my father's family that we communicated with. Staying in touch with him and his family was easy because he was a minister at the church we used to attend in Philadelphia. I told her that I wanted to talk to my uncle and requested that she give me his phone number. She did. I left her and went upstairs to my room to call him.

My uncle was the smartest man I knew. Besides the fact that he could speak Japanese, he was like a human almanac. Any question I asked, he knew the immediate answer. And on the rare occasions that he didn't, he'd call me back within twenty minutes to provide it. Aside from hearing his annual lie about how he was going to give me money for my birthday, I enjoyed talking to him. When I got him on the phone, he was happy to hear from me. We spoke briefly before I heard a faint voice in my spirit say, *"Here's your chance."* I guess enough time had passed since my Dallas trip to the Christian youth camp, and it was time for me to make good on my promise to God. Our conversation was nearing its end when I told my uncle that I wanted to write to my father. He was surprised but glad to hear it, for he loved his little brother and pitied the lack of relationship that he had with his children. He told me that he knew that my father would be pleased to hear from me, and he gave me the address where to reach him. As he was reading off the address to the correctional facility, he offhandedly started spelling the name that my father was incarcerated under. I found that peculiar and could not wrap my mind around the notion that my father was locked up in jail under an alias. There was no point in inquiring how this was even probable, because, based on the information that my mother shared with me, I concluded that he was stealing identities.

I went into work the next day with the information about my father still fresh in my mind. At the bank, I had access to a very sophisticated system where I could enter anyone's name and could obtain his or her social security number, date of birth, address, and the addresses and names of neighbors. I needed to see for myself exactly what my father was up to, so I keyed in his birth name which gave me his social security number. To my surprise only one address appeared—his house on Warnock Street. I took it one step further and entered the alias my uncle provided me. This time, two social security numbers appeared on my screen—my father's and his victim's. Acute levels of disgust permeated my soul. I hated the fact that I shared his bloodline and was one of two of his descendants who carried his last name. How could he do this to someone? Did he not have a soul as well as an active conscience? Once I was able to get past the evidence on my computer screen, I was able to unearth additional truths about who I was as his daughter. It explained without having to literally explain the root behind the queer thoughts which entered my mind—thoughts about selling social security numbers and lucrative account information that I had access to at the bank. I felt abnormal while scheming on how I could obtain the accounts from the computers of other associates to prevent it from being traced back to me while I was strolling by or assisting them with their accounts. Until I looked up my father on the bank's tracking system, I never understood my personal battles and all that I was capable of illegally accomplishing. I would question myself, *Flora, why are you thinking about this?* Or I would ask some close associates if they ever thought about how much people would pay on the streets for a good social security number? Every person I asked responded emphatically "no." Why was I so different? Why did I think this way? I couldn't understand how I or why I concocted such detailed and villainous thoughts. But staring at my father's information on the company's computer screen, I had my answer: His tainted blood runs through my veins.

Although this was true, I stand firmly on this erudition: the blood that Jesus shed for me for salvation, forgiveness, and covering is more powerful than any inherent wickedness. Right there at my cubicle's desk I prayed. I asked God to forgive me for my thoughts and for him to help me to not put them into action. I urged him to take full control of my mind. A new desire blazed inside of me that wanted to put all of the intrinsic evils of my father to good use. Whatever it was that he stood for, I stood against. Where he schemed to get money illegally, I would plan to obtain it legally. Where he went out of his way to bring hurt into people's lives, I wanted to help people. I was my father's daughter, but I was determined to not be like my father; that much was well within my control.

When I made it home that evening, I went straight into my bedroom with the agenda of actively furthering my steps towards forgiving the man who gave me life. I grabbed a tablet and began constructing a three-page letter to my father. I addressed him informally by his first name because the title of daddy I had already given to my grandfather. In the letter I listed my accomplishments, letting him know all that he missed. I told him about his son, my brother, who he never raised and how he was the star on his football team. I told him that I met my sister without his help, and I told him that I forgave him for all that he did to my family. I tri-folded the letter and stuffed it inside of an envelope. I turned the envelope over and addressed it to the phony name of an inmate locked up inside of a jail in Camden, New Jersey.

****

I fell. There I was in a jump circle in front of my competition, the cheerleading coach, and then current D.S.U. cheerleaders and I fell. I wanted so dearly to present the coach with my very best Toe Touch. I recalled instructions that my high school coach gave us for executing a quality toe touch. She said that one should sit in one's jumps, and when it's done properly, one should almost feel a falling sensation. Well, I didn't just feel the sensation; my booty felt the ground when I did not bring my feet down in time. The small gymnasium echoed laughter at my expense. I was confident that I was not going to receive a phone call welcoming me to the squad after that embarrassing number. Many of the ladies whom I was competing against came over to me and complimented me on my high jump. They unanimously agreed that my height and technique was there despite my undesirable landing. *Kind words for the girl who took herself out of the competition by falling on her ass,* I thought. I made the drive back home regretting my attempt to cheer on a collegiate level and felt ashamed that I held the mustard seed belief that I had what it took to make a college cheerleading squad in the midst of me knowing that I wasn't that good. What a fool I made myself out to be.

When I arrived at our development, I bypassed my mother's home and drove straight to the community mailboxes. I doubled parked my car, turned off the ignition, and jumped out. The hot summer air was stifling. Plunging the key that was paired with our residence into the keyhole, with one firm turn I unlocked the box. I grabbed its contents without a preview and tossed them angrily inside my vehicle. It did not take long for me to drive the short distance to my mother's house. I parked the car in its reserved space and began to gather the scattered mail. One envelope was addressed to me in a familiar script. I looked at the return address and it mirrored the alias of my father. My mood shifted instantaneously. The unsuccessful cheerleading tryout was now a distant memory. I stared at the envelope anxiously and lacked the will to get out of my vehicle. My palms perspired and moistened the envelope that I clutched. Cautiously, I tore it open and removed from the white manipulated paper two yellow legal-sized pages that contained my father's words. He wrote back to me. He cared enough to respond. Maybe he wasn't so bad after all. I read his letter several times before I finally got out of the car, and each time I read it, I grew fonder of the man I once hated.

I entered my mother's house feeling surreal and handed her the mail for the day. As she filtered through it, I told her to look at the letter that was addressed to me. Before she even read it, she immediately recognized the handwriting. Her body started to quiver and her voice quaked as she said, "Flora, what have you done?"

I told her that I wrote to him because I needed to get in contact with him. She cut off my words and said, "That man now knows where I live!"

I tried to reassure her that we were still safe. I told her that I misled him into believing that he was mailing the letter to my grandparents' address instead of hers. That information did not bring her comfort. After eleven years, she was still afraid of her abuser and feared for her safety. She began pacing around the house and praying to God in a loud voice. I started thinking about the possible consequences of my actions. Her fear scared me. Was he more dangerous than I knew? Nonetheless, he was my father. He wrote back to me, so he obviously cared about me. I thought that this was just another ploy of hers to make everything all about her.

No…no… she would not take this from me. I deserved to hear his side of the story. Everything that he'd done was done to her and not intentionally directed towards me. She would not and could not stop me from communicating with my father. I was now eighteen—a grown woman who was free to make her own choices.

I ran upstairs to my room and drafted my father a second and final letter. Just as I finished licking the postage to place on the envelope, my cell phone started to ring. I answered it and was alarmed by the sound of the female voice in my receiver.

*"Hello, can I speak to Flora?"*

*"This is she."*

*"Hi Flora this is Karen—the coach from D.S.U.'s cheer squad."*

*"Oh! Hi Miss Karen.*

*"Girl, do not call me Miss."*

*"Ha ha ha. Okay.,"* I giggled nervously.

*"Well, I'm calling to tell you that you made the D.S.U. cheerleading squad, and we were really impressed by your performance."*

My mouth fell open so wide that a fly wouldn't have had any problems introducing himself to my tonsils. I was speechless.

*"You will need to report to campus on August 1st to begin cheer camp—"*

*"Excuse me, Karen."*

*"Yes."*

*"Um. On August 1st, I'll still be on vacation in Florida."*

*"When are you coming back?"*

*"On August 3rd. Will that be a problem because I really do want to cheer?"*

*"Well come to camp on August 3rd as soon as you come back."*

*"Okay, not a problem."*

Was I in a dream because things like this just did not happen in my world? I was about to be a college cheerleader. Someone saw something in me that I did not see in myself. I was going to college for free. And, I was starting to form a relationship with my father. I leapt up and down for joy and ran screaming throughout the house. My joy was contagious, even my mother caught the bug. She had no choice but to fake like she forgot all about her present situation and join in on my excitement. For once, my life was starting to look up.

# PART FOUR

*Show us what you got (Hey Hey)*
*Don't waste no time*
*Hornets are hot (whoa)*
*Will shock your mind*

# CHAPTER TWENTY ONE
## *IT TAKES A HORNET...*

I t took us twenty-four hours to travel from Delaware to Florida via Greyhound. The worst part was that we had to ride another twenty-four hours just to return home. The drive was miserable. We had to stop at various bus depots and remove our bags from the carrier only to transport them onto another bus. The convenient restrooms on the passenger vehicle gave off a foul stench every time its door opened or closed (we should have taken a note from history and refused to sit at the back of the bus). My mother got into an argument with a fellow traveler whom we did not know. She reported to the bus driver that the man was smoking on the bus. The guy cooperated and put out his cigarette but made a public announcement to other passengers that our mother was a snitch. When we got off of the bus to switch onto another Greyhound, he'd yell (while pointing) outside and inside of the bus station, "Listen up everybody, here comes the Snitch!" I supposed she thought that if she told him that she was a police officer, he'd curb his enthusiasm, but that didn't happen. He went from crying out "She's a snitch" to "We got ourselves a pig on this bus." I think that he was even calling her names in his sleep right in between each snore.

The exhausting family vacation did not settle the growing anticipation for my upcoming move. My eagerness continued to build with every passing day. I never felt happier than I did on the morning that we returned to my mother's home. I leapt out of her car, ran into the house, and started packing my belongings. My mother asked, "Flora, where are you going?" I ignored her a few times unintentionally as I hurried past her, continuing to pack up my car and clear everything out of my bedroom, minus the furniture.

She asked again, "Flora, where are you going? We just got here."

This time I replied, "I'm on my way to school for cheer camp. I'm already late." Just like that, I left without supplying her with a forwarding address, dorm name, or telephone number. My Chevy Corsica was packed to capacity, and I was on my way to start my new life at Delaware State University.

Unpacking my car was the last thing that entered my mind when I first arrived to campus. I thought that running to the gymnasium to meet my squad was top priority. When I walked in I immediately noticed that I was not properly dressed. Everyone was uniformed, even the male cheerleaders who were better known as stunt men. I was wearing plaid "class of 2001" boxer shorts, sneakers, and a tee shirt. Everyone else was wearing red skimpy shorts and white tee shirts or sports bras. The coach approached me and directed me to the stores that sold the appropriate cheer camp attire. I was not allowed to participate while out of uniform. That was just a little embarrassing. Later, I returned in uniform and the coach told me to take my place and spot a stunt that was already in the air. No proper introductions were given to acquaint me with the rest of my squad.

Welcome to college.

Cheerleading camp was the most physically daunting task that I had ever experienced. Every single muscle in my body was in pain. Eight hours of our day, five days a week for four weeks before the start of classes our time was monopolized by cheerleading. We ate breakfast, lunch, and dinner as a squad. Once practice concluded, we returned to our dormitories only to continue practice independently. My days of cheering strictly for fun came to a screeching halt—this was a sport and we trained as athletes. Our coach made it clear that we had more bodies than uniforms. If we expected to travel with our squad, we had to compete for our spots. Unless you were a flyer, no one's spot was guaranteed. Traveling was a huge deal. Athletes took flights around the country and were given per- diem. In addition, they stayed in the best four- and five-star hotels. In the airports, restaurants, malls, hotels, and games uniformed cheerleaders, especially, were treated like celebrities by locals. I competed as best I could until I was injured during practice. We were working on a new stunt where a flyer is tossed through the air like a cannonball. Well, the human cannon landed right on my head and knocked me clear off of our mats. My head hit the solid gym floor with full force. When I came to consciousness, I had a crowd of cheerleaders surrounding me and applauding. My captain, May, said with a radiant smile "So you've been injured. Now, you're officially a D.S.U. cheerleader." My coach instructed me to go to our athletic trainer who was assisting the football team on the field. My brain felt like ground beef that had been knocked clear out of my skull. My head was spinning and putting on a tee shirt to cover up the sports bra that I was practicing in did not even come to mind. I walked onto the field and told the trainer what just occurred. He asked me a series of questions before reaching into his bag to hand me medication. I looked away from him briefly and noticed that the football team stopped practicing. All of these huge young men in padded uniforms and helmets were staring at me conspicuously. I focused my attention back on the trainer who was handing me my medicine and walked off of the field and back in the direction of the gym.

That evening for dinner, I grabbed a lunch tray and a plastic cup and headed over to the lunch line. On my way, random guys said, "Hi, Flora."

Who were they, and how did they know my name? Walking to the cheerleader's section of the cafeteria after retrieving my lunch it was the same thing but from different guys. I felt weird. I definitely did not like this mysterious attention. I had only been on campus for two days and only associated with my squad, so how did they know who I was? I sat down with my fellow cheerleaders and some of the senior girls on the squad started right in on me.

"Yeah, I heard that when Flora walked onto the football field earlier she stopped practiced."

"Um hum…yeah," another girl said. "I heard the same thing."

I didn't tell my squad about that happening. I walked over there by myself how could they have known?

I sat there quietly, unresponsive, until another one said, "Girl, football players have been asking questions about you already."

"Well, you can tell them that I have a boyfriend," I responded.

"That's good," she said. "I just want you to be careful. It's real easy for a girl to get a reputation around here."

Even though I had been trying to push Champ away for the past few months because I felt that he deserved better than I had to offer, I was thankful that I had him for that moment. I was glad that he attended the same school to keep other guys at a safe distance. During that conversation with seasoned squad members, I made it my business to steer clear from dating athletes. I would associate with them because I cheered for them, but that was where it would end.

As the weeks progressed, the squad began to separate into cliques, and I did not fit into any it seemed. I hung out with a few individuals independent from their groups, but none of them I deemed as my friend. I started longing for someone familiar. I called up He-sh and asked if he could come see me, but he claimed to be having car trouble. He-sh and I had become intimate over the summer. Although our encounter was romantically planned, the outcome was unexpected. We needed to answer that burning question of "what if?" while simultaneously quenching our compelling lustful desire. He-sh planned a romantic beach getaway for our first time together. We drove to Ocean City, and he paid handsomely for our hotel. Away from people who knew us, we were free to behave as a couple. For that day, we were a couple. We played in the sand, held hands on the boardwalk, and made out on the Ferris Wheel. Before giving myself to He-sh, I was willing to marry Champ and become his un-happily married wife, but I felt an urgency to sample another prior to making that life-long commitment. Who was better suited for my experimentation than my friend who genuinely cared for me and who had become almost like my boyfriend in secret? Once we crossed that line, things were never the same. We took long, leisurely strolls through parks, he rowed us in a boat on a lake, and there we sat gazing into each other's eyes. We spoke on the phone every night for hours and professed our love for one another. I even talked about him to some members of my squad, but I was careful to never reveal his name. Instead of calling him He-sh, he elevated to the status of "Side Jawn." So, when my "side jawn" was unavailable to provide me with physical comfort in my deserted dormitory, I called up Champ. Champ said that he had been really sick since I left for Florida, and his stomach was bothering him at the time, so he couldn't come until classes resumed. Even with two men in my life loving me, I still felt alone and empty, for their physical presence was only a band-aid on an open wound.

> *Be courteous to all, but intimate with few, and let those*
> *few be well tried before you give them your confidence.*
>
> —George Washington

# CHAPTER TWENTY TWO

## *SAME KIND*
## *OF DIFFERENT*

Freshmen returned to school a week before the general student body. Members of fraternities and sororities, student government, and athletes (who were already there) all came together to ensure that the freshmen had a fantastic time during their freshmen week of festivities. One evening, I was sitting on the window sill of my dorm room alone talking on the phone to Sharonda. She wanted to know how college life was thus far, for she was preparing to begin her senior year of high school. Just as she asked the question, a crowd formed outside of my dorm. I told her to hold on for a minute because something was happening right now. Several young, bald men wearing fatigue pants and gold boots marched directly in front of my dorm. They yelled out a few things that I couldn't make out before stripping butt naked and hopping in their gold boots. Sharonda could hear the entire ruckus outside and wanted to know what was happening. All I could tell her was that I was in heaven. Any place where men voluntarily put on a live nude performance in front of my window was a place where I wanted to be. I ended my conversation with her and found one of my squad-mates. She and I decided to take a walk around the campus which was covered with people.

On our stroll I recognized a familiar face—it was the boyfriend of one of my friends from high school. My girlfriend gave me the heads up that her man was attending the school and wanted me to keep an eye out on him. My squad-mate and I walked over to him and some of his football teammates. He and I conversed briefly before one of the other guys asked for our names. She said hers was Candy Coated and I gave them my rap name—Big Nita. Big Nita was a name that I acquired at Central. I used it as my tag when I rapped. It was fitting because although I was a small girl, I had a lot of heart.

The following morning, I arose for 6 a.m. cheer practice. When I entered our practice gymnasium, I found our squad seated in a circle. I squeezed in, and one of the captains announced that it was important for them to talk to us new girls about the reputations that we were getting around campus.

Another senior squad member said, "Damn, already? You girls have only been here for a month, and school hasn't even started yet."

One of the captains said, "Flora, last night you and Candy were out talking to some football players and told them that your names were Big Nita and Candy Coated—."

Candy immediately interjected by coming to her own defense and said that Candy Coated was her nickname from home, and I told them that Big Nita was my rap name from school. Some of the squad members felt that those two names sound like names of strippers and from that we were well on our way for being dubbed "hoes." My first evening going out socializing and touring my campus resulted in a round floor squad discussion. I did not flirt with anyone, kiss anyone, or sleep with anyone—all I said was my name was Big Nita, and I was already being labeled. The school was different, the people were different, but the bullshit remained the same.

During the first week of school, I attended a Miss Freshman interest meeting. I received a packet outlining the specifications and deadlines. Before I could be considered a candidate, I had to receive a pre-determined amount of signatures from my classmates showing their support. Despite all that occurred in the last week, it was not the time to shy away from people, especially the male populace. I gathered my signatures and immediately started the campaign. I selected three of the best pictures of me to use for various flyers to hang around campus. I went door to door, along with my boyfriend, in the male dorms allowing its residents to pick their favorite picture to display on their doors. Guys didn't care about the speeches, they voted for the candidate who they thought looked the best. One of my competitors resided in the same dormitory, so our dorm was split in half in terms of supporters.

I sat down one evening to write my speech, and I thought that it was pretty good. But it didn't stand out. I believed that I needed something to set me apart in the event that the other candidate had a speech that rivaled in quality. So, I decided that I was going to rap. Yeah. That seemed like a good idea. I would recite the first part formally and then I'd let Big Nita wrap up the ending. The speeches were scheduled for September 11, 2001, and I woke up already to go. I was hype until I found out they'd been canceled. They were canceled because two airplanes struck the twin towers in New York City. I didn't quite grasp the magnitude of the event until I saw New Yorkers around my campus running and crying. Then, I turned on the television to see the event replay on the news. There were talks about it being a terrorist attack, and no one knew where the terrorists would strike next. Classes were canceled, and we were encouraged to remain indoors. Against all warnings, I decided to drive up to Philadelphia to visit my great-grandmother, Big Mom-Mom, who was gravely ill.

I arrived to Parrish Street not knowing what to expect. My mother had forewarned me that Big Mom-Mom was unresponsive but I didn't believe her because Big Mom-Mom always had a response to everything. Her being sick didn't concern me at all because she was frequently sick and hospitalized. And every time, in true Big Mom-Mom fashion, she bounced back and returned home unchanged. It wasn't until I saw her for myself that I believed. The woman who lay on the hospital bed in the dining room looked nothing like my spunky great-grandmother. She looked like one who was preparing to meet death. Her eyes were shut tight and her once round, full face was sunken in. She'd lay there opening her mouth only to receive ice chips. She wouldn't eat any food. The heavy set woman was now frail and sickly.

My older cousin sat at her bedside and sung her spirituals. My grandmother was wiping tears from her own eyes. It was as if she was already dead. I came. I saw. I left. I never wanted to see her again like that. During my drive back to school, her last words to me repeated in my mind: "Baby, get your education. Education is the one thing the white man can't take from you. If you don't do it for yourself, do it for me."

At the time, I had made her the promise that I would. She was distraught over my great aunt (my godmother), not allowing her to attend my high school graduation. She wanted to be there so badly, and I wanted her there. But after my commencement, I visited her in her bedroom. She cried and made me make her that promise to finish my education for her. I took those words back with me to my college campus.

A few days passed before our speeches were rescheduled. They were held in the Price building auditorium. The hall was filled with freshmen girls—all friends or supporters of the three Miss Freshman candidates. The room also hosted the newly elected class officers and the reigning class queens: Miss Sophomore, Miss Junior, and Miss Senior. The university queen, Miss D.S.U., was the mistress of ceremony. We, the three contestants, sat on the undecorated stage for all eyes to see while Miss Delaware State University eloquently delivered her opening address. Looking out into the crowd, I saw many familiar faces, but focused on none. Instead, I entered into my zone, pretending to be alone in the crowded space. I rehearsed my speech in my head until I heard the sound of applause. Miss D.S.U. had just announced the first candidate to present her speech. I felt temporary relief when my name was not called and hoped that when my time did arrive I wouldn't forget my words. I watched the first girl walk up to podium. With every click of her heels, my heart raced faster. I listened to the monotone delivery of her speech and my tension immediately decreased in magnitude. It was terrible. It was so awful that I no longer considered her to be competition. I looked over at the other contestant, and we shared a smile; it was almost as if we also shared the same thought. The first young lady returned and took her place beside us as Miss D.S.U. announced the second contestant. The girl seated next to me stood to advance to the podium. Her speech went exceptionally well. She had proper voice inflection, eye-contact, and poise. Her black skirt suit was appropriate, her speech had substance, and the strong applause given by the crowd as she concluded showed that they, too, loved her. Although I was intimidated, I was not going to show it. I knew that if I was to lose it would be to a worthy opponent. Last to deliver my speech, I presented it just as I practiced before the ladies who shared my hall in my dormitory. The first half of my speech matched the second contestant's in style and substance, but the second half—my rap—was the run that won the game. I smoothly transitioned into it, and my audience ate it up; they went wild as they presented me a standing ovation. I was the talk of the campus: the new cheerleader rapped her Miss Freshman speech. Random people stopped me in the halls and in the cafeteria to ask me to spit it again for them.

My peers definitely enjoyed it, but not the reigning queens, Miss Junior specifically. She wanted to know "Who is the ghetto chick up there rapping?" Well, that ghetto chick was the winner of the title of Miss Freshman. I couldn't believe it. In such a short period of time, I had yet another dream come true. I felt infallible in my quest to becoming the most popular freshman. In fact, after my victory, I lost ownership of my own name and was redefined as my title. Everyone around campus, aside from my squad, referred to me as "Miss Freshman."

September ended, but not before ushering in a chill that came in the form of a 5 a.m. telephone call. It was my mother. She was sobbing heavily on the phone:

"Flora."

"Yes, Mom. What's wrong?"

"She's gone."

"Who's gone?"

"Baby, she's gone. Big Mom-Mom's gone. She passed away this morning."

Silence.

"I'll call you back with the funeral details. Okay?"

"Yes, Mom."

"Flora, are you alright?"

"I'm fine. Call me back. Okay"

"Okay., Baby"

I was numb when I received the news, partly because I was awakened from my sleep and partly because it just didn't feel real. I was due in to cheer practice in less than an hour, so I stayed awake to prepare. I did not plan to tell anyone at the school but Champ because I didn't want sympathy. I went into practice with every intention of attending to business as usual. We stretched on the floor in a circle but for some reason, the girls were more talkative this morning than usual. I did a poor job at outwardly masking the pain that I felt inside. Someone took notice and asked me what was wrong. The moment they asked, others zeroed in on me with concern. It was like my pipes had frozen, and they were trying to turn on the hose. I had not yet wept over the news of my great-grandmother's death, and, being the queen of avoidance, I tried to push it out of my mind. But, the longer they probed, the more my pressure increased until my pipes finally ruptured. The moment I heard myself say "great-grandmother died this morning" it was impossible to plug up the leak. I grew angry. I was angry they made me cry. I was angry that

I was appearing weak. And, when they tried to show me their support by attempting to hug me, I pushed away. I drew back and scooted myself across the gym floor towards the door. I got up and ran out. Behind me, I heard laughter. Laughter. I made a fool of myself in my moment of pain, and they responded by laughing.

From that moment, I was no longer a part of that squad. It took me back to high school when I just cheered with minimum socialization. It was just a club that I belonged to, but I was not really a part of the club. My spot became insignificant, and I stopped trying to compete. Just when I believed everything was going my way, I sobered from my momentary intoxication to notice that nothing was going my way at all—so is life.

*Out of the night that covers me,*
*Black as the Pit from pole to pole,*
*I thank whatever gods may be*
*For my unconquerable soul.*
*In the fell clutch of circumstance*
*I have not winced nor cried aloud.*
*Under the bludgeoning of chance*
*My head is bloody, but unbowed.*
*Beyond this place of wrath and tears*
*Looms but the Horror of the shade,*
*And yet the menace of the years*
*Finds, and shall find me, unafraid.*
*It matters not how strait the gate,*
*How charged with punishments the scroll*
*I am the master of my fate:*
*I am the captain of my soul.*

*—"Invictus"(1875) by William Ernest Henley*

# CHAPTER TWENTY THREE
## *CONTROL*

I underwent a spiritual transformation after the death of Big Mom-Mom which consequently affected my attitude and outlook on life. Up to this point, I read my "Women's Devotional Bible" regularly and prayed daily; however, after Big Mom-Mom's death, I stopped reading the manual that houses the basic instructions before leaving Earth, and my prayer life equally suffered. I just wanted to free myself from everyone and everything with rules and restrictions. I felt claustrophobic being enclosed in a world of asphyxiating people who acted as four walls tightly closing in. The more I withdrew, the more persistent Champ became. He was there for me during her death, but I did not want him to be. I didn't want anyone to be. Even though I refrained from speaking the words, my behavior made my feelings evident. I tried to celebrate his nineteenth birthday with him. I told him to drive to Philly, so I could buy him new Timberlands. I needed the drive to be quiet, but he persisted in trying to uncover the source behind my change. I asked him repeatedly to shut up, but he refused. He just kept pushing the issue until finally, while he was driving eighty miles per hour on Route One, I sat up and punched him in his jaw simply because I needed him to shut up. He swerved the car and spoke words that I tuned out for a few minutes more before ultimately giving me the peace that I needed at the time. I decided that day that it was not healthy for me to remain in his company. Anytime I unromantically put my hands on someone who I am supposed to love, it is time to end the relationship. Domestic violence is wrong on all accounts. It matters not if the abuser is male or female. Two days after his birthday, I did just that—I ended it. He did everything he could to change my mind—he called my phone non-stop, waited for me after my classes, waited in the lobby of my dormitory, called other residents requesting them to sign him in or open the side door for him—but there was nothing he could do to get me to alter my decision.

Once I informed my side jawn about my break-up, he automatically assumed that he was receiving another promotion. Wrong. I got rid of him, too.

Immediately, I started to date. I didn't need any time to heal from the relationship because I didn't want to be in it for a considerable amount of time. Now, when I say "date" I mean just that. Some people get it misconstrued. If I dated someone or "talked to" them (as its commonly called), that means, in my interpretation, that we went out on a date or two in the traditional sense, and there was nothing more that went beyond a peck on the lips. Now, if I said that I "messed with" someone then that's equivalent to messing around or fooling around, therefore, assuming that we had sex would be a safe assumption. I dated two guys briefly before being introduced at a campus comedy show to the one who would be my second real boyfriend.

He was a senior who just finished celebrating his twenty first birthday. According to him, his party was the talk of the campus; strangely enough, I didn't hear of it. He was surprised to find out that I wasn't in attendance. After the show, he asked if he could take me out to a movie. I saw no harm in it, so I agreed, and we exchanged telephone numbers. I went back to my dormitory excited by the unanticipated encounter when I overheard some of the girls talking about a Que one of them was dating. The door to the room was wide open, so I invited myself in. The ladies welcomed me as I took a seat on the bed nearest the door to listen to the conversation filled with silly laughter. After about twenty minutes of listening to the gossip, I stood in preparation to leave. One of the girls asked—

"Flora, where you goin'?"

"I have to get ready for a date," I replied.

"Ooooh," they exclaimed in unison while exhaling girlish giggles in between asking "Who is he?"

Good question. I didn't know the boy's name. I told them as much. And they, of course, looked at each other and laughed at my ridiculousness. How was I going on a date with someone whose name I didn't bother to know? In fact, I knew nothing at all about him, least of all his name. I had never even seen the young man before that evening.

I said, "Wait a minute. I think he wrote it down with his phone number." I took out the slip of paper he gave me, and, sure enough, there was his name. I said it aloud, and an elephant immediately appeared in the room. A full minute passed before anyone was willing to speak. They all just sat there exchanging various looks. I looked around, too, trying to figure out the problem. When my eyes connected with someone's, they'd turn away to look at someone else, or they'd stare off into the ceiling, or glanced down at the floor. In an attempt to end the awkwardness, I finally asked—

"What?"

One of the girls jumped up in excitement and asked me if he was a Que.

"A what?" I replied. Then another girl included herself into the interrogation style conversation with questions regarding his physical description. The first girl told me that he was the guy they were all talking about when I entered the room. The more she spoke, the more wired she became. She jumped up and down and clapped her hands together as she attempted to explain. The other girls used this as their opportunity to chime in and give me their unwelcomed fifty cents. Many of them joined her in the jumping and hand slapping. They were so loud I couldn't hear everything she was trying to tell me. I did hear her mention that she was talking to him and advice not to deal with him because "he's a no good dog." I told all of them that I had no intentions on sleeping with him, and he was not that serious to me; I was just going to catch a free movie—hat's it. The gentleman in question happened to call to give me the movie times just then.

The moment I said, "Hold on ya'll a minute. That's him now," the girl who claimed to be "talking" to him started having a jealous tantrum, jumping even harder than before and taking breaks by nervously pacing the floors while her entourage was now putting in their seventy-five cents. I didn't have time for the drama. And, according to him, I didn't have much time to get ready, so I showered and threw on a football jersey with a pair of jeans and Timberlands and met my first real college date outside in the parking lot of my dormitory.

He pulled up in a nice green Camry. As I walked towards the vehicle, I could hear his automatic locks unlock. I stood there next to the car. He rolled down the window and told me I could get in. I continued to stand there. He opened his driver's side door and stood out of the car and said "It's unlocked."

I told him that while he was already out of the car, he could come around and open my door. His eyes widened with surprised, and he gave off a pleasant smirk of approval before coming around to honor my request. Despite me not being dressed to impress or not taking time to put on makeup in an effort to put my best face forward or even me not having remote interest in the young man outside of watching a free movie, it was important to set my standards on our first official date. Once inside the aromatic vehicle, I put on my safety belt and tried to relax as much as I could with a stranger by listening to his soft non-suggestive music. As he pulled out of the parking lot, he told me that anytime I wanted to go some place, I could call him and he'd take me.

I asked, "For what when I have a car?"

He was amazed because freshmen weren't permitted to have vehicles on campus, but I was not the ordinary freshman. The majority of freshmen did not contest the rule, while others tried to find an upper classman who was willing to register their vehicle under their name in order to grant them the freedom of parking on campus. Not I. I walked into the security building with the confidence of an upper classman and requested to register my vehicle. With no questions asked, the worker retrieved my documents and payment and approved my request.

When we arrived at the Dover Mall, he had apparently already caught on. He came around to the passenger side of his car and opened my door. He also opened the door to the mall. I checked him out thoroughly, unlike before at the comedy show. He had straight, unstained beautiful teeth, relatively good conversation, and a mature and sophisticated dress accompanied by grown man music. He wasn't like most campus guys who would pick up a young lady with his rap music blaring. Instead, he played the jazzy, soulful music of Donell Jones.

After he purchased our tickets, I decided to tell him about the dorm room drama. I was curious to see his reaction to my knowing that he was talking to two girls who lived in the same dorm on the same floor, directly across the hall from each other. He didn't appear shocked by my knowledge but contrarily expressed some very strong, less-than-polite feelings about the girl he was allegedly talking to. From our conversation I found out that she had attended his wild party. I didn't particularly care for how he spoke of her, but I was also determined not to allow either of them to ruin my night of a *free* date.

We watched the movie, grabbed some food, and afterwards went back to his dorm room. It was my first time inside of the upperclassmen dormitory called the "New Dorms." It was much larger than my campus dwelling, and it was the only co-ed living quarters on the campus. I was tense about going to his room until he unlocked his door, and I stepped my first foot inside. It was very well lit, and one of the girls from my dorm was in there with his roommate, the same girl who had introduced me to him at the comedy show. She and his roommate were just in there eating and watching television. Seeing this brought instantaneous relief. The four of us laughed and joked and had a great time.

At the height of our enjoyment, I noticed the time; it was quite late. It was the kind of late where the only thing open was legs and since it wasn't that type of party, I said that I should be heading back to my room. He said okay and agreed to walk me back without applying any pressure, but my dormitory acquaintance urged me to stay over. She giggled and said, "We can have a slumber party."

I was in an awkward position. I was stuck between thinking W.W.M.D. (what would my Momma do?) and Momma ain't here so have fun. I looked to my date, Frat-boy, for an answer.

"I don't mind," he said as he shrugged his shoulders. "If you want to stay, I'll sleep on the couch, and you can have my bed." I agreed.

The next morning, we walked the short hallway leading from his room to the elevator. We boarded it and rode it down to the first floor. He opened the front door, and we stepped outside together. The pathway leading to the dorm split into two distinct parts. Before departing, we shared a warm, friendly smile, said our good-byes, and he assured me that he'd be calling. Frat-boy chose to take the path to the right, and I the one to the left. As I was treading my path, I noticed Champ walking with a few of his friends. We locked eyes, and his were filled with tears. He had observed me parting ways with Frat-boy. To make matters worse, I was wearing a jersey of his that he gave to me. I automatically knew Champ and his friends thought the worst. They believed I had slept with the young man and with good reason—I was walking out with him early in the morning, and my hair was disheveled (from sleeping without my hair scarf, for I had no intentions on spending the night when I accepted the date). I felt horrible, but, at the same time, I didn't feel I owed him the courtesy of an explanation. He and I were no longer in a relationship. His friends consoled him by putting their arms around him and urging him to continue on his path to class.

Later that evening, my mother called me. She asked what was going on and wanted to know why I was acting so wild. I had no clue what on Earth she was talking about until she asked who I spent the night with. I asked her if Champ called and told her these things, and she said "Yes." That bastard! I know he was hurt, but he took things way too far. She told me not to get upset with him. He had my best interests at heart. He wanted me to be careful because the guy that I was with was a player in a fraternity, and those fraternity guys prey on young girls. If I wasn't black, I think my face would have turned bright red, but I wasn't black enough for it to turn to a deep shade of purple. It became difficult for Champ to witness me begin a new relationship with my frat boy, so he transferred schools at the end of that semester.

My frat boy did not allow the rumors he heard from his inner circle to deter him from pursuing a relationship with me. He knew first hand that I wasn't the whore that people gossiped about because he was having a difficult time "hitting it." I would spend the night with him and he with me, and we both saw each other completely nude, but no sex transpired for a long while.

And, if I had my choice, it wouldn't have happened for an even longer time. I thought that in spite of what I had heard about him and his brothers, he was harmless. He made me feel at ease when we were together, and I was just enjoying his company and friendly conversation.

Frat-boy was very curious and observant. He wanted to know while already knowing the answer if a lot of guys tried to talk to me on campus, and he wanted to know why my last relationship ended after three long years. Even though he was three years older than me, his longest relationship hadn't extended past six months. I was transparent with him about the details of my past relationships. He knew I had only two partners before him. I told him openly that I cheated on Champ and that, after we broke up, Champ confessed that he also cheated on me—twice, with two different individuals. Frat-boy said that he never acted unfaithfully; he'd rather break up with a girl than cheat on her. With this understanding, I was beginning to feel safe with the idea of lending him my heart; however, the fact that I admittedly had been unfaithful disturbed him. He believed that if I could do it before, I could do it again. He was right. I could, but I was unwilling.

He also had a problem with my chosen attire. My jeans were always tight, and my shorts and skirts were really short—not short enough that my cheeks hung from them, but short enough that they prohibited certain movements. People perceived me as easy because of the way I dressed. Read my words…I could care less. I stopped caring about what others thought a while ago. I felt like since I was a cheerleader my body was already subjected to the eyes of the campus and old men spectators. We practiced in next to nothing, and jumped around with half of our behinds out anyway. Gawking no longer bothered me as long as the beholder did not make the mistake of touching me. My physique is out of my control, it was a gift of genetics; so why should I have to cover up my butt when I wear sweat pants and skinny, flat booty girls do not? My breasts are very small, so I saw no harm in wearing a low cut shirt; I didn't have any cleavage to pop out of it any way. Still, he didn't appreciate the extra attention. And, when I modeled in a risqué fashion show on campus, he told me that if I participated in another one, we were over. I loved my Frat-boy, and I had no knowledge of fraternities or sororities until I met him.

Other people made a big deal about his Greek affiliation, but I could care less. One night when I was in my dorm room, I heard continual barking outside of my window. I continued reading my book without bothering to look out to see what it was. After the noises ceased, the landline phone in my dorm room rang; it was no one other than my frat boy. He only called the room when he wanted to ensure that I was in my room, especially late at night. He asked what I was doing, and I told him reading a book. He said that he noticed my light was on, so he stood outside of my window and called me. I told him that I didn't hear anyone calling my name. He said that it was him barking to get my attention. That was the most outlandish thing I had ever heard. I told him that I didn't respond to dog barks and if he wanted me, he should have called my name. Yeah, that was Frat-boy.

I often mocked his fraternity because I thought they were way too serious about their "organization." I didn't know any better; I was a dumb freshman. Even though he was a devout member of his fraternity, I loved how he didn't fit the status quo. He was content in retaining his individuality. He was intelligent, athletic, social—an all-out well-rounded person, and, like Champ, he was skinnn-y. He was my ideal man, but I couldn't let myself trust him fully, despite him proving himself trustworthy. My hang-ups with my father and then learning that Champ cheated on me while I was feeling unworthy of his adoration caused me to be ever-suspicious. I played foolish games in an effort to make him confess what I hoped was the truth—that he was unfaithful. I wrote myself a phony letter and hid it in a place where I knew he would look. If he told me that he was going to a party, I found a reason to pop up to the party without him knowing. I had other females call his phone on three-way to come on to him, so I could hear his reaction. My game playing and our trust issues put a toll on our relationship, and the summer of his graduation, we mutually ended it.

Our break-up did not extinguish the love that had ignited my heart for him. He professed that he did not feel comfortable living in another state while I had an apartment. He thought that it would be unfair for me not to enjoy college on his account. Well, if enjoying college meant sleeping with a lot of guys, then I didn't want that sort of entertainment. We once tried to give our relationship another shot, but he later said that he didn't want to be in a relationship because he wanted to focus on graduate school. I understood. I told him that I would wait for him until my college graduation, and I meant every word. Every time he came into town, whoever I was dating was immediately dropped so I could make accommodations for his stay. One time, he came without giving me prior notice. I had a nice, gorgeous, professional black man drive his B.M.W. from Washington D.C. to take me out that very same weekend. The moment Frat-boy notified me that he was in town I didn't return one single phone call from my displaced D.C. visitor until after Frat-boy's departure. I dated after Frat-boy for sure, but I never dated a member of his fraternity out of respect for him. I befriended many of them, but I never dated them. Even though he and I were no longer in a relationship, I wanted to continue sleeping with him because I didn't want my number of sexual partners to increase. I was already on over half of one hand.

But, he eventually thought that it was a good idea for us only to be platonic. I was devastated, but I was still hopeful of winning him back and earning his love through my devotion. I wanted desperately to become his wife. I loved him. I loved his family. And, I believed whole-heartedly that I had found my one true love.

The worst things were for me in the relationship department, and it became harder to endure the drudgery of school in my sophomore year. Every place I went on campus, every guy I attempted to date, and almost every conversation I held were constant reminders of the one I loved but could not have. When Janet Jackson recorded "My Ex" on her *Damita Jo* album, I was convinced that she was singing my reality. The truth of my relationship failures was getting the best of me. Dean's List recipient, student worker, college cheerleader, campus tour guide, member of student government, and a faithful attendant of just about every party at our school and others within a sixty mile radius, yet I was still bored and unfulfilled while wearing many colorful hats. No longer did I hold the motivation to continue school for myself. If I was to finish, it had to be for a greater purpose.

My tolerance for men decreased substantially, and I befriended women who philosophized that, as long as they had no kids and no diseases, it was okay for them to have as many sexual partners as they desired. After all, they were *"grown ass women."* I didn't adopt the philosophy, but it sure was starting to make sense. I put so much of myself into two relationships that went south and was not sexually promiscuous only to receive the reputation for being such anyway, so what was the point? I might as well live up to all of the hype. I became more flirtatious than I've ever been and very forward with men. I was no longer going to play the good girl role because it didn't pay well. If there was a guy I liked, I went after him. But, as much as I desired to become sexually free, I couldn't. My scruples constantly got in the way. Every person I slept with, I required some form of a relationship. For instance, if we weren't officially boyfriend and girlfriend, I had to see us heading towards that direction. He had to put in time and express some want of a future between us. I could not consent to a one-night-stand.

Even though I managed to steer clear of football and basketball players as well as members of Frat-boy's fraternity, it still came a point where I didn't recognize myself and felt a need to regain control. I entered into the process of re-assessing who I was and who I wanted to be and what it meant to be Flora. I knew that I wasn't who people said I was, but I wasn't all that I wanted to be either. There was so much I wanted to accomplish, but I felt my chosen career path of being a high school English teacher and my rearing confined me. I wanted to do something big, something great, but I couldn't quite figure out what it was.

One day, while I was walking to class feeling empty inside, a guy stopped me to hand me a flyer. I looked at the piece of paper that was placed in my hand and recognized a familiar face. The face was of the captain of my cheerleading squad and the flyer was advertising for models. EUREKA!!!! I could be a model. I was pretty enough, and I was in the best shape of my life. I thought I found a path that I wanted to take.

> *"Anyone who has never made a mistake*
> *has never tried anything new."*

> —*Albert Einstein*

# CHAPTER TWENTY FOUR
## *ALL THAT GLITTERS...*

With the flyer in tow, I drove to downtown Dover, circling the block several times in search of a modeling agency that didn't exist. Stopping for a red light, something grabbed my attention—a barbershop with an address that matched that the flyer. I changed my course of direction, made a right turn, and parked on a corner beside the building. I sat in my car for several minutes debating whether I would go in. This couldn't be legit. A modeling company... run out of a barbershop? To abate my curiosity, I decided to go inside but resolved that I would not pay them one dime of my money. What harm was there in *hearing* what the "company" had to say? When I walked inside of the shop, several men were seated in barber's chairs, each wearing a black barber's cape, and each one stared at me intently. I ignored their stares and inquired to the barber who sat closest to the door the whereabouts of Ed (the contact name on the flyer). He didn't speak. He used his thin, black comb to point in Ed's direction. I walked over towards the guy who introduced himself as Ed. He was dark in complexion and was as cleanly shaven as could be expected. A large mass accompanied by several blisters protruded from the left side of his distorted face. It was difficult for me to look directly at him without feeling a bit queasy. He politely asked me what's up, and

I told him that I was given a flyer and wanted to check out what it was about. Ed finished up his client's head and led me to the back of his shop.

Behind the enclosed wall of the barber section was a photo studio containing various backdrops and props along with tall fluorescent lights. Further back was his office. In the small, stifling space, Ed had me fill out a brief questionnaire which did not exceed a quarter of a page. I handed the completed form back to him, and we began to discuss what I was looking for in the modeling industry and my past experiences. I told him that I did some modeling as a child, nothing major—I was the winner of several church fashion shows here and there and did a screen test for a cracker commercial and was a pre-contestant for the Miss Junior Teen Philadelphia competition. But, as an adult, I was interested in being in magazines. I knew that I was too short to do runway, and I struggled with the catwalk in on-campus performances. He told me that he was a photographer with connections and could make that happen. He took out his portfolio and had me look at some of the shots he had photographed. The pictures, to my inexperienced eye, looked of a high quality; he definitely was gifted; however, many of them were entirely too indecent for my taste. There were pictures of scarcely clothed girls in mesh, or sheer, or in bathing suit attire lying on large rocks by a beautiful body of water, in parks, and in bath tubs. These neatly catalogued pictures compelled me to make it abundantly clear what types of photos I was unwilling to take: Nude. There was no way in hell I was getting naked in front of someone who looked like the Loch Ness monster. I felt comfortable in my own skin, but was uncomfortable with the idea of baring it all to the world. The world was only worthy of seeing small sections at a time—a thigh here and there, my midriff, some cleavage in training, a flash of a cheek if I did a really high jump, but that's it.

I told him explicitly that I was not looking to model in *Playboy* or *Hustler*; I was not that type of girl. He said that he understood my position and proceeded by pulling out his price list. The imaginary tune to "Here comes the bullshit" played instantly in mind. I listened with closed ears to him read off his different photo packages. My indifference to his sales pitch was obvious—my hand propped my head, my eyes wandered or continuously checked the time, signaling my near departure. He ended that conversation and transitioned into another one by asking me about school. He asked if I knew certain people on campus. I knew everyone that he mentioned: the cheerleader on the flyer, who he said he had known since she was a little girl, and a well-known campus model. He said that he wanted me to come back to do some test shots and to be one of his models. He said that I would join a team, and we'd travel and model at different events. The idea seemed cool; at least we weren't still talking about *me* paying *him* money, and it would afford me the opportunity to test his legitimacy.

The following week I arrived to his shop ready to go. He handed me a black baby tee shirt to put on that read "Ed's Models" in bold red letters. He had prepared his low-budget studio for the photo shoot—big, bright lights were on and the selected backdrop hung from near the ceiling and extended across much of the floor all the while men awaited on the other side for their hair cuts. Once I came out of the bathroom wearing the tee shirt, he got a fresh idea requiring a change in venue. He wanted me to take the pictures outside in the northern chill. The weather was cold, the winter was approaching, yet I had to make like it was spring while I stood in front of a gate that I used as my prop. Ed directed my every motion. He had me to grab the black iron in my left hand and slowly squat in front of the metal. All of my motions were slow and deliberate so he could get the best shot. For another pose, Ed had me to press my body against a cold brick wall. I raised my right arm, allowing my hand to press against the hardened red and brown clay while my left, slightly bent arm and hand gently touched it. Cars drove by at a snail's pace, trying to see what was going on and who was the girl of photographic importance.

After a couple rolls of film, Ed told me I did well and said he'd call once the film was developed. His phone call came the next week. When I arrived at his shop, I noticed a poster hanging on the wall that wasn't there previously. It took a little time for my faculties to apprehend the recognizable image on the poster as me. It was huge. There I was on a poster with my name running across the side of it in large, decorative print. The gentlemen in the front of the shop being serviced seemed to make the connection well before I could, for they sat there looking at me, then the poster, then back at me, in an exertion to confirm their suspicion. Ed came out from the back and immediately asked if I liked it. In an attempt to downplay my excitement, I simply told him I was pleased. We walked to his office where he pulled out a stack of five-by-seven shots. He sorted through them and allowed me to take whatever ones I wanted. He complimented me by saying that I took a lot of "hot" shots that he could use. He said all of this before he started rambling off his packages again. This time I didn't rely on body language for him to get a clue. I told him directly and honestly that I was not interested in purchasing any photographs. Period. Ed grew quiet and his eyes softened in that moment. He looked at me and said that, in order to model, I would need a portfolio, and before I completely blew him off he told me that he was willing to take my pictures for free. *Free* was not a word that I frequently said "no" to. I saw no harm in him giving me free pictures to build my portfolio, so I kindly accepted his offer without inquiring about the underlying cost. Ed pulled out another form equal in length to the questionnaire I completed earlier and asked me to sign it. Without perusal, I graced it with my autograph. He assured me he'd stay in touch and contact me about various modeling opportunities.

Ed contacted me weekly, and I was beginning to dread his calls. Sometimes he would call to see how I was doing. Other times he'd call to request to take me out to eat. Often times when he called my cell, I'd ignore him. But, he'd always leave a message about a potential gig which obliged me to reply. I was beginning to see why he so generously photographed me pro bono, and the suggestion made me feel quite uncomfortable. I heard tales of girls sleeping their way to the top; however, I never mixed business with pleasure and, with Ed's looks, our relationship was only destined to be one of business. I was unwilling to go where my talents alone couldn't take me. One day he called and asked if I was available to come over to his shop right away. He said he had someone—a business contact—there who he wanted me to meet. My classes were finished for the day so I drove by. When I went inside, a hefty brown-skinned fellow was in his barber's chair.

Ed said "Yo, Flora. I want chu to meet Bill. Bill saw ya pitcha and wanted to meet chu."

Bill *claimed* to be a CEO of a very well-known Midwest rapper's clothing company. He said that he was interested in me being one of his models. I didn't believe him. Why would this CEO be in Dover, Delaware of all places and not in New York or Los Angeles? And why would he get his hair cut in Ed's barbershop of all places? The wool wasn't going to be pulled over my eyes. Bill said that he had a house or family in the area (I don't really remember which) and he stopped through from time to time. He wanted to know if he could get my number to discuss business. I gave it to him and the entire time Bill was putting it in his phone, Ed looked at me with a grimace.

Bill called later that evening and asked if I could pick him up from his house and take him to the train station in the morning. I did, and he compensated me two hundred dollars that he peeled from a roll of hundreds and gave me two complimentary tee shirts from his clothing line. Then, he began calling me bi-weekly just to see how I was doing. Then, he called propositioning me to be his girl; according to him, he just wanted to let me know that once we became official, he'd be coming by my campus to pick me up in his Hummer, and the college kids were gonna talk and start sweating me because of the fact that I had a rich man. All of the attention from my peers was never going to happen because his arrogant behind was never going to be my man. Were my panties supposed to just fall after seeing he had money? I couldn't believe that some women actually fall for weak game like his. Did I wear an invisible sign that screamed I'M FOR SALE? I was especially irritated with Ed for arranging our meeting.

Come to find out, the jerk was who he claimed to be. Bill arranged for some of us models to model at his partner's rap concert at the Wachovia Center in Philadelphia. I didn't tell a soul because I knew no one would believe me. But, that night, I felt of such high importance. We were rushed in by security in front of a long line of patrons. We were escorted to our seats, and afterwards we had male fans trying to track us down to get our attention. I truthfully began to think that I could grow accustomed to the lifestyle. What would my father think if he happened to pick up a magazine featuring the daughter he never cared to know? How low would he feel? Or, could he possibly feel proud in spite of his absence. I wanted to know. I wanted to do something big, something huge that would smack him in his face. He hurt me.

I had tried to take the steps towards forgiveness and he hurt me again. I wrote to him and he wrote back, but soon thereafter the content of his letters shifted; they became more and more concerned with the actions of my mother. I felt used. He tried to use me to get to her. My mother was right all along. So, I stopped writing him. And, now, his daughter who he didn't feel was so pretty was well on her way to becoming a professional model. I didn't want to write to him any longer. I needed to see him face to face. He needed to see me and my pictures. And, the next photo shoot that Ed arranged for me could be the very vehicle that I needed to gain both fame and my father's remorse.

Ed told me that he had a reputable photographer that he wanted to use for my next shoot. He said the guy freelanced for *Essence* and other popular magazines. He instructed me to select wardrobes for the shoot that would display my range as a model. I didn't have time to shop; therefore, I had to rummage through my drawers and closet in search of possibilities. I selected a black-and-white spandex dress with horizontal stripes that my mother had given me. I only wore it in the house because it drew undesired attention to my butt, but I found it fun, flirty, and appropriate for a front shot. Then I thought I should model a bikini, so I packed one in my duffle bag. Then, I thought I'd do a seductive black-and-white shot where I'd blend masculinity with femininity by wearing a black Kangol style hat, a white business dress shirt, a black tie, fish nets with laced boy shorts, and black, quarter-length shoe boots; I got the idea from my part-time jobs as a waitress. I always thought in spite of the masculine attire, I looked kind of sexy in my restaurant uniform. Lastly, I packed makeup and costume jewelry to complete my various looks.

It was dusk by the time we arrived at the photography studio in Wilmington. My level of anxiety grew once I walked inside and saw that it looked legitimate. Slim, the main photographer, shook my hand without a smile. He was short and had what appeared to be a glass eye. One eye was blue while the other one was brown. A camera hung from around his neck. He asked if I could do my own makeup and instructed me to do a heavy brow. After my facial artistry was approved, he wanted me to douse the remainder of my body in baby oil and come back out so he could see my wardrobe. I went back into the bathroom to change into my first piece. I chose to put on the long, spandex striped dress.

When I walked out, Slim said, "Uh huh." He stared me up and down and motioned for me to come closer to him. Once I did, he grabbed a pair of scissors and immediately began to cut my dress. I was too taken aback by his aggressiveness to protest. He cut it and made it look fitting for a Tina Turner rock concert. I wasn't wearing any undergarments with the dress to give it a proper fit, so I now I was very uncomfortable with its new length. He cut the front too short, and I had to play with it to keep it from revealing my hidden triangle. He could tell I was nervous and asked if I preferred any music to calm my nerves. I requested Lil' Kim or Trina. Both artists' lyrics made me feel like I didn't have to be reserved just because I was a woman—I could free myself. At the time of the photo shoot, while I was alone with two order-barking photographers armed with cameras, I needed to feel like I was "Da Baddest [Chic]" and needed to take on the attitude of "I got it goin' on wha wha…."

For the second scene I wore my bikini. The shots were relatively simple and took the least amount of time out of the three, but, for the third scene, Slim and Ed transformed me into a photographer. I stepped out of the bathroom wearing the oversized white dress shirt accessorized by a loose fitting black and white tie, the lace and fishnet undergarments with the black hat and black shoe boots. Only two buttons on the shirt were buttoned up. I intended on showcasing my second best asset—my tight midriff. I knew the look I wanted to achieve and exited in full confidence. Slim loved the look, or so it appeared. He high-fived Ed and told me to come to him. When I walked to him, he took control over my wardrobe *again*. He unbuttoned the only two fastened buttons on my shirt. I told him that I didn't have any adhesive to make the shirt remain closed; he told me to work it with my hands.

Once he achieved the look he desired, he left me and began creating a photo studio set. He instructed me to sit on a stool and act like I was trying to operate the camera. He also told me to pull up, suck in, stick out, turn, caress, raise my chin, lower my chin, adjust my eyes, etc.

When I was done with the shots, Slim looked over at Ed and said, "I think you've found yourself a winner."

All in all, the mentally draining shoot lasted well over three hours. I went in there not knowing what to expect and left out not knowing if I ever wanted to experience that again. I definitely was taken outside of my comfort zone.

Two weeks later my modeling portfolio was complete. I have to admit, Slim did a fantastic job. I almost did not recognize myself. I looked beautiful, and the pulling in and sticking out gave the illusion of an exceptionally large and perfectly round rear end. The way I manipulated the shirt, made my breasts even appear to be perkier than in reality. While looking over the pictures in Ed's office, he mentioned that he was in contact with several magazines, and it looked as if I had a good shot of making it in. At hearing this news, it became increasingly difficult for me to remain seated. I burned with excitement. This was the opportunity I was waiting for. He spoke of one magazine in particular he was really pushing for, but its name didn't send any bells ringing. His phone rang. He asked to be excused before taking the call. While he was engaged in his phone conversation, I started looking on a table he had sitting against a wall in his office. It featured the magazine Ed had just mentioned. I thumbed through it, and it contained strongly suggestive pictures of black women that accentuated their breasts and backs sides. It seemed like eye candy for inmates. As soon as Ed ended his conversation, I asked if that was the magazine he was talking about, and he affirmed my suspicion. I told him that I wanted to be *Jet*'s beauty of the week and told him that I'd like him to parade my flirty and playful pictures over the ones that I took just to exhibit my range as a model. He acted as if he fully understood me. He gave me my free pictures, and I was on my merry way.

"Give them an inch, and they'll take a mile" is what wise people typically say. The saying proved true in Ed's case. After the photo shoot with Slim, he'd call to ask if I'd model at area car shows and the like. He did not understand the image that I wanted to put forth to the public. Time after time, I rejected the opportunity to stand around a car wearing next to nothing. I made it clear at our very first meeting that I wanted to be in magazines, not car shows. After the photo shoot, my respect for Ed diminished. I loved my photos, don't get me wrong; nonetheless, they weren't something I'd like to display outside my home. Immediately, Ed posted the most revealing pictures of me on his website. At the time, I didn't mind because Edsmodels.com was not getting a lot of viewers. It did, however, confirm that he and I did not share the same vision for my modeling future.

The results of Slim's vision were not the pictures I envisioned taking to bring pride to the heart of my daddy or absentee father, yet I was willing to give a career in modeling just one final chance. I took Ed up on an offer to be featured in a music video. When I met Ed at his shop, two other young women were waiting to accompany us to the shoot. After the two and a half hour drive, we finally made it to a warehouse in Baltimore. The girls and I were rushed to the dressing area to meet with the wardrobe director. She requested to see every outfit we brought and accessories—shoe, belts, purses—everything. She picked the ones she felt best suited the theme of the video and directed us to someone who was to brief us on what we were expected to do.

The video shoot took seven long, exasperating hours. Many of the girls present were featured in videos before. The professional video models were stand-offish from those of us who were new to the industry and only associated with the artists and film crew. The girls, new and seasoned, were like camera vultures. One minute they'd be standing off to the side, but the moment they saw the camera they did their best to keep or steal its attention. I didn't like the aura of the place. I stood off to the side associating with the people behind the scenes, like the publicists, costume designers, and photographers. I jumped in to participate in my scenes when called, but as soon they were over, I went back to my corner to finish picking their brains. I asked them questions about the staging of a music video, like if it is customary to shoot women with a lighter complexion apart from those who are darker, for I observed this action taking place at this particular video shoot? The female publicist shook her head in a shared disgust, as if she already knew what I was getting at. The models at this shoot were hungry, and I wasn't hungry for modeling enough. In fact, the few modeling courses I tasted were enough to leave me feeling not full, but satisfied.

*"Defining myself, as opposed to being defined by others,
is one of the most difficult challenges I face."*

*-Carol Moseley-Braun*

# CHAPTER TWENTY FIVE
## *REDEFINITION*

Summer marking the conclusion of my sophomore year was eventful. I spent three weeks visiting my uncle in Japan, was featured in a low-budget music video taped in Baltimore, and exhausted two weeks in Florida visiting Frat-boy. The tropical visit hurtfully confirmed the incompatibility between the two of us. When he took me to visit Magic Kingdom and nothing majestic occurred, I started accepting the fact that we simply weren't going to be. While watching a beautiful show in the Orlando attraction, I couldn't help but to notice the allure of it all. There were fireworks, beautiful music, couples all around us kissing and holding hands, and then there was Frat-boy on his cellular phone. At the ending of his conversation, I asked him at what age did he see himself married? His response: "By the age of twenty six."

For him, that was only two years away which would have put me at the end of my senior year. His timing would have played perfectly in my life's plan had the fact of his not taking any strides in pursuing a meaningful relationship with me not been a major factor of concern. His answer to my question compared with his ungentlemanly behavior let me know where I exactly stood in the order of importance in his life. I had traveled to Florida to see him, as he requested, and he returned me to the airport on a bus without even offering to assist with the fare. I traveled to Florida to see him, and he was unwilling to pay for my meals or entertainment. Where I took four steps, he took one. Like back when he was in college, we were still traveling on two very different paths and mine required me to release the dream of him.

I sat alone in my campus apartment after returning from Florida and took a serious self-inventory by notating my attributes, goals, and abilities. My awareness of all I had to offer a man was vast; however, as a recipient of their "benevolence," I was left quite unimpressed and annoyed. Therefore, my measure of any potential suitor became stricter. I came up with ten standards for a man and resolved that, if any man did not measure up to those commandments, he was unworthy of my time. To keep myself on track, I needed to have the results of my self-assessment in my face constantly, so I posted them on my printer. I placed the obituary of my great-grandmother on the wall near my computer to ensure that I'd honor her dying wish since I lacked the desire to finish school for my own personal benefit.

My bonus extracurricular activity of modeling only enhanced all that I did not want to become—superficial, self-absorbed, and predatory. Needless to say, junior year required a shift of moral focus. I found my moral compass and adorned my walls with various scriptures pertaining to the fruits of the spirit as well as to womanhood, motherhood, and those that presented the ideal wife. Since "charm is deceptive and beauty is fleeting…," I sought to achieve a new look to match my new attitude. Walking into a popular Wilmington hair salon and requesting them to cut the poison out of my lengthy, chemically processed hair was my first step. When the stylist was through chopping, all that remained from my long mane was two and a half inches of soft, thick, alien tresses. I looked into the mirror and it reflected a stranger. I thought to myself, *Wow, so this is the real me.*

I did it because I wanted people to look at me differently; no longer did I want them to see me externally but to appreciate all that I had to offer in the depths of my being. I did it because I needed to view myself differently. But, change is never easy; the adjustment to it is the worse. Trying to un-school oneself from learned behaviors and perceptions is a mentally daunting task, especially when one transforms themselves into something contrary to the self-loathing cultural essence of beauty. I often found my eyes fixed on the mirror image of me to which I was unaccustomed. The end result was tears and anger while having to face myself, learning to appreciate myself, and hoping to one day fully love myself. I looked into the beveled mounted glass and wondered what was it about me that not even my father could love? Feeling low, I elected to elevate my spirit by seeking my living rainbow, my grandmother. She always knew what to say or do to brighten my day, for she always made it her business to affirm my importance in her life.

I pulled into her driveway and opened her front door. As I walked into the foyer, I quickly gave my routine glance into the living room. There is was, just as it has been since I lived with her in the sixth grade—the grand organ. The splendid piece is a symbol of her unwavering love for me. Once I told her that I'd like to learn how to play the piano and the next thing I knew she had me enrolled in lessons and spent thousands of dollars on an organ for me to use to practice at home. Although the organ is a slightly different instrument from the piano and, besides the fact that I never learned how to play either, I always appreciated her kind gesture. The sound of "Hey Grandbaby!" broke my momentary daze. The words came from the eat-in kitchen which had a clear view of the foyer. At her kitchen table, beaming without the benefit of her dentures, sat my grandmother. Beaming she was until she took notice of my hair.

"Baby," she said with concern while clearly stating the obvious, "you cut off all of your gorgeous hair—*mmm mmm mmm*"

I ignored her elderly sign of disapproval and took a seat on the sofa in front of her heavily draped family room windows. She thumbed through the newspaper with her oversized rose-colored eye glasses resting on the tip of her nose when she matter-of-factly mentioned her recent reading of the paper and seeing a sheriff's sale on my father's duplex. Her observation sparked a conversation with my father as our central topic. I shared with her the details of my writing to him and she was surprised to learn that I knew his whereabouts. She asked me if I wanted to see him, and I responded honestly. And in true CJ fashion, my grandmother said, "Let's hit the road Clyde because I'm ready to ride."

Just like that, without premeditation, we were off to a Camden, New Jersey jail to see my estranged father. In the car, she declared the details of our little visit were to stay between me and her. It would be just another little secret that me and her shared.

The old girl winded up taking several wrong turns in the unfamiliar New Jersey turf, but, after a couple of hours, we made it. The anticipation felt like an out of body experience. Rage, eagerness, sorrow simultaneously overwhelmed the many things I wanted to address with him.

My grandmother looked at me and said, "Take your time baby. I'll be waiting out here until you're done." She realized my meeting him was something that I'd have to face alone. I nodded my head, grabbed my purse, got out of the car, and walked inside the building. I approached the guard's station and signed a visitation request for a name that wasn't my father's before taking a seat at a vacant oblong table in the visiting area. The apprehension caused my nervous bowels to secrete embarrassingly odorous gases. This made me grateful to be alone while waiting for my father who was not suspecting a visit from me of all people. During my rank and uncomfortable wait, I noticed a woman approach the clip board I had signed. She asked the guards a question that prompted one of them point in my direction. The veins in my forearms and hands emerged as I prepared for some jailhouse visitation drama. The scowling woman said my father's name and asked if I was there to see him.

Immediately I stood up to defend myself against an imminent attack and declared yes. The heavy set woman's tone was aggressive as she introduced herself before asking "And who are you?"

I matched her demeanor as I said, "Flora! His daughter!"

The guards stepped from behind their post in preparation to defuse a budding altercation. But there was no need for them to take action because the moment I spoke my name, her eyes widened, and she threw her arms around me in a strong embrace. The strange woman released me, grabbed my hands, and sat me down to tell me that she was a friend of my father's. She said she heard a lot about me and my sisters. She knew I was in college, but was unsure which one I attended. My enthusiasm did not equal hers. I was still recouping from our initial greeting. I austerely told her Del—State.

"Get out of town!" she said. "My daughter Shaliese goes there, too."

I knew her daughter. We lived in the same dorm during our freshman year. She seemed very nice from what I gathered from the couple of times we spoke to each other, despite my not believing that she voted for me during my Miss Freshman campaign. While the mystery lady jabbered on, the man of the hour appeared. Aside from his attire, he looked the same as I remembered him. He appeared to be both surprised and exultant to see me, and the woman looked equally elated just to take witness of our blissful reunion. She told him she'd stop back by to see him later to give us some time together. The meeting had made me forget everything I intended to say. A different feeling overcame me—joy. He was calling various inmates over and introducing me to them as his daughter. It felt good hearing the man with whom I shared semblance refer to me as his daughter Each of them boasted about how much they respected him.

He said, "You see this, Flora," calling me by my childhood nickname, "I'm like the god-father around here."

He followed those words by pulling out a wad of money and peeling me off fifty dollars. FIFTY DOLLARS after fourteen years.

Out of everything I had planned to say, all of my accomplishments that I planned to boast, and everything that I intended to do, at this point I decided there was no use. It became abundantly apparent he had not changed. I made up my mind that, for the remainder of my visit, I would share as little as possible in order to guard my heart against the sociopath who sat before me. At this point I felt disappointment. He dominated the conversation while I gave only brief, vague replies. He told me that he knew this day would come because I would have questions about who I was because of his blood that flowed in my veins. He told me that I could expect to feel inexplicable things and emotions that he could teach me how to control. My eyes began to swell as he feigned empathy for my sensations; nevertheless, I refused to allow one to fall in front of the psychotic, egotistical bastard. He mentioned his knowledge behind his paternity and that his father was now a pastor who went on to marry and later raise all of his children born from his bride. As he told this story, I could see the pain masked by anger in his eyes especially when he tried to act as if his family history was insignificant.

I sat there and studied him—the contortions of his mouth, the movement of his eyebrows, and the look of shock in his eyes when I told him that I knew the story and remain in regular contact with the man who is believed to be his biological father. He then stressed the importance of me having a relationship with my sisters—my sisters, not him— and gave me my oldest sister's phone number since she and I had fallen out of touch.

About the spousal abuse, he spoke briefly. He said that I needed to hear his side of the story. The sharing of his side never came. Even so, there's nothing he could say to explain away what my young eyes witnessed and what I lived—the beatings, the blood, the constant moving, the eternal fear. An apology for my trauma never came. And even after giving him my phone number, I only received one phone call from him.

Needless to say, our meeting was not the beginning of a beautiful, long-lasting relationship.

Two hours passed before I went back to my grandmother who fell asleep waiting in the hot car and asked her to take me home. I thanked her for taking me to do what I had to do. She didn't ask many questions about the nature of our meeting; she just drove me back to her home. That day she taught me the importance of putting others before myself while remaining true. My grandmother hated my father, but she loved me. Although she made it known how she felt about him by her refusal to speak his name, she never spoke badly of him in the presence of me or my brother. She loved me enough to acknowledge that I needed to start getting closure. She loved me enough to take me to see the man who had harmed her daughter. And she knew herself well enough to remain in the car.

1. *Sticking to a purpose in spite of difficulties, obstacles, or discouragement*
2. *Never giving up on what one has set out to do*

# CHAPTER TWENTY SIX
## *PERSEVERANCE*

Women join sororities for many reasons. Some join in search of sisterhood. Others join because they have friends or relatives who are members. Even more join to become closer with their boyfriend who may be in a brother organization. I joined my sorority because of its illustrious history. Social organizations tend to blend together to the extent that, aside from their calls, symbols, and colors, it is hard for an individual to make clear distinctions from one to the other. However, the crux of the founding is essential. I marveled how my founders were advocates of change and forward movement. I respected how they went against what was popular in order to achieve a greater common good. They were women of courage and distinction, and I wanted to be a part of an organization that welcomed such strength. Voraciously, I read every piece of literature that discussed the service organization. I memorized the names of its founders, its chapters, its symbols, its tenets. I ensured that I met and exceeded all of its qualifications for membership. But despite how well I looked on paper and how well I could interview, I still had to gain approval from its young female chapter members. Dear reader, please keep in mind that interacting with females on a personal level is not my strongest attribute; nevertheless, earning their favorable vote became my primary goal during my junior year.

Apparently, I struck a wrong chord with one its undergraduate members, and she sought to destroy any chances of me ever receiving membership through her chapter. All of the ladies I met who were members on campus admitted to having heard of me. Many were apprehensive about even trying to get to know me because my reputation preceded me. Others candidly said that they didn't like me or didn't want to know me because their sister held such strong views towards me. I wracked my brain trying to figure out what I did to be treated with such disdain. *Did I sleep with her boyfriend? Did I hit her dog with my car? Did I torment her as a child?*—I ran through my mind and nothing rang true. Yet, in spite of all of the rejection, I remained persistent. If they hosted an event, I was in attendance. I continued to speak to each of them in passing even if they ignored my greeting. The chapter members' disinterest in me did not reduce my desire to join the organization. Eventually, some of the members began to come around and took a genuine interest in trying to get to know me. Some of them gave me advice on how to win the others over. One lady in particular would call my room to give me words of encouragement. She'd say, "Don't give up no matter what it looks like." She revealed to me in her few outward acts of kindness the beautiful face of genuine sisterhood.

Trying to join the sorority kept me on constant high alert. I became conscious of my actions because I was walking on sorority egg shells. Everything I did and every association I held was put into immediate question. I was asked by members of the fashion club on campus to model in another risqué fashion show and one of the sorority members advised me not to do it. She did not want me to solidify doubts in the minds of members who were already questioning my campus reputation. I had serious problems with my roommate that I wanted to resolve by laying hands upon her head, but a member of the sorority said that they couldn't have anyone associated with them who was starting fights around campus. She told me that when you're in a sorority you lose your individuality. Every action that you take reflects on the organization as a whole.

Then my two best friends on campus who also had questionable reputations were a matter of discussion and that is where I drew the line. I may be many things and I may not be many more; however, I need no one's confirmation to the degree of my loyalty. Those two women whom I befriended are two of the most genuinely loving and generous people I know. Their kindness has been taken for weakness and their hearts have been mishandled by males in search of a conquest; however, they are unworthy of the labels placed on them by jealous, gossiping strangers. My friendships were not a reflection of a character flaw; therefore, they were not something I was willing to alter under any circumstances.

Winning the majority vote for membership intake from the collegiate chapter members made me feel like there was nothing I couldn't achieve. It is, indeed, one of my biggest accomplishments. I went from being the underdog to one that many were rooting for and as a result, my self-confidence tripled in magnitude. I attained my goal in spite of opposition and difficulty. The level of difficulty I had to overcome in my pursuit for membership made me appreciate the sorority even more. But there was yet another barrier. I had to form relationships with a host of other women that the organization approved for membership intake. One of the women was Shaliese, the daughter of my father's friend. One evening, many of us excited candidates were sitting together in a small room talking and studying our intake material. We were going around the room sharing our backgrounds since we were to become sisters. When it came my turn to speak, I shared with them vague details of my upbringing—where I was from, the number of siblings I had and their names, what parent I grew up with, and the fact that I had an abusive father.

With that, Shaliese chimed in and mentioned contemptuously that my father had hit her mother, too. The air was sucked out of my lungs. The walls of the room closed in. My new sisters were becoming increasingly blurry. The moisture fled from my mouth. I had nothing left to say. What could I say? What was appropriate? I'm sorry for my reckless father's behavior? I wondered how he had impacted her life. It was bad enough knowing all that my siblings and I had to endure but to contribute to the destruction of lives outside of his own bloodline was revolting.

"How many more children?" I asked myself.

She acknowledged that she knew my oldest sister and explained the true nature of our parents' relationship before announcing, "I hate your dad." That was her introduction to the sharing of her own story. My heart was breaking, and I didn't know the ladies well enough to let them in. I was embarrassed for my father as much as for myself. That icebreaker laid the first brick to a wall that I began to build up against them—my sisters. The first opportunity I got I removed myself from that intimate setting. I turned my phones off to avoid being reached by them and retreated back to my room to reflect on the evening's events. From that night forward, I became known as disagreeable and stubborn. I rejected the sorority ideal of collectivism and regressed to being about the individual.

> *"Character is like a tree and reputation like its shadow. The shadow is what we think of it; the tree is the real thing."*

> —*Abraham Lincoln*

# CHAPTER TWENTY SEVEN
## *PANDORA'S BOX*

S tudying abroad is a great opportunity that many overlook in higher education; conversely, it is also one that I had the benefit of taking full advantage. Working in the department of residence life gives a student the opportunity of meeting diverse students from all over the world. One summer afternoon, a Mexican young lady who appeared to be of traditional undergraduate age entered the housing office accompanied by a tall, dark-skinned young man. Mexicans were not very common at the historically black university, so, regardless of her height not even exceeding five feet, she stood out like an Asian running back. I tried to make her comfortable by conversing with her in her native tongue. My gesture was well received. It was her first time in the United States, and she came to Delaware State to improve her English during the school's first summer semester. I told her that I was a Spanish minor and would love to one day travel to Mexico. I had traveled there once as a child with my grandparents, but my memory of the trip is vague. She boasted that it is a beautiful country, and I should come to visit. She even extended an invitation for me to stay at her home with her *familia*. I told her not to joke around with such a matter because I would actually come. She insisted that her invitation was sincere and wrote down her telephone number and address in Morelos as confirmation.

I took her personal data to the school's foreign exchange office and sought additional information about the program. I told them that I was very interested in becoming a foreign exchange student. The school was excited about my willingness to travel abroad. The director said that she did not have many interested students in the program. I retrieved the requested documents from her and told my grandmother about it later that evening on the telephone. Two weeks later, grandma bought my ticket, exchanged a thousand dollars into pesos to take care of my leisure expenses, and told me I was flying into Mexico City the following week.

Cuernavaca, located in the Mexican state of Morelos, was breathtakingly beautiful. Its weather felt like eternal spring. During my daily walk up and down its hilly streets, I removed my mind from the problems I left in the United States. Problems like breaking my rule about football players, for instance. In the seven weeks of my stay, I wholeheartedly embraced Mexican culture—I made friends, climbed the Aztec pyramids, saw Diego Rivera's original work in the Palacio de Bellas Artes, attended intimate family events, ate traditional meals, Salsa danced in various *discotecas*, drank exuberate amounts of Tequila and cervaza during all hours of the day. Other than from my local friends, I didn't receive many phone calls or emails, but, I didn't fail to remember my loved ones back home. To make sure they knew I sorely missed them, I spent a couple hundred dollars on souvenirs for the majority of my line-sisters and my immediate family. My stay in the country was eye-opening, pleasurable, and, most importantly, drama free.

I was different when I returned to *Los Estados Unidos*. For starters, I saw one of my professors in Walmart and kissed him—in fact, I kissed everybody as is customary in traditional Mexican culture. It became increasingly difficult for me to speak solely in English, especially when I got passionate about a subject. I even went as far as seeing every Mexican as my brother or sister. When I was in the country, *mis amigos y familia* told me that I was an honorary Mexican, and I truly took that to heart. I even sat in a parking lot at Delaware State University bumping *"Sa Sa Sa, Ya tu Sa, Ya tu Sa"* by Climax like he was the Mexican Ludacris.

Unfortunately, not everyone was interested in hearing the details of my travels, especially not on campus. And my line-sisters in particular could not wait to tell me that I was involved in a campus-wide scandal. The pictures I had taken for Ed during my sophomore year resurfaced in my senior year. The pictures were never a huge secret. The women who were closest to me on my line had seen them in my bedroom. But the problem came with the connotation of the website. Ed decided to rebrand himself by choosing a very suggestive domain name which sent the wrong message in conjunction with my picture. Although my picture was not taken in distaste, the other models featured on the site were a different story. I tried to explain to my sisters that they were only modeling pictures, and it wasn't that big of a deal because I was not nude or even semi, but they did not share the same opinion. One sister actually told me that she worked hard to maintain her reputation and was not about to let it get ruined because of me. There are no individuals, only the group. The actions of one person reflect on the whole, and many of my big sisters did not welcome the reflection. It appeared that a lot transpired in my absence that triggered a spark, but my pictures just fanned the flame. I left serenity only to be ushered into chaos, and I did not like it. But what did I expect? Where there are females there's bound to be trouble. And it seemed like where there was Flora there was an impending disaster.

I tried to play down the hype as much as I could. Politically on campus, the pictures were not a good look. By this time I was a captain on my cheerleading squad, a member of a prominent sorority, and Senior Class President. At the end of junior year, I was elected to class office. Like one who matures, my goals and campus dreams evolved over the years. I desired to move away from positions that encouraged pageantry and set my eyes to one whose memory held significance and longevity—senior class president. My main goal was to speak at commencement; however, that was a gift only bestowed upon the class president, not the university queen. Also, due to my scheduled student teaching cooperating experience, I would be unable to sufficiently fulfill the duties and meet the demands of Miss Delaware State University. Therefore, class president was a superlative position for my lifestyle.

Despite my best effort, people would not move past the excitement caused by my dated modeling pictures. One afternoon I was in the library conducting research when one of my line-sisters ran up to me and said, "Flora guess what? I just left the computer lab, and I saw a couple of guys that had you up as their screen saver. Your picture is all over the place!"

I felt flattered, and I told her. Out of all of the beautiful women in the world, in the entertainment industry in particular, those guys chose me to look at regularly for their screen saver. Contrary to how they thought I should feel, I appreciated the compliment. To appease my sisters, I contacted Ed and asked him to remove my picture from his site. He refused. I tried to reason with him by telling him I was scheduled to student teach in the Spring, and I couldn't have something like that coming back on me. He didn't care. Then, I decided to play hardball by telling him that I did not authorize it for the new site, and I'd be contacting my attorney in reference to the matter. He welcomed legal action because he informed me that I signed away my rights to the pictures; therefore, he owned them and could do whatsoever he pleased with them. I hung up and immediately phoned my attorney who had recently won my accident settlement and informed him of the situation. He took a look at the site and said that he had no interest in touching the case. I was screwed. The picture was just the ammo gossipers needed to brand me as a hoe, ending all speculation. I guess my modeling portfolio did actually come with a price.

On Thursday evenings, I had late class that went from 6 p.m. to 8:45 p.m. Half way through, my instructor permitted us to take a ten minute break. Instead of relieving myself, as I needed to do, I spent one Thursday evening's break on the phone with my prophyte. I called her to address rumors I'd been hearing about me and my line sisters. During our conversation, she made it quite clear that she did not like me, and I made it equally clear that I could care less. She went on to say that she disapproved of our conduct after we crossed and became official members of our sorority. Then, she became specific and mentioned that several of us were being called "hoes" around campus. Her statement enraged me, for she was never around me and my sisters after we crossed, I was. And, in my presence, none of us did anything to cause this type of speculation. I thought she was lying. She had to be making this entire thing up, so I demanded answers.

"Who?" I asked. "You keep talking about these alleged hoes on my line, so who are they?"

She sniggered at my question before stating bluntly,

"You. You're one of the hoes."

After the phone conversation with my prophyte, I needed time to regroup. I had just come back to the country, and I was being attacked over something that was beyond my control. Plus, I didn't even look anything like the two-year-old pictures anymore. I was thinner and my hair was natural, but none of that mattered. They were going to believe what they wanted to believe about me regardless of the truth. I felt as if I worked hard trying to prove myself to this group of women for nothing. For a while, I wasn't feeling any love from my sorority, and I definitely wasn't experiencing any sisterhood. Consequently, I told my line-sisters not to contact me with concerning to any sorority event outside of the one I had already committed myself to, for I was taking a social sabbatical. They laughed when I told them, thinking it was said in jest when it was indeed stated in earnest. I needed to time to figure out how these got this far. Why did people perceive me this way?

On the eve of August 31, 2004, at the height of my sorority/campus drama, I wanted to get out and do something non-Greek organization-affiliated. It was the day of my best male friend's birthday, and I wanted to help him celebrate, so I brought a line-sister along who had grown to be more of my friend than a Greek affiliate. She and I attended his party, but there was another party going on simultaneously down the hall that she wanted to check out. I didn't want to go because there was a host of fraternity guys there that I was trying to avoid, but she didn't think that there'd be any trouble. Wrong. I ended up engaging in a highly intense dispute with a frat guy that left me shaken up. My sister encouraged me to go home, and we walked to our cars to do so, but something changed my mind. I told her I was not about to allow some asshole to ruin a night that I planned to enjoy. She asked me what did I want to do next, and I told her just walk around and pick on people until I felt better. She laughed, but agreed. As we were walking she spotted a guy from one of her classes whom she had a crush on. The guy was a very popular athlete around campus; nevertheless, I never formally met him, only heard of him and much like myself, his reputation preceded him. I asked her if she wanted me to hook her up. She played bashful, so I became assertive. There were three men I never saw before standing together in the direction my sister described while trying to identify the guy. Each one of the men wore Mardi Gras beads around his neck. She was reluctant to point, so I tried my best to follow her un-detailed description. When we approached the festive men, one of them walked off to engage momentarily in another conversation. I asked the two remaining guys if they knew E —everyone called him E which was short for Emmett. The smaller of the two spoke up and said that E was over there— the guy who walked away. I thanked the men before asking if they could call him over for me. The taller guy glowered when I asked the small request of them; meanwhile, the small dude did me the favor. E responded to his signal, ended his conversation, and came straight over. The moment he took sight of my sister he walked past his friends and me and went straight to her.

*Damn that was easy,* I thought. The two of them were taken in conversation and shared laughter, and I was left awkwardly standing there with two complete strangers and one of whom did not look too thrilled to have my company. I decided to ignore him and strike up a conversation with the smaller fellow. I asked if they were freshmen and to my surprise, they were seniors. *He is way entirely too small to be a senior,* I thought. I asked why I didn't know them and why they had not been in attendance to any of my class meetings. I was, after all, Senior Class president, and it was my duty to encourage all senior participation. The skinny dude said they were all on the baseball team and had no knowledge of any senior events. Well, luck came knocking at their door that evening. I ran down all of our past and forthcoming affairs with their corresponding dates. I asked the skinny one his name and where he was from, since he was the only one talking, the other guy just stood there looking on like a retarded mute. I, in return, volunteered my name and told him I was from Philly, despite his refusal to inquire. The silent friend peculiarly stepped away from me and his teammate and began buttoning his shirt up to its collar. He also adjusted the fit of his black hat embroidered with a black-and-white Atlanta Braves insignia. His teammate let out a chuckle and repeatedly shook his head at his now-distant friend. The silent guy found his voice and decided to finally acknowledge my presence. He looked at me and said, "I bet you'd like me if I wore my shirt like this." Who would have known that the mute with attitude possessed a sense of humor? He was poking fun at the urban attire of Philadelphia's men in a silly attempt at being flirtatious. His gesture was cute, so I smiled and walked over to him and began to fiddle with his shirt's collar that he happened to accidently flip while trying to be a comedian.

I said "You almost got it, but you'd have to fix your collar first." After I corrected his appearance, he called to his boys alerting them that he was ready to leave. He grabbed himself and informed everyone that he had to piss. The friendly, thin ball player looked at me to apologize on behalf of his friend. He told me that he was a little drunk because they were out celebrating his twenty-first birthday. That explained why all of them were wearing Mardi Gras beads, in Delaware, in September. The drunken, formerly silent comic stumbled off into the direction of the street. E and the slender gentleman went running after him. Meanwhile, my sister and I started heading back to our own vehicles. I don't know what is was, but I couldn't take my eyes off of the intemperate birthday boy. I found it attractive how he acted as if he wasn't paying me any attention.

I looked over at my sister and said, "He's kinda cute."

She grew excited. "Who?" she exclaimed.

"Him right there with the patchwork on his jeans."

"You want me to hook it up?" she daringly asked.

"Naw. I'm good," I replied.

"Alright, well I'ma go get his number," she said.

"Well, I'm going home. I'm tired. I'll see you later on tomorrow."

"Alright then. Bye."

"Bye."

I drove the short distance to my apartment glad that I did not let the altercation with the frat guy ruin my evening. Once in the door, I undressed, turned off my light, and crawled into bed.

*Ring. Ring.*

"Hello," I said half-awakened.

"Girl, what are you doing?"

"Trying to sleep. Why? What's up?"

"Oh. Nothing. I wasn't ready to go, so I went back upstairs to the party."

"Okay., but I thought you were going to go talk to the guys."

"Oh. Yeah, I did. I did."

"So did you get E's number?"

"Ha. Ha. Ha. Noooo. I'll just keep lookin' at him in class and smilin', that's all. But um, guess what."

"What?"

"Martin wants you to call him."

"Who the hell is Martin? I don't know no Martins."

"Yes you dooo," she insisted. "Martin is the guy who you said was cute. You know—birthday boy."

"Farah! You didn't!"

"Uh, Yes, I did. I told you I was going to get his number."

"Yeah, but I thought you meant E's number, not the other boy. I said he was cute, but I didn't say I wanted to talk to him."

"Ha. Ha. Ha. I was talkin' about getting Martin's number the whole time. But, Flora listen, he's really sweet. He's from North Carolina, and he really likes you."

"Now, I know you're lying. That boy don't like me. He barely said two words to me for the hour we stood outside talking."

"Yes he does. He started smilin' when I told him you liked him. Just call him."

"Girl, I don't have that boy's number."

"Uhhh, yes you do. Grab a pen."

"What!"

"Just write it down." I grabbed a pen and proceeded to write down the number that she read twice to verify. Then I repeated it back to her because she wanted to make sure that I actually wrote it down.

"Alright, I'll give him a call tomorrow."

"No, you can't."

"Why not?"

"Because he's expecting you to call tonight."

"You know you play too damn much with this."

"Ha. Ha. Ha. I know. Bye."

I lay in bed in utter astonishment not knowing what I was going to say to this boy with a warped sense of humor. I picked up to dial his number and after only two rings he answered.

"Hello, is this Martin?" I asked.

"This is him."

"Hi, Martin. This is Flora. I met you a few hours ago and wanted to apologize for my sister. I didn't ask her to do that. But, any way I wanted to check on you to see that you got in the house okay. You seemed pretty drunk."

"Yeah, I got in alright, but ummm I got to talk to you lata or somethin' 'cause I gotta piss. I'm about to piss all over this fuckin' floor. Bye."

Click.

"What a dick," I said out loud to myself, "Now this asshole is going to think that I like his nasty ass. There's no way in hell I'm callin' this boy again."

I got out of my comfortable egg-crate covered, full-sized bed and threw his number in the trash can. I was heated. I lay in bed for several minutes trying to get over my anger so I could fall back to sleep when my phone rang. I answered it in anticipation of Farah being on the line just calling at 2:30 a.m. to see if I kept my word. I couldn't wait to cuss her out while giving her the details of his crudeness. But when I answered, Farah's voice dropped ten octaves—it was Martin. This time he spoke like he had some sense. I suppose he pissed out his intoxication. He began the conversation with an apology for his improper telephone etiquette and also for calling me at such an inconvenient hour; however, he said that he felt that if he didn't call me back that very night then he'd lose the opportunity of ever talking to me again. He told me that he liked me a lot and had since our freshmen year.

My mouth dropped open in my dark bedroom with only the green light from the telephone's keypad to illuminate it. Until only a couple of hours ago, I never knew that a Martin from North Carolina existed and attended my school, and yet he had liked me for four years. He told me that every day he and his teammates would sit in the education building which housed the vast majority of my classes. And each day I would walk by him, never stopping to look in his direction. He said that I always seemed focused. I was impressed by the details of his observation. Many people that I share this story with find it creepy and stalker-esque. Believe me, I have had my share of creepy guys with stalker potential in college—there was the one guy who called my room phone every time he saw my bedroom light turn on. Then there was the other who left weird letters on the windshield of my car, telling me how he wanted to take me on a vacation to France. However, Martin's sentiments I found to be very charming. I told him that his hunch was correct. If he hadn't called me back that night, I wouldn't have spoken to him again. I even confessed to throwing away his phone number. I admitted how I felt about his behavior and that Farah had no right to pursue his phone number in the first place on my behalf.

I said, "I told her that I thought you were cute. But, I didn't say that I wanted your phone number."

With this truth spoken, Martin gained the assurance he needed. "So, you think I'm cute?" He totally disregarded everything else that I said. "I think you're cute, too. In fact, I think you're beautiful."

Put me in the box and wrap me up—the sober drunkard had me sold! By the end of our two-hour long 4 a.m. discourse, I learned that he lived in the apartments directly across the small parking lot from mine and on the same floor as me. In fact, our balconies faced each other. Every day for four years when I walked to class, I walked past him. Every time I stepped out onto my balcony, I never wondered who lived in the apartment that mine faced. I knew the people living beside him and everyone living beneath him, but I didn't know the one that I failed to notice contained the man who would become such an integral part of my future. What I was looking for in Magic Kingdom was right across the parking lot.

*My Love Song*
*I awake in the morning and sing of your love.*
*Songs of praise that continue throughout my day—You*
*my summer's day, who lights a fire*
*during my winter's eve*
*the melody of my heart, who serves*
*as my instrument of love—*
*Shower me with affection.*
*Kiss me with lips sweet as nectar,*
*—equally full of promise.*
*Our love is the chorus of my life,*
*and every day we write a new verse....*
*I sing to the world my favorite song of love— You*
*My Love Song.*

# CHAPTER TWENTY EIGHT
## *MY IMPERFECT TEN*

Sorority drama only brought Martin and me closer. The less time I spent with them, the more time he and I spent together in spite of our agreement to maintain a friendship in lieu of a titled association. However, it took only one month for us to redefine our status of availability. Martin made it abundantly clear that he was not afraid of a commitment and only conceded to the idea because of my insistence. It was as if he lived the male version of my life. He too experienced his share of hurt in previous relationships ranging from infidelity to having to end an intimate involvement against his wishes after investing himself entirely into its success. With this knowledge, I grew exceedingly confident that Martin would never cheat on me because he knew firsthand what it felt like to be emotionally wounded. He and I even had the same number of past sexual partners. Contrary to his memorable first impression, he was very well mannered, a true gentleman who only portrayed the very best of intentions. Whenever he spent the night over at my place, he'd sleep on the floor, or if I'd insist that he join me in my bed, he'd place a pillow in between the lower half of us while we cuddled. He exhibited a high level of self-discipline and aligned perfectly to my ten standards. Martin supported me in all of my endeavors—whenever I cheered, he was in the stands; whenever I had a speaking engagement, I could find him listening intently in the audience. He brought a fairytale ending to my tenure at Delaware State University. And to think that I could have had him and the happiness that he brought all along. After all, I held his interest for four years, so what could have possibly prevented him from expressing his attraction to me from the beginning?—rumors. A female confidant, who he considered to be like an older sister, advised him not to talk to me because I was a known hoe on campus. She told him this during my freshman year, during the time when I came to school with only two sex partners, during the time when I was involved in relationships. Where did this female, who I never met or heard of until I met Martin, obtain her information? From a friend of Champ's, a friend that was with him on the morning after my first date with Frat-boy. Everything comes full circle.

The lesson to be learned lies in the irony of she who judged me is also guilty in having a tarnished reputation. Only God is a proper judge, for only He is omnipotent and omnipresent; everyone else are mere members of a self-righteous jury, ready to convict and condemn off of only hearing what one purports as fact.

Martin took a chance on me despite admonitions from Champ's inner circle. And, whenever he had doubts, he brought his concerns directly to me for clarification. I didn't have any skeletons in my closet. My life was an open book. I always held the philosophy of showing my worst self in a relationship prior to revealing my better qualities. It is my belief that one must give a person the right to choose who he or she truly desires to be with, for better or for worse. If I reveal my worst qualities first, and the person sees them and chooses not to accept them, we'll save each other a lot of unnecessary heartache down the road.

Martin knew about my hang-up with Frat-boy, he knew about the people I dated on campus, he knew about my prior arrests, he knew that I had a problem with flatulence, he knew that I spit, he knew that I exercised fluent use of profanity, he knew about my modeling misadventure, he knew that I had a tendency to become explosive and impulsive when angered and was generally a difficult person to deal with. From the meals I routinely prepared for him, he learned I was an excellent cook. From the trips and events he asked me to accompany him to and that I agreed to attend, he discovered that I am firm believer in keeping my word. Martin knew that above all of my career aspirations having a God-fearing, closely knit family was at the forefront. I made Martin a promise that I would never cheat on him and break his heart like the girls in his past and told him I was willing to sacrifice my dream of teaching abroad to move to any location of his choosing after graduation to enable us to continue being together.

Martin listened to me while hearing others and made a well-informed decision to take our relationship to the next level. He had a general idea of what it meant to be involved with me; I, on the other hand, stood at a slight disadvantage. While I told Martin everything, he shared with me the minimal. When I made promises to him in regards to our future, he remained reserved all the while promising me nothing. These things I was willing to accept without any notion of their future ramifications.

Atlanta, Georgia is where Martin chose for us to live. He always wanted to return there since he had to leave as a small child to live in North Carolina with his mother. He yearned for the opportunity to form a stronger bond with his cousins and to be near enough to see his grandmother, whom he had strong affections for, regularly. When I agreed to move, it didn't register that Georgia was not central to both of our families. I was leaving my loved ones for my boyfriend to be closer to his. I don't think he even recognized the degree of sacrifice on my part. At the time, I only had two concerns: 1) not returning to my mother's home and 2) being with Martin—wherever he was I was willing to make my home, despite the lopsided arrangement. In April, I flew to Atlanta and got a job teaching English at a high school in Atlanta's metropolitan area. Additionally, I rented a townhouse in Dekalb County for Martin and me to begin our post-undergraduate lives together. He and I were scheduled to move in during mid-July. When I called Martin from Atlanta to tell him about the place I secured as our future residence, he started talking peculiarly. He mentioned how he didn't like the idea of playing the role without having the part. Then, he asked how I honestly felt about marrying him. My heart pounded nervously while I processed his insinuation. I told him I'd love to marry him; however, I didn't see any need for us to rush into it. In theory, I always desired to be married. That's what I was raised to want—to become a wife and a mother. However, the idea of practicing marriage brought to mind such permanency to one whose entire life had been about change. Change I learned to embrace; the notion of permanency is what frightened me.

As my relationship with Martin continued to flourish, people from my past crept back into my life. Champ and Side Jawn both contacted me out of the blue. And, Frat-boy, whom I heard from only once a month at best prior to my involvement with Martin, began calling me more frequently. I loved Martin, this is true, but my heart still desired closure from my previous relationship with Frat-boy. While seventy-five percent of it was occupied by my affections for Martin, the other twenty-five percent kept a small window of hope open for Frat-boy to get his act together; for his amended behavior was beginning to show promise. I convinced Martin to go forth as planned and illustrated how our move to Atlanta wouldn't be any different from what we were already doing in Delaware, spending every single night together although we each retained our own apartments.

*****

One person I had not expected to resurface was my father. Near commencement, I started seeing my father more regularly with my oldest sister. When his jail sentence was complete, I called him on a few occasions from unrecognizable phone numbers. He'd answer and we'd hold a brief conversation. I went out on a limb and invited him and my sisters to my graduation since they all lived nearby, in the Philadelphia area. I informed them all that I'd be speaking at the commencement ceremony. All three of them agreed to attend. My father said that my invitation meant a lot to him and assured me that he wouldn't miss it for the world. His acceptance made me happy, and I even put down my guard long enough to say, "Thanks Dad," instead of customarily referring to him by his first name.

I informed my family that my father and sisters would be attending my commencement. My mother's youngest brother and my grandparents congratulated me on taking steps towards reconciliation. As for my mother, she didn't have anything to say other than "Okay.." I tried calling him again to confirm his attendance two days before commencement. He didn't answer. I tried calling again the day before and still no answer. I even left a message with the date and time again. Nothing. I called my oldest sister, and she said that she hadn't heard from him and last she knew he was coming. Graduation day came, and I spoke in front of hundreds of people. My oldest sister and her family, my mother, my grandparents, my distant cousins from Philadelphia to Virginia, my sorors, and my boyfriend Martin were all there to share in the celebration of my great achievement—the first of my great-grandmother's descendants to graduate from a four year college. My father, however, was not in attendance. He didn't pick up a phone to say he wouldn't make it. He never called to give a rationale for his absence nor wrote a letter of apology. I received what I always received from him—nothing. So, why on Earth did I ever expect anything different? He showed me his worst, and I accepted it—Foolish me.

I wanted to accumulate additional funds before our move in July because the school year in Atlanta did not begin until August, and my new school district only paid its teachers at the end of each month. Therefore, I needed to have a little cushion for financial security. Besides, Martin had to finish his summer employment before he could join me, and that wouldn't be until August. I needed shopping money to keep me company while I was alone in the southern state. I took a job as a summer school teacher at a small high school in Delaware that paid twenty-eight dollars per hour. That supplied me with the capital I needed to live comfortably until my full-time employment began. I tried another business venture of auditioning for a movie in New York while visiting one of my best friends, the former Miss Junior. Miss Junior and I had become close when I was Miss Freshman, and we both escorted our reigning Queen into a bathroom located in the student center to give her more than just a few pieces of our minds. We were like a match made in heaven. She brought out my bougie side, and I brought out her inner ghetto. Miss Junior moved to Connecticut after graduation to pursue a career in television production. She sent me weekly emails of casting calls, even though I told her I had no interest in being in front of the camera. But, I took her up on her offer for auditioning for this role because it involved our sorority.

I made the drive up there with two of my other sorority sisters who shared interest in auditioning for the parts, Shaliese and Rasheedah. Rasheedah and I made it to the second cut and were just grateful for the experience. After our fun-filled day in the Big Apple, we made our way back to Miss Junior's luxurious apartment in Connecticut. When night fell and all agreed it was time to turn in, Rasheedah and Shaliese slept in the living room, and I retreated in the bedroom with Miss Junior. As she and I prepared for bed, I shared with her a secret concern that I had been trying desperately to put out of my mind without much success. I confided in her that I couldn't shake the feeling that something abnormal was happening to my body. She told me not to worry and that it happens to her all the time. Still, I felt uncomfortable with the possibilities.

As soon as I made it back to Delaware, I dropped off Rasheedah and Shaliese and drove, alone, to the pharmacy where I made a first time purchase. Returning to my empty apartment with the package in tow, I opened it and read the directions before I took the longest and most difficult three-minute test of my life. In fact, the test was so positive that it didn't even take the full three minutes to produce the results. PREGNANT the screen on the applicator screamed at me. Reading the word on the screen's solemn gray background was like reading that I had been sentenced to death. Life as I knew it was officially over. I grabbed the phone to call Martin but when he answered, I couldn't speak. The phone became a two hundred pound weight that I dropped before sprawling onto the floor, wailing all the way. I hooped and hollered and cried and prayed an unintelligible prayer with my face buried in the hallway carpet for what felt like hours until Martin's hand gently touch my back. Although I was capable of producing sound, I still was unable to create speech. All I could do was point in the direction of my bedroom. My master bathroom light was on; the packaging was still on its floor and the test which still flashed the results was still on its vanity. Martin came back out into the hallway. He picked me up and carried me to the living room sofa. He gave me a strong, comforting embrace, and I felt a solitary tear hit my cheek that was not produced by my dry eye ducts. He told me he was happy about the news and assured me that everything would be alright.

The next morning we lay in my bed and discussed our unknown future. In our confused discourse, one thing was apparent: we both wanted to give our child more than our parents had to offer—a stable home environment and two attentive parents. Martin looked into my eyes, and I knew what was next to come.

"Flora, I'm about to ask you a question."

"Okay."

"I need you to be absolutely sure when you answer me."

I took a deep breath before nodding my head in agreement.

"Will you—wait a minute. Before I ask you this, you need to know that if you start crying I'm gonna to punch you in your nose."

"What?" I asked stunned by his unexpected remark. While I stared at him with a slightly opened mouth and a forehead wrinkled with disappointment, he finally asked his question.

"Will you marry me?"

With my forehead still wrinkled and mouth still ajar but this time in disbelief of the unromantic proposal, I unenthusiastically gave a reply—"Yes."

There was no ring presented and it definitely lacked the element of romance, yet it was my marriage proposal, nevertheless.

The nurse practitioner who confirmed my pregnancy through a blood test told me that I conceived approximately two days after my college graduation. That explained my missing cycle in June and the increased tenderness in my breasts. When I made it back home to give Martin the confirmation, we immediately phoned our parents and presented them with the double announcement. In addition, we called our exes. Breaking the news to Frat-boy was the most difficult call I had to make. My heart emptied when I told him good-bye. Visions of me wearing a white dress down the aisle at our wedding vanished with the click of the receiver. Despite my strong affections for Martin, I wasn't excited about the idea of becoming Mrs. Season. I felt like I was fulfilling a moral obligation to our unborn child and to God. I couldn't stand to make any more phone calls delivering the news and pretending to be happy about my circumstance, so I sent out a mass email to everyone worthy of knowing and continued trying to accept the next phase of my existence. Providence has a special life bill that I read called plan reformation. I can't say that I particularly enjoyed its progressive stance; nevertheless, I fully render myself to its revisions of my life's plans.

# PART FIVE

*"Know what is in front of your face, and what is hidden from you will be disclosed to you. For there is nothing hidden that will not be revealed."*

—*Gospel of Thomas*

# CHAPTER TWENTY NINE
## *REVELATION*

Pregnancy is a beautiful experience that I hated every agonizing minute of. There's nothing like feeling life grow inside of you and seeing evidence of its existence obtruding through your stomach in an effect that makes one question whether or not they are actually human or have been unconsciously morphed into an alien. Afternoon sickness can be reserved for someone other than me. Charley horse cramps at three o'clock in the morning can remain a trait for the unconditioned athlete. And watching a tight four-and-a-half pack of abdominal muscles reduced to an ever-growing mass that forewarns others that you were once engaged in sexual activity is cruel and unusual punishment. But, what is even more torturous is telling a young woman that she is expected to wear a wedding dress and walk down the aisle while others gaze first to see if she dared to wear white, and secondly if they can actually see the fruit of her transgression.

At each bridal fitting, I was larger than the previous. I had to purchase my wedding gown in the size that I expected to be on the date of my wedding, a wedding that I did not want to have. I wanted us to simply state our nuptials with a Justice of Peace and have the ceremony five or ten years later to renew our vows.

But, no. Martin wouldn't have it any other way. He insisted that we have a traditional ceremony while I was stuck with all of the planning for the event that was three months away. Picking my friends was the easy part. I only had four, and any one of them could have easily been dubbed my Maid of Honor. In fact, if I had been thinking more clearly, I would have made the executive decision of giving them each the coveted position. However, I chose not the one who I knew the longest but the one who could most effectively execute the duties.

Like a wonderful production producer, former Miss Junior needed to know all of the details. She asked for my wedding colors. I told her I didn't any. She asked about the style of bridal gowns; I told her I hadn't picked them out. She asked about hair style and jewelry preference; I told her I didn't have any. She asked where I was registered; I told her I wasn't. But, my dear "Sistah Friend" did not give up on me. Everyday she'd call or email me ideas and forced me to make decisions regarding my own wedding. I finally decided to make my wedding colors crimson and champagne which proves I wasn't in my right state of mind, because my favorite color, for the record, is green. She purchased a domain name and a creator for a website that featured every detail about the wedding. Little did people know, the information on the site was as much for me as it was for them. Everything was moving at high speed, and I was just trying to hold on. I desperately wished that someone would pull the reins to make it all slow down.

In the midst of planning the celebration of our union, my relationship with Martin was experiencing a mild case of turbulence on our Georgia home front. While I was battling the nine month flu and working ten-to-twelve hour days as a first year teacher trying to familiarize myself with the new curriculum, Martin was at home unemployed and creating additional bills for me to pay. Quickly, I watched my account dwindle from thousands to mere cents. I didn't even have money enough to purchase more than five maternity outfits. We were living month to month off of a paycheck that came only once a month. We agreed to him getting one credit card to take care of personal expenses, like my wedding ring. Without my knowledge, he obtained three credit cards and ran up balances well into the thousands without having employment to repay what he borrowed. Having worked for five years, while in high school and college, at a Fortune 500 credit card company that had been featured in *Forbes* magazine, I warned him about the dangers credit card misuse. I informed him that having one was almost necessary to establish credit, but not to spend more than he could pay back. When using credit cards, one must have a plan for repayment. He did not heed my caution. Instead, he sought the advice of his "sister" who also worked at a credit card company. I would come home exhausted and would have to cook and clean. She knew the full scope of his credit woes; I, on the other hand, was just finding out. I encouraged him not to keep secrets from me, especially in regards finances, and I sacrificed more money in an effort of trying to help him get back on track. The way I saw it, we were about to get married and have a family. His money would become mine and mine his, so what he did with his money had a direct effect on our family. If there was any way to help him, I was obliged to do so.

However, the more I tried to help him, the more resistance from him I received. I wanted to call off the wedding, leave, and return home, but I remembered what home was like. Miserable— even more miserable than my then-current state. I didn't want to raise my child alone. I saw what being a single parent was like. But, what's a relationship when you've lost respect for the man you're with and you're the sole benefactor of the family? I worked so hard and worried so much that I couldn't even enjoy my pregnancy. In fact, I blamed my pregnancy instead of my reckless behavior for my predicament, and I saw it as the only thing binding me to a man I was about to marry but was just getting to know.

My subjection to stress increased in correlation to our rapidly approaching date of doom. My family financially contributed all that they could towards our wedding while his family did not voluntarily contribute anything. When we went to them for assistance, we were told to have our guests eat sandwiches at the church for our reception. Getting one thousand dollars for a six thousand dollar wedding was like pulling teeth. Ultimately, the remainder of the bill was forked over to us by my family just one week before we were scheduled to take our vows. Martin and I split the bill. He placed half on his credit card, and I placed the other half on mine. Our wedding was the beginning of both of our credit problems. Afterwards, we couldn't even afford to go away on a honeymoon. People unsympathetically called me with grievances wanting to know why they didn't receive an invitation or why so and so's name wasn't mentioned on the website that I had no significant part in creating. I was ready to crack at any minute. The weekend of our wedding things didn't get any easier. I reserved a beautiful restaurant at Penn's Landing, in Philadelphia, for our bridal party dinner. The restaurant was exquisite. Its prime location afforded patrons the luxury of overlooking the Delaware River while they dined. I knew that it was my future in-laws first time in my historic city, so I wanted to leave them with a grand impression. The only problem is only my soon to be father-in-law and his date were in attendance. The flight of my mother-in-law's family was delayed and arrived while we were all enjoying our second course, and my mother-in-law and her boyfriend decided at the last minute to not show up at all until our wedding day. Never mind tradition, never mind the preparation of me and my family, never mind how it looked to have the groom sit at a family dinner, that's meant for the families to get acquainted, without the presence of his family. On the day of our wedding, one of Martin's groomsmen was under the influence of marijuana. He reeked of cannabis all weekend, but I thought he had enough decency to be sober for the ceremony. Wrong. Another groomsman arrived with an Afro. A freaking Afro in my wedding pictures! And, two other groomsmen arrived with their girlfriends, so they refused to ride in one of the three limousines that my grandparents rented for our wedding. Above everything else, the thing that disturbed me the most was that Martin acted as if he didn't see any problems with any of it. He was singlehandedly allowing other people, people who were close to him, to ruin our wedding.

But, when I stood at the doors of the sanctuary holding my brother's arm, none of that mattered. All the feelings I had about him, his family, and his tacky groomsmen disappeared. My baby didn't move in my stomach during that moment; she decided to allow her mommy to enjoy her moment. Despite the happiness others tried to take away from that day, joy was there. I walked half way down the aisle before my daddy stepped in to take my arm. He led me the rest of the way and presented me to my husband. Before me stood a man wearing a white tuxedo. A man who always had the best intentions even when he messed up. A man with a pure heart. Tears flowed down his cheeks as he received me and a look of certainty gleamed in his eyes. This time I knew I had not made a mistake. He was the man I was destined to marry.

People came from all over to partake in our special day. My cousin Mia flew in from Egypt and sang at our ceremony; my husband's maternal relatives flew in from Georgia; my cousins and my mother-in-law drove from North Carolina; and my father-in-law flew in from Alaska. Friends that we hadn't seen in years arrived. And Martin's baseball teammates as well as my sorors came out in droves. It was truly a special reunion. So many familiar faces sat in the audience, but neither my father nor my sisters were in attendance. But the Lord works in mysterious ways. One of the officiators of my wedding was the man is who believed to be my paternal grandfather, a man whom my father has never formally met. And his son, who is also a pastor, assisted in the officiating. My grandfather and my uncle gave my husband and me their blessings; I believe that was my wedding gift from God.

Our reception was a blast. Even though my father wasn't present, I did not miss out on my father-daughter dance. My grandfather—my daddy—danced with me, and it looked like it was the first time he danced in all of his seventy years. My grandmother told me that he didn't even dance with her on their wedding day. This confirmed that I am my daddy's little girl. I also danced with Martin's father who I met for the first time the day before, and Martin danced with both his mother and mine. The reserved Martin read me a poem he wrote for me and immediately then after my bridesmaids and I pulled him into the middle of the floor and serenaded him through dance to Destiny's Child's "Cater to You." My sorority sisters then surrounded me and honored me with a tribute that is only reserved for special occasions. The music was good, until my cousin, the DJ, had to leave to service a party that was actually paying for his talent, and my other cousin without DJ experience took over "the ones" without "the twos". The bar was free for the entire evening, so many of the guests were high off of the spirits, and the food was edible—none of that fancy-smancy stuff. When the time came to depart, Martin and I hopped back into our limo which dropped us off at the hotel. Martin said he needed to grab his luggage from one of his groomsmen's rooms prior to heading to our bridal suite. I waited outside the guys' room for him for several minutes before heading alone to our room. When I walked inside, everything was breathtaking. My family decorated the room prior to our arrival. Champagne was on ice. Flutes with our names and wedding date rested carefully beside it. Confetti and rose petals were all over the large circular bed. While waiting in the room, I decided to surprise Martin. I quickly undressed and slipped into my seductive maternity bedroom attire reserved for the occasion. I hopped onto the bed, positioned myself where I could be in clear view of the door, and held an erotic pose. The room was still, the lights dimmed, and the ice for the champagne melted. After forty minutes, I grabbed my phone to call Martin. When he answered, loud music glared in the background, and he was laughing. I asked calmly, "Martin where are you? I've been waiting for over forty minutes?"

"Ha. Ha. Ha. I'm in the car with Carl." Carl was the same groomsman who was high in front of my family the entire weekend.

"You're with Carl. Well, why are ya'll in the car? I thought your stuff was in his room."

"It was. I got it. The fellas and I headed out to get something to eat. We're about to go to Wendy's.

"Get something to eat? Get something to eat! We spent four thousand dollars on the reception. You should have already ate!"

"I didn't eat anything. I forgot. I was drinkin' the entire time."

"Martin, I've been sitting in this room waiting for you after I stood outside of their door. This is our wedding night. You're not supposed to be with them. You're supposed to be with me!"

"Alright. Alright. I'm on my way back now. I'll be there in like ten minutes."

So, this is what my marriage is going to look like.

# CHAPTER THIRTY
## *BITTER SWEET*

I wanted the day that I delivered my first child to be absolutely perfect. I wanted to present my best physical self for the very first time my daughter was to lay her eyes on me. I wanted her birth to be recorded, and I planned on making her watch it on every birthday starting at age twelve as a method for promoting abstinence. I did much to prepare for her birth. I kept a journal chronicling when I first learned I was carrying her in my womb and planned on completing it on the day that I gave birth. I decorated her nursery and prepared my heart to give her unconditional love. Martin was very much involved in the process for he was equally excited about our first child, in spite of the fact that she was a girl instead of the coveted male child. He would often lean in very close to talk to my stomach and the baby would often move vigorously in response to his voice. We would joke that she was trying to kick him in his face. Martin attended many of the major doctor's appointments with me and went along on the tour of the hospital so we'd be better prepared when the time actually came. But nothing can really prepare you for that moment.

On my cue, my mother stood over me and styled my hair and painted my face. She then retreated to the sofa positioned across from my bed in the delivery room. Just that fast her role shifted from mother, to cosmetologist, and now to film director. She picked up the recorder and began filming the memorable event. Martin took his place by the nurse to assist with the birth.

Martin grabbed the heel of my left foot and brought that leg into my chest. An assisting nurse grabbed my right heel and did the same.

The nurse said, "Flora it's time. Are you able to push?"

"Now that I have my epidural, I can do whatever ya'll need me to. Just tell me when to stop." The three nurses in the room all laughed.

"Alright, now. I'ma hold you to it. Now, I need you to start pushing. One, two, three—good that's enough. That was real good, but now I need you to do it again. Ready? One, two—."

"Wait." I said. "Mom, the light to the camera went out."

"Flora! You don't stop pushing for that. I can still see what's goin' on. Keep pushin'."

"Mom, I think you should plug in the camera. I don't think that it's still recording."

"Flora, what are you doing?" asked Martin. "The nurse is ready for you to continue pushing."

"Alright. I'm ready now. Sorry nurse."

After twelve long hours of labor, I gave birth to my seven pound daughter.

The little girl who invaded my dreams for the months leading up to the delivery of my daughter was a pretty dark skin girl with kinky black hair. Aside from the hair which I assumed she got from Martin, she reminded me of my baby pictures. That little girl was who I was expecting. But the infant girl who suckled my breast and rested peacefully in my arms was white with silky, curly black hair. Even though she had green blotches on her hands and feet, in my eyes, she was flawless. Was this white baby really mine? She had to be. No one had left the delivery room yet, so she couldn't have been switched. I stared at her hard trying to detect my features in her. I could see that she had Martin's head and his grandmother's nose, but it was her feet that confirmed her maternity. Both of her feet were identical to my right foot; the one that I call "my ugly foot." Martin likes to tease and say that my toes are throwing up gang signs, playfully mocking their distortion. I kissed her little feet and smiled. On her, they looked good enough to be featured in a Jergens commercial. My baby was breathtakingly gorgeous, and I couldn't take my eyes off of her. I fell in love instantly and was in utter disbelief that she was mine for keeps.

After the nurses took her away for bathing, dressing, and observation, Martin was still grinning ear to ear. I thought he was still in shock over the experience. I smiled too and asked what he was smiling about. I wanted to hear it in his own words.

He said, "I'm proud of myself. I promised my sister that I wasn't going to cry, and I didn't. She teased me because she told me I was going to cry at our wedding. And I did. So, she said I was going to do the same thing at Shaniah's birth, but I didn't."

The smile that was pasted on my face in waiting for him to say something fatherly, romantic, or even loving disappeared. I lay in that bed with a sore vagina from birthing his first child that had undeniably his head, and he wouldn't allow himself to show emotion because of a promise he made to a wench who wasn't even his real sister. I let him know how foolish and juvenile he was, and my disgust for him steadily augmented. While my mother was sitting on the sofa silently listening to me lay into him while still on the delivery bed, I asked her to let me see the footage. I needed something to take my mind off of the spectacle standing before me. She dropped her head as she told me that the recorder died from lack of power just as the baby's head was crowning. Both my husband and mother alike were trying to sabotage my experience.

Martin's paternal sense went into overdrive the moment we walked into the door of our home. Like the alpha male, he paced our home with his chest puffed out in pride. High levels of testosterone bled through his pores. My mother did the unthinkable on our first eve home as a new family—she threatened his cub by requesting permission for the baby to sleep with her at nights. Martin immediately came upstairs to me and ranted while I lay in the bed suffering from post childbirth pains.

The audacity of her actually thinking it would be acceptable to sleep with his child on the first night that she entered our home. How dare she want to deprive us of our parenting experience? She had two children, so she had two chances to experience what it is like to sleep with her very own children on that first special night that they are brought home. No! Absolutely not. He was not going to have it, so he refused her to even be left alone with our daughter for the remainder of her visit. I was too mentally and physically drained to play mediator. If the baby slept with us, I didn't care. If the baby slept with her, I didn't care just as long as I could get my sleep.

Without arguing, I consented to my husband's decisions. I was in no condition to contest. My bottom, dominated by pain, throbbed. My engorged breasts were knotting and excruciating. It seemed like overnight I went from a semi-full B-cup to a double D. I loved the appearance of my newfound voluptuous twins, but I could do without the intolerable discomfort of having more supply than demand. At this point, I desired to nurse and was unwilling to dry out my milk completely, so as a remedy my mother suggested that I rest my bosom in warm-to-hot water to relieve the pressure and allow the milk to seep out on its own; this way I could still lactate at the baby's request. That method was not working fast enough for me, so she and I proceeded to wring my breasts out and milk me like a cow over my bathroom sink. At that point, I had no dignity left. My mother took control of my left breast, and I handled my right.

While we stood over the sink grabbing my breasts with both hands in a repeated downward motion, slowly milking me until streams of the nutritious fluid flowed in the white basin, my mother looked at me and said, "Flora, you're not going to like what I have to say, but Martin has strong similarities to your father."

What would possess her to say such a vile and contemptuous thing? Her words, in my mind, were malicious. She was trying to draw a wedge between me and my husband. She knew

I never wanted a man who had any characteristics or other resemblances to my father. Her words stung and my rage and eyes simultaneously began to swell. She said this to me while I was unclothed, disoriented from pain. She knew I was vulnerable. For that moment, my mother became my enemy. *She's just jealous*, I was convinced. *She's angry because I'm married, and she wanted to be. She's upset because Martin is showing affection towards our child, affection that my father never gave to hers. She's furious that we have a home—a nice home—and were doing well, relatively, without her.* I silenced my mother at once. I told her that she was to respect my husband in his home, and I wouldn't tolerate anyone talking about him to me—not my mother, not my friends, not even his own family. No one. I made it brutally clear I wanted her out of my house, and the remainder of her stay was uncomfortable for us all.

Depression kicked in shortly thereafter and lasted for a period of three days. During those bleak hours, I lost any desire to leave my bedroom and left Martin and my mother to dwell in the warzone alone. She'd make sly remarks towards him and shoot him dirty looks, and he'd make sly remarks back then come upstairs to tell me that his in-law respect tank was running on E. Whenever Martin mentioned the baby, I began to cry. He had to resort to using formula for her because I cried whenever I tried to nurse. I didn't want to see her. I didn't want to hold her. I didn't want to hear of her. But, oddly enough, I never ceased loving her.

The night before my mother returned to her Delaware residence Martin's mother arrived. We only had a two-bedroom house, so we gave up our room to his mother. Martin slept on our loveseat, and I, the new mother with a still-sore vagina, slept on our sofa all the while she rested comfortably on our king-sized pillow top bed. As soon as my mother left, she moved into our guest room and immediately wanted to know how she could be of service. She did our laundry and cleaned our home. I was grateful that she came. When night fell, Martin came to me and said that his mother wanted to sleep with the baby, and he told her already that it was okay. I didn't understand the discrimination for a few days prior he was in an uproar over my mother's request. He attempted to justify himself by saying that his mother only wanted to keep the baby to help me out so that I could rest because once all of the help left, we were on our own. The point was valid, but his actions seemed to be unjust. He noticed his unfair treatment towards my mother, but he didn't try to rectify it by denying his own mother, like he did mine, the privilege of keeping her first grandchild. Although my mother wasn't my favorite person at the time, she was still my mother, nevertheless, and I retained my childhood sense of needing to protect her—from everyone but me. How I treat her is between me and her, (we've come to have an unspoken understanding) but that doesn't give someone else the green light to take on the same actions, for they do not share the same relationship, nor had the same experiences. This may sound absurd, but it my attitude about my family.

Later that evening, we lay in our bed alone together staring into each other's eyes. Martin thanked me for the first time for giving birth to his child. He said that was something that no other woman offered him, and recognized the sacrifice of my body I made on his behalf. He told me there was nothing another woman could ever possibly do for him that would equate all that I've done. With these words, I temporarily forgot about his maltreatment of my mother. With these words, I became sure that he would be forever faithful to me and our child. In these words, I heard hope.

Nevertheless, Martin's insanity continued to thrive after his mother's departure. When my grandmother called and made mention of her watching our baby, he told me that she could never watch his child. First my mother and now my grandmother, I didn't understand. He said that he didn't trust her because I always say that she's crazy, and he doesn't know how she is with children. He did, however, as he mentioned, know how his own family is with children. Being raised in the church, I was brought up to believe that the woman is to submit to the headship of her husband. However, I believe that this should only be done when the husband is fulfilling his roles of provider and protector. This was not my case. Therefore, as the mother of our child and the financial head of our household, I needed to make an executive decision by letting him know that our daughter would not solely be subjected to the care of his family. Like all families, mine certainly has its share of dysfunction and much of that has to deal with personal choices. But, we are not a clan that abuses children. We are loud, obnoxious, and sometimes rude. We fight others and each other, but we know how to come together in a time of need or celebration. We are proud, strong, and zealous. My family is an acquired taste, much like myself, and he made the decision to marry me, even after seeing where and who I came from. Both of our families would play a shared role in the life of our child; however, he and I had the leading role. He understood and shook his head in acquiescence.

# CHAPTER THIRTY ONE
## *BOUNDARIES*

Approximately one month after the birth of our daughter, Martin landed a steady job. The income he brought in was decent; however, it demanded him to work twelve-hour swing shifts. Neither of us was comfortable with the idea of placing our infant in childcare, so we alternated caring for her. After I came home from work, we literally only had one hour to share with each other before he had to leave for the start of his shift. When he returned from work at seven o'clock in the morning, I was getting dressed and preparing to depart for school. Needless to say, he was unable to provide adequate care for an infant while he yearned for sleep from working twelve consecutive hours. To worsen matters, his employer was condescending, disrespectful, and, to put it plainly, rude. I was concerned about him working security alone in the heart of Atlanta. He often complained that crack-heads would break into the scrap yard he was securing to steal copper. Most nights I called Martin during his shift to make sure he was safe and staying awake. I wanted to be on the phone with him while he made his rounds in case I needed to call 9-1-1 on his behalf.

But, as time would tell, often nights after Martin hung up the phone with me at twelve o'clock in the morning, he would pick it back up to dial his sister. I was often silent about the nature of their relationship because I didn't want to appear jealous; however, there are certain boundaries in marriage that should not be crossed, especially when I had never met the girl.

When Martin and I dated in college, he told me about how close they were. They were so close that she felt comfortable enough to request money from him whenever she needed a new weave ponytail. I told to him on several occasions that I wanted to meet her. If there was going to be another woman playing an integral part in his life, I needed to meet her. I was even willing to forget about all the things she said about me without even knowing me for Martin's sake. Each time, she refused.

One night, while he was over my house, she needed to pick up money from him that he owed her. I told him to invite her over to pick it up. She declined. I told him that he could leave the money with me, and she could get it from me later, but she also said no to that offer.

Another time, she called him while I was over at his apartment. She said she was in the neighborhood and wanted to stop by to watch a movie. He told her I was there but invited her to join us, and she did not take his offer. So, since I did not actually know the woman my husband was engaged in conversation with during ungodly hours, I told him that it was inappropriate and was to stop at once. It was my place as his wife to make such a request. No conversations should go on with members of the opposite sex who are not family past nine o'clock when you are married. After I told him that, he felt that it was imperative that she and I speak. One afternoon he told her that very thing on the phone. She agreed to hold a conversation with me, but this time I was the one to decline. While she was still on the phone, Martin called me a dick-head for my refusal to talk to her. After all of the times I extended an olive branch, he called me, his wife, a dick-head.

Then there was the case of his ex—the one who was never officially his girlfriend but was romantically involved with him all the same. I found out accidentally one evening he had off from work that he'd been calling her while I was at school. While he was sleeping on our loveseat, his mobile phone rang. I couldn't make it to answer it in time, so when I flipped it open to see who called, I noticed he had a missed call from one of his male friends from North Carolina. However, the rest of his call history was in clear sight. Curious, I strolled through his history and noticed several calls made from his phone to a blocked number. "Why would he block his number to call one of his friends?" I wondered. The situation seemed odd, so I decided to investigate. It was my first time ever checking his phone, and I was more nervous than a kid playing Hide and Seek. My stomach did acrobatics during the long ominous flight up our eight stairs. Lightly I shut the door behind me once I made it securely into our bedroom. I dialed the anonymous number from his phone and hoped to hear a male's voice that would confirm my insecurity and make me feel horrible for doubting his fidelity, but, as I suspected, a soprano voice reverberated in my ear. I wanted to hang up and sob into my pillow as a sign of grief over a broken heart. But, I needed answers—from her. There was no time to play into my emotions.

I had only seconds to respond to her twice stated hello, so I said "Hi, is this Charlotte?" using the first name I could think of. The woman with a North Carolina phone number politely said no. I apologized and told her that I meant to call Charlotte but was just curious to know whose number I dialed because I had it in my call history?

She giggled and said "Bebe."

I then said, "Hello, Bebe," in an emphatic tone, "Do you know my husband Martin Season?"

She hesitated for several seconds, probably debating whether or not she should hang up before answering my question. "Yes," she finally said.

I then asked her how she knew my husband. Her reply of they were friends who went to school together was quite ambiguous. I needed their friendship defined. I inquired if he was her ex-boyfriend, and she said convincingly that he was never her boyfriend. I thanked her politely for her time and hung up the phone.

After leaping down several stairs and landing thunderously, I awoke sleeping Martin. I stood over the loveseat with clenched fists where he was still laying down and asked him forcefully with disorientated eyes who was Bebe? Slowly he began to rise as he looked at me with caution and delivered to me an identical answer. "She's just my friend from high school." It was like they rehearsed it. My jaws began to tighten, and I paced back and forth like a tigress. What made everything difficult is Martin never told me the names of any of the girls he had been with. He gave me bits of details but always avoided divulging names. He tried to calm me down by saying that their conversations were nothing and assured me that she wasn't a threat because she was married and lived in Connecticut. He only called her because he had been considering entering into the military and wanted her input about her particular branch. EUREKA! That's it. The longer he spoke, the clearer things became. I started piecing together various stories he told me during the time we dated. I remembered him telling me about a girl who left to get married while he was still seeing her. I also knew that he lost his virginity to her. And, I knew that the coquette moved to Connecticut and was in the military. She called him once before when I traveled to watch him play baseball in Florida and after that he changed his phone number at my request to eliminate the possibility of being contacted by exes. But now he was the one calling her. I guess I wasn't specific enough in my request. I asked why he blocked his number, and he claimed it was to prevent her from calling him and upsetting me. But he had to think I was stupid. I can smell bull manure from miles away. He blocked his number to prevent her husband from knowing that he was calling his wife. All I could contemplate was the fact that despite my strong affections for Frat-boy, I respected our marriage enough not to contact him. When I married Martin, I had forsaken all others. Yet, he could call her constantly while I was at work, while he was supposed to be watching our daughter. The inkling of her giggling at the sound of our daughter's coos or cries drove me to the brink of insanity. The gall—to call her in my house (that I paid for) and to disrespect me in front of my daughter. You mean to tell me that I gave up Frat-boy for this non-sense? I birthed him a child, I paid to move him to Georgia, I cooked for him, bought furniture for her to rest comfortably on, cleaned his house all for him to call his ex, a woman who denied being in a relationship with him, a woman who got married to someone else while he was still boinking her was beyond belief.

The military. He told me he would never consider joining the military. Now, he's calling her for military advice when both of his parents spent over twenty years in the service, while he had cousins and an uncle who took up arms to protect our country. The direct insult to my intelligence infuriated me. I retreated up to my room to think and made the mistake of playing Destiny's Child's "Through With Love" song. With each beginning verse, my rage intensified. He stood at the bottom of the stairs calling my name until I whirled a twenty pound dumb bell from the loft. It missed him, but that didn't stop me from flinging another one in hopes of hitting him instead of the plastered wall that it landed through. Throwing his clothes down the steps and demanding that he leave my home at once wasn't enough for him betraying my confidence. I wanted to cause him physical trauma. I picked up a baseball bat that he kept stored in our bedroom and waited for him to enter. He never did. So, to bring myself temporary gratification I went to work on his entertainment center and television and hoped for the opportunity to go to work on him. By the time he finally came upstairs my anger was beginning to subside. The bat that I clenched was now feet away from me on the debris-covered floor. He looked around the room until his eyes finally found mine then told me that his family was downstairs and he was going to stay with them. I said okay and then suddenly felt ashamed. What did I do? How could I allow myself to lose complete control like that? What if he did enter the room while I was plotting my attack? I could have seriously hurt him. Or, the tables could have turned and he could have seriously hurt me out of self-defense. How was I ever going to be able to explain this to my daughter? The reason why she had to grow up without a father is because daddy exercised bad judgment in making a phone call. A phone call. I was ready to throw my marriage away over just that. As I sat alone with an infant in a house that I destroyed but had to rebuild, no gratification existed. I was lonely and realized that I wasn't through with love but willing to give it a second chance, and even a third and a fourth if that's what it required.

The aftershock of our highly publicized marital spat revealed not only our true colors but also our family's personal outlook on marriage and ours in particular. The day following the altercation, I spoke with his concerned mother. She had every right to be concerned for I had threatened bodily harm to her only child. She was also upset over my destruction of property that she purchased and gave to us out of her good will. She couldn't understand what aspect of the situation was worthy of my becoming upset.

She said, "I mean don't you still talk to your male friends?" Her question surprised me because she made it sound like it was no big deal as if it was normal and acceptable for a married person to engage in such tempting behaviors. I informed her that I severed all ties to my exes the moment Martin and I became engaged. I also shared with her my philosophy that there is no room in a marriage for ex-boyfriends and ex-girlfriends. If I wanted to continue a relationship with them, I would have remained single. She then went on to let me know how fortunate I was that Martin even considered marrying me and that he only did it because I was pregnant. Guess she had no idea that months before my pregnancy he and I discussed our future and prospective names for our children. And that he and I agreed to having four in total. And that he inquired about my interest in matrimony exactly one month before I conceived our child. Then he had other relatives advising him to just end it. They said he was too young to be going through this.

Reader, tell me this—what adult age is the right age to experience the peaks and valleys of a marriage? At what age should one commit him or herself to another person? People fascinate me. It is acceptable in Western culture for one who is eighteen or older to honor their commitment to the military. No matter how much they may dislike the arm services, they will be a stench in the nostrils of their country and community if they up and quit before completing their term of service. People will tell them, "you took an oath to defend your country and you must honor your commitment. Suck it up. Finish out your term of service." However, when it comes to the sanctity of marriage, when it comes to honoring that lifetime commitment made to another individual in the eyes of God and man, divorce and breaking marital vows becomes socially acceptable. Married couples are told, "Well, if you're not happy, you should leave." Absurdity. Imperfect people in search of that perfect person are the most delusional of them all. There will always be someone who looks better, or makes more money, or is more or less affectionate, but that is not what the union of two people is about. Marriage is not trial and error. It is only perpetual trial and in that trial called marriage there is bound to be error of some degree; however, one must try and try again until the trials become habitable.

I thank God for my family for when I called my divorced mother to complain about the situation, she refused to listen to me. She said that is your husband, and you two are to work through it. When I called my grandfather and requested him to bring me home at once, he told me to truly think about all of the consequences of my projected actions. He said although he was willing to grant my request he wanted me know that marriage takes work and it wasn't going to be easy, but he believed that we would work it out and be alright. Martin and I learned in premarital counseling that in order for two people to become one there must be boundaries for friends as well as family. Hearing that wisdom is easy; however, applying it takes much effort.

# CHAPTER THIRTY TWO
## *GROWING PAINS*

amily, career, and homeownership are universal priorities. At the age of twenty two, I already attained my family and secured my dream career. The pursuit of my final goal of homeownership by the age of twenty three was just underway. I was approved for a home mortgage and purchased a 2,700 square feet four-sided brick home with half of an acre of land in the Georgia suburb of Newton County. It wasn't love at first sight for me, but it had the potential to make me fall in love. The bones of the house were great. My cement driveway could hold eight cars and although my home lacked the coveted white picket fence, I accepted a chain-link one around the perimeter of my backyard as a compromise. My master bedroom contained his and her closets and inside our master bath was an additional walk-in closet for the two of us to share. Three bedrooms, two full bathrooms, a living room, dining room, eat-in kitchen, bonus room, over-sized laundry room, walk-in pantry, attic, two-car garage, bay windows, and French doors were all of mine to have at twenty three years of age. With a little paint, a few updated appliances, and minor aesthetic renovations, my first home would be ideal. And, I could pay it the attention it needed over a five–to-ten year span. That is how long I anticipated living in the house before considering it for an investment property.

Martin selected the house. It wasn't my first choice. He fell in love with its master bathroom. He appreciated how the extra deep garden tub separated the his-and-hers sinks. He liked the idea of keeping his side messy without having to hear me nag. He also liked the idea of my hair not being all over his sink or its surrounding floor. My first choice for a home was completely updated. It had a jetted Jacuzzi in the master bath, a formal dining room, a foyer, and curb appeal. When I walked into its front door, I could see myself living and entertaining in the home. Not so much so at my Newton County property. But I purchased it nevertheless because it's what Martin preferred. Despite him choosing the house, he never felt like it was our home. I tried to include him as much as possible in the mortgage process; however, he lacked interest in most of it. Then, he would become upset whenever he was probed by his mother in regards to its purchase and was unable to intelligibly answer any of her questions. He hated having to say, "I don't know. You'll have to ask Flora. She's handling all of that." Truth be told, he opposed us purchasing a home. Homeownership was my dream. No one in my family owned a home at my age. My mother didn't purchase her first home until she was in her forties.

When Martin and I became engaged, we made pacts. The first pact was that divorce would never be our option. The second pact was just because we were getting married fairly young, that didn't mean the pursuit of our dreams ceased. We agreed to always encourage each other to pursue our dreams. Just because he decided to give up on his dreams didn't mean I had to do the same. Martin hoped to play professional baseball, and for a while, it looked like he had a pretty strong chance. But, unfortunately, that opportunity didn't come for Martin in college. And, as much as I encouraged him to attend try-outs for nearby professional teams, he refused. He said that he would have considered pursuing professional ball if he didn't have a family to consider. But, I knew that if he didn't pursue it, that "what if" question would forever linger in his mind. I didn't want him blaming me or our child for whatever he failed to accomplish. And, that's exactly what happened in spite of all of my encouragement; in spite of me offering to pay for his travel expenses to try-out. So, I didn't pay much attention to his feelings, for it was my money and my dream, and it would be my home for my daughter. All of the bills were placed in my name, and the moment we moved into my dream house our marriage was on the brink of disintegration.

Moving into our own home allowed Martin and me to see a different side of each other. When things needed servicing, we didn't have a maintenance man to come over to fix it as we did with properties we rented. We became Mr. and Mrs. Fix it. The effects of Martin growing up without his father in the home became increasingly apparent for he was unable to fix anything, and he was without a clue for whom to call in the event that things needed special attention. I grew up with only my mother also, and I learned to be not only handy but resourceful, so I didn't have a problem with picking up the slack in this area. But, Martin was also extremely lazy. He didn't like to take out the trash, mow the lawn, or rake the leaves. When he selected the house, the first area of concern I had was the amount of land that came with the house and its upkeep. He said that when he lived with his mother, he cut her lawn all the time and didn't have any quarrels about cutting grass. He said that all he needed was a self-propelled lawn mower, so I bought him one. But, when we brought it home from the store, not only did he not know how to assemble it, he also didn't know how to start it. I tried to show Martin different things and explain to him why something wasn't working and how to fix it, but he became angry. After a while, he stopped trying and left everything up to me without even offering his hand to assist. I felt like I was both wife and husband and saw that, aside from sex, Martin really didn't have anything to offer me.

Our arguments increased, and some had the potential to turn violent. For a while, I wondered if my mother was correct in her assessment of Martin because I was beginning to fear that he would one day hit me. A few hours after we moved into our new home, Martin picked up his boot and threw it at my head in the midst of an argument. A month later, he jumped in my face and told me to "do something" when I wasn't even trying to fight him. And another time, he grabbed his baseball bat and motioned like he was about to hack my car. I am the first to admit that I have a violent temper, but it takes a lot for me to get to my breaking point. Typically, I explode after I allow things to build up inside of me for a prolonged period. But, it didn't seem like it took too much for Martin. Just one push of his button— BOOM! When he became angry to avoid hitting me, he would break stuff. One day I challenged him to break or destroy something that he bought, something that would cost him money to repair or to replace instead of me—there was nothing. Instead of us talking out our problems, I was often left alone for hours while he retreated to be with his family in Georgia. I had no friends and aside from him and our daughter no family whatsoever in our city, our county, or our entire state. In premarital counseling we were taught to not discuss our marital problems with our family, so I refrained from venting to family or friends. No one truly understood all I was enduring in our first year of marriage.

My body was resilient after the birth of my first child. In fact, it was even better than what it was before I had the baby. Externally, I looked fabulous. Internally, I felt like a failure. I gave all that I was taught to give. I cooked and served him his dinner, cleaned our home, gave up my vehicle to him when his died, gave him money whenever he needed it, and gave him a child, all the while not asking for anything in return, yet I could not make my husband happy. Our sex, the one other thing that kept us together, became scarce. My husband paid me no compliments and gave me very little attention. We only spoke to each other in regards to the business of our relationship: what time are you picking me up from work, this is what our daughter needs, these are the bills to be paid this month, it's time to go grocery shopping again, etc.

I still went to work with a smile on my face each day, but, during my planning period, I would lock my classroom door and cry my heart out. I cried about our financial situation. I cried about the state of my marriage. I talked to God during these times and acknowledged my sins to Him. I knew our marriage wouldn't be easy because we went against His will while we dated by fornicating and shacking up, but I never expected it to be this mentally exhausting. In that first year of my marriage alone, I began to learn the true definition of long-suffering. I had first period planning during my first year of teaching, and one day I couldn't make it through the preparation of my lesson, for the burdens of my heart weighed down my spirit. Someone came tapping at my classroom door, so I did my best to straighten myself out. It was the other young English teacher from across the hall. She was recently divorced from an abusive husband who left her penniless and with her credit in shambles. She told me that she had a dream about me the night before, and the Lord impressed upon her heart to give me the money she had reserved for tithes and offering. She also said,

"I don't know what's going on, but stay with your husband. Trust me. I'm divorced, and there ain't nothing out there. Ya'll have a beautiful little girl, and unless he's putting his hands on you, you stay put with your husband."

What could I say? She already spoke the concerns of my heart without me having to mention a word. Tears streamed from my eyes as I humbly accepted her check for three hundred fifty dollars. She turned around to walk out of my classroom, and I couldn't help but to rejoice. I fell to my knees and praised him from whom all blessing flow.

All of life needs attention of some sort to exist. Flowers need the attention of the sun and rain in order to survive, but I was isolated from all of my family and friends when I needed people most. As a result of not frequently seeing one another, our phone conversations were a rarity. I sacrificed all of my relationships for someone who was not taking care of me at all. The men at my job paid me plenty of attention. Every day I went to work, they did not withhold any comment of admiration; however, I'd wear the same outfit home only with retouched makeup, and I'd hear nothing from my husband. To make matters worse, we'd visit his mother and he'd compliment her on her hairstyle, so I knew he was capable of producing such a thought.

Eventually, I started calling and emailing Frat-boy again. He was all but too eager to hear from me. I'd tell him I was leaving my husband, and he'd tell me to just come to Florida to be with him. He said what I wanted to hear, and it pissed me off. It upset me that Frat-boy had to lose me in order to appreciate fully appreciate me, and it dawned on me that my poor excuse for a husband would probably be the same way. The reality was I wasn't a love-smitten teenager or college student who could just dump her stupid boyfriend. My life was more complex than that. I brought a child into the world that deserved the commitment of both of her parents. I invested my money into a home, in a state where I had no one. My credit cards were maxed out. I couldn't just pick up and move even if I wanted to. I felt trapped.

Seldom did we have people over our home. Martin's friends would come into town, and he'd drive to wherever they were to meet them. He said he didn't like people in his space. I, on the other hand, love to entertain and holidays or special events are my excuses to invite people over to show off all that God has blessed me with. It was also a time where much-needed laughter was brought into our home.

We celebrated with family and my co-workers in our house our daughter's first birthday. The event was a great success. After the last guest left and the birthday girl crashed, I went to use the bathroom and to bring an end to my growing suspicious. I came back out and showed the results to Martin—PREGNANT. This time, I was actually happy about the baby in spite of its un-expectancy. I thought it was just what we needed to bring us together. Things would be different this time. I knew it. *This baby is conceived in wedlock, so it is definitely blessed*, I thought. I saw this unborn child as a ray of hope in a very dark hour. Martin did not share my views. When I told him about the baby, he lowered his head and rubbed it roughly. "Fuck! Shit man," was his reply.

He looked at me and asked what I wanted to do. Abortion. Was he inferring that I should have an abortion when we're married? What exactly did he mean by "what do you want to do?" I told him flatly that we were keeping it. I tried to explain to him the blessing, but he only saw my pregnancy as a curse.

Apparently, Martin planned on using the military as a means of leaving me. It would train him, pay for his move, and provide him with money to support his child. I never understood until I delivered him the news about me carrying his second child why he was so adamant about joining an institution that he loathed, why he was willing to have me sacrifice my career and the home that I recently purchased. He saw it as his escape, a clean cut way to sever ties. He told me that he felt he got married immaturely and that when he met me he was just starting to live, just starting to get the attention from women that he so long craved. He said that it was nothing that I did *per se* and that I was a great wife, but he felt like he needed to sleep with more women. His number, although it could complete two hands, was considerably lower than his friends and other males that he knew, and he saw that as a problem.

In all of my years of studying and teaching the English language as an art form, I am unable to accurately articulate the pain, the anger, the confusion, and the feelings of inadequacy as a woman and as a wife that I felt at that moment. Every ounce of self-esteem I had this one being single-handedly demolished. The thought of a piece of him living and developing inside of me repulsed me. Out of all of the Sundays I listened to my pastor and youth ministers speak on the subject of marriage and how to be a Godly husband or a Godly wife, I never heard them talk about how to remain in a marriage with someone who does not want you and not because of something you've done but because of something that pollutes his soul.

A problem I can fix. If he was to tell me that I needed to lose or gain weight or change my hair or even change my attitude, I could do it. I was willing to be that selfless. But I could not change who I was; I could not be another woman. I started thinking about the stacks of magazines he kept—magazines that I had the opportunity to be featured in. I thought about the caliber of friends he had, especially the one in particular that came to Atlanta. That friend—the groomsman under the influence, the one who tried to take my groom away on the eve of our wedding— knew what kind of car my husband drove, yet Martin always asked to use my vehicle to see him because it looked better. It dawned on me that they were spending time with other females together. I asked Martin about this, and he didn't deny it. But he also just wanted me to know that, in spite of his feelings, he never cheated on me, never even kissed another woman since we've been together. I was willing to fight for my marriage, but not alone. Basic training might be our much-needed separation, so I made the suggestion that if he still had the same feelings while he was there, I would agree to a divorce. Twelve days later he was gone.

*No man is an island, entire of itself*
*every man is a piece of the continent, a part of the main*
*if a clod be washed away by the sea,*
*Europe is the less, as well as if a promontory were,*
*as well as if a manor of thy friends or of thine own were*
*any man's death diminishes me, because I am involved in mankind*
*and therefore never send to know for whom the bell tolls*
*it tolls for thee.*

*-- John Donne*

# CHAPTER THIRTY THREE
## *SEPARATION*

Being alone in Georgia with a toddler was tough. Even though he had relatives that lived in the state, they didn't have much to do with me outside of him. Many would drive by the exit for my home on their way to or from Atlanta and wouldn't even call or stop by to see how I was managing. The unwelcomed changes to my body as a result of my pregnancy were occurring faster the second time around, and it made work unbearable. I was also left with the challenge of getting rid of my home. I no longer wanted to live there and grew to hate what it represented. I wanted to rid myself of it and its memories. Since we hadn't even lived there for a year, we had no equity in the home. Also, aside from painting two rooms, we didn't make any of the necessary changes to make it competitive on the market. I needed to get away and be around people who cared. My mother and father in-law called to check on me regularly, particularly my mother-in-law who lived two states north. I decided to drive the five-and-a-half hours during Spring Break to visit her to get a change in scenery.

I arrived to her home in the middle of a storm. Lightning flashed. The thunder crackled. She immediately came outside to grab my daughter. I grabbed the baby's diaper bag, my purse, and a small box of her toys and carried them into my mother-in-law's recently built house. It was only my second time there. She was strongly against us purchasing our home. She thought it was foolish. When she came over, she was very critical of our outdated appliances. I guess she had to find something wrong with our home since it was larger than hers. Shortly after we settled into our house, she put hers on the market and bought a larger home for just herself. I sat my belongings down and informed her and her boyfriend that I was going back out to get our suitcases. Despite their knowing I was pregnant because I was already showing, and even though it is common knowledge, especially for one who has already experienced motherhood, that the first trimester is the most critical, no one offered or made any motion to assist me. I made two trips to bring our bags into the house. Once I got settled, she and I chatted for a while about Martin. We both saw some promise in him while he was in boot camp. He wrote the both of us and told us things he never previously said. He told me that being away made him realize how much he loves me and that I am the only woman he wants. He promised to make every effort to show me once he got back home. He told his mother how much he loves and appreciates her and how she is the best mother in the world. She teased and said that he sound like a nigga in jail but guaranteed he would forgot all about those things once the torment of boot camp was complete. I told her I sure hoped not and intended to hold him to his word.

My stay with her was not as relaxing as I anticipated. It was downright uncomfortable. One day while on her way to work, my mother-in-law gave me permission to park in her driveway, so I did. Later that afternoon, her home telephone rang several times; I figured it was her trying to reach me. I answered and it was her boyfriend who had moved in with her once she purchased the home. He asked me to come outside and move my car so he could park inside of her two-car garage. My car only blocked one entrance to the empty garage, yet he found it imperative for me, a guest, to move so that he could park in his usual spot despite the availability of other parking options. Then when he came in the house, he didn't speak. He walked straight into their office then came out and asked if I was on their computer. I told him that I tried to use it to access the internet. I wanted to find a park or something to take my baby to. He said that I didn't need to use the internet for that. I could have used the phone book, as if I knew where that was. He took it out of the decorative table that rested against the entry wall and flung it on the couch. I made up my mind that I would make it my business to not be in their home alone with him anymore. I grabbed my daughter and got in my car and drove until I found a mall. I shopped until I was certain my mother-in-law was back home. She wasn't happy that I left. She felt like I did it intentionally. I did, but not for the reasons she suspected.

When I returned with my daughter, she said, "I thought you went shopping. Where's your clothes?"

I told her that I left them in my car. She mentioned she wanted to see them, so I went back out to retrieve them. I was enthusiastic when I showed my maternity clothes to her until she called each and every outfit ugly. I jumped on my phone and contacted older cousins I hadn't seen or spoken to in years who lived in that state, and I made arrangements to see them. I wanted to do all I could to stay out of that house. But while I was there she told me that she didn't like my hair cut, that she thought longer hair was more flattering on me, then she kept talking about how having two babies in diapers was crazy and didn't make any sense, as if I had much of an option.

Then she wanted to know how the selling of my home was coming along and when I told her that it wasn't she'd say, "See don't you wish you'd listen to me and not bought that house. I bet you regret it now don't you."

I was so happy when I finally left. I made up my mind that not only would I make it my business to not be in her home when she was not there, I was making it my business to not be there period if my husband or someone other than my children wasn't accompanying me.

I drove to Georgia wishing that I would have spent that time with my grandparents and mother. While driving, I dialed my mother. I shared with her the difficult time I was going through and she said, "Now you see what I had to experience as a single mother."

It was almost as if she was happy that I was miserable. I didn't comment; I just continued to drive. Then she started talking about my brother's high school graduation. She wanted to know if I would be in attendance. I assured her that I wouldn't miss it for anything in the world. She expressed concerns about his future. She said she couldn't afford to pay for his college, so she was considering selling her home to take care of his debt. Was she for real? Did she forget who she was talking to? I am her daughter—the one she refused to even sign the FAFSA for, the one who she would call to ask for money while I was going to school and working to support myself at the same time, the one who she offered nothing. All of my life I excused her behaviors and said I understood. Even though I didn't like it, I understood that although I was a teenager, I needed to give her money for the bills because she was a single parent. I understood that I was the only one with chores because I was a woman who would one day be somebody's wife and therefore their servant. I understood every time she denied me of something, or take away a new gift that my grandparents purchased me and replace it with her used one. But, I didn't understand this. It was blatant favoritism. There was no excuse for her willingness to sell her home for someone who wasn't even a good student, for someone who'd rather quit his job than to help her with her bills, for someone she had already given so much of herself to and she wasn't appreciated for it. For years I held in my feelings, only expressing them only in my diaries. For years I defended her when my grandmother, or cousins, or aunts talked about how she favored my brother over me, or how she didn't have her priorities in order. But, this time—the first time in my life that I tried to tell her how I felt about the injustice—,she dismissed me. She hung up the phone and wouldn't even allow me to finish my respectfully sincere thought. When I was a child she once told me, after her mother hung up the phone on her as she was attempting to express herself, that it was one of the rudest things that can ever be done to someone. When she hung up on me, her daughter whom she spent countless hours pouring her heart out to, me—her daughter—who carried her burdens in my youth, she rejected me and the fact that I have feelings. I wanted to ball up my fists and pound her. I wanted to beat her until I could no longer see. . I didn't desire to visit or to speak to her again.

Depression set in when I returned home. I heard my baby crying for hours, crying until she fell asleep from hunger or the need to have her diaper changed. I heard her cries, but my body wouldn't allow me to do anything about it. I sat there, lying on the couch, tuning out the television. I thought about how worthless I was, how unloved. I felt betrayed by every single person close to me and that life was not worth living. I contemplated suicide but didn't have the physical strength to get up to do it. While I lay there sobbing with a blanket pulled up to my chin entertaining all of my anxieties and insecurities, a large, black spider appeared on my abdomen. I thought I was hallucinating or perhaps in a dream until I saw it moving faster and faster towards me. It wasn't until it made its way to my chest, staring me maliciously in the face, that I mustered up the strength to fight back. I threw the blanket onto the floor, stomped it, punched it, threw a dining room chair at it, yelled at it, cussed it, and released all of my emotions onto it. I stripped myself of all of my clothes until I stood naked in my living room. I rigorously shook out my hair and jumped repeatedly up and down. Finally, I moved the blanket. I shook it, turned it, and there was no trace of any spider. As I stood bewildered looking at the areas where I expected it to be, I only saw my daughter sitting in her high chair without food, looking back at me intensely. I knew then that it was important for me to remain strong for her and the baby in my womb. No one else mattered.

When school recessed for summer, I drove twelve hours to Delaware to spend the remainder of the time Martin was away with my family. My mother's brother agreed to let me stay with him to limit my interactions with my mother. When I reached "The First State" at ten-thirty in the evening, I called him to let him know I was nearby. He told me he didn't think I was serious when I initially asked him to stay and his wife thought it was a bad idea because their home wasn't quite ready for guests. I was infuriated. I planned to stay in Delaware for two-and-a-half months; I couldn't afford to reside in a hotel the entire time. My grandparents' home wasn't conducive to a toddler, and, meanwhile, my daughter was growing very restless in the back seat from our twelve hour drive. With my toddler's piercing shrills penetrating my ears, I had nowhere else to go in the familiar territory but to my mother's.

Without any foreknowledge of my arrival, my mother opened the door and was excited to see us. The feeling, at least on my part, was not mutual. I dreaded staying with her. The unfavorable stench of dog filled my nose as I entered into the simple house that I lived in for only a year prior to going off to college. I didn't look forward to sitting on her tattered sofa or bathing with rags that she called washcloths. My in-laws had better. I, at twenty four, had better. But, my mother never seemed bothered by the condition of her humble home; she always welcomed me back to it with opened arms. This time was no exception. The moment she saw me she embraced me warmly as if I never stopped speaking to her. In her mind, all was truly well. As I meandered from her foyer towards her living room, I stopped to admire the carpet that comforted my feet. It was creamy in color—a definite step up from the blood orange covering that once barely sheltered her floors. I commented on its inviting appearance then looked back at the entrance way where the dog tracked mud. I remembered a time where my mother wouldn't allow an animal or her children, for that matter, to destroy her home. She retained a certain pride about her dwelling place. She'd always say, "It may not be much, but we're going to take care of what God gave us." Every Saturday, she'd have me to clean the baseboards of the walls, scrub the kitchen floor on my hands and knees, vacuum the rug, clean the bathroom, but now dog hair covered the baseboards and tracks of mud were on her brand new carpet. I entered into her living room expecting to see the deflated tattered pleather she called a sofa and loveseat but instead saw chocolate microfiber furnishings. My eyes widened in surprised, and *"Oooh"* unintentionally expelled from my lips as an expression of satisfaction in my mother's baby steps in home improvement. The sparkle that beamed in her eyes reflected her pride in herself.

She ran into her basement to bring up a pack-and-play pen for my daughter's accommodations along with a baby walker and several toys. My mother jabbered on for what felt like hours instead of the realistic several minutes. The newfound comfort her living room furniture brought hastened the effects from my twelve-hour travel. I excused myself and informed her that I really needed to get to sleep. My mother acted as if she understood my physical condition and insisted that I sleep with her in her bed. I agreed because I didn't have the strength to make up her sofa bed, and my brother destroyed the day bed in what used to be my bedroom, and his room, in which he still dwelled, needed to be quarantined and was, to my estimation, uninhabitable.

Quickly, I undressed and crawled into her bed. It didn't take me long to find a sleeping position that satisfied both me and my growing fetus. All was quiet and all was well as I found myself falling asleep. Almost as quickly as my trance began the darkness ran farther and farther from me until I was unwelcomed by a beaming light, a blaring television, and the rushing sound of my mother's voice. She asked me questions which I managed to limit the answers to no more than two words. Despite my brevity, she would not stop talking while I was trying to fall back to sleep. I told her politely using my smallest voice that I was tired from my long drive and wasn't feeling very sociable. She ignored me and just kept right on talking. I tossed and turned and buried my head beneath the covers—all of my signals she overlooked. My need for sleep, my request for rest, and her blatant disregard enraged me. Leaping out of her bed to put back on my clothing, my mother sounded concerned when she asked where I was going. I threw my purse over my shoulder and responded through tightened lips and clenched teeth, "To sleep in my car where it's quiet." On the driver's side in my Mazda 6 is exactly where my fetus and I rested for the remainder of the evening until early morning. When I went inside of her home again, I think she got the point.

My grandmother was happy to hear I was finally in town and drove immediately over to see me. As always, I was equally excited about seeing her. Until the birth of my daughter, she was my favorite girl. We sat in my mother's kitchen and caught up. While we were talking, my grandmother noticed a magnet on my mother's refrigerator; it read *"Sons have a special place in a mother's heart."*

My grandmother said "Humph. That's nice. Where's the one that talks about a daughter?"

Hearing this, my mother went off. She accused my grandmother of all sorts of stuff relating to her own childhood. The entire time she ranted, my grandmother listened quietly. I, on the other hand, couldn't be so gracious. I jumped to her defense and told my mother that she had some nerve to try to call my grandmother out on her stuff when she wasn't even willing to listen to her own daughter's gripe. I noticed the magnet before, but it bothered me that other people could clearly see what I was only beginning to learn. I packed up my belongings from her house and left. I didn't know where my baby and I were heading. I just knew that I certainly couldn't stay with her.

My daughter and I bounced around a few places before ultimately ending up at my grandparents' home. Although I was still getting paid from the school district, I decided to work to take my mind off of Martin. Since he completed military Basic Training, he did just what his mother predicted—he reverted. In technical school, he was given certain freedoms that weren't permitted during basic training. He was allowed to travel off-base, party, and hang out, and Martin did all of the above. He didn't talk to me during the day because he was in school and at night he called only to say that he'd talk to me tomorrow because he was going to hang out with some friends—people he only knew for a few weeks. It was as if he completely forgot about me, his promises, our child, and the child I was carrying. To me, it seemed like tech school was the equivalent of him having a second college experience even though he was one of the oldest enlisted there. Once when I flew to the training base to visit him, he kept me locked up in the hotel room the entire time. This was disappointing because I heard of these restaurants he frequented and it seemed like he was having so much fun, yet when I came to visit I was confined. I asked to know the reason behind his behavior, and he said it was because he didn't feel like seeing anyone. Oddly enough, he was talking about him not wanting to see the same people he dissed me for regularly. I happened to meet someone he attended technical school with during my short stay when he took me to the store to satisfy a craving. At the McDonald's, there was a young woman sitting there with a guy. Martin was about to walk by her until she noticed him. Mechanically, he grabbed my arm and walked over and introduced me as his wife.

She said, "Martin! She is so pretty! You have a beautiful wife. And, I didn't know you had another baby on the way. By the way, this is my husband."

Come to find out, she was one of his friends— a friend who never saw my picture; a friend to whom he never bothered to mention that his wife was expecting. I tried to open up and talk to him about his actions. I encouraged him to keep his focus, to remember that his purpose for being there wasn't to party but to learn. He didn't see things that way. He accused me of wanting him to be a hermit. He said that, after all of the stress he went through, he deserved to have fun. Fun—that word was as foreign to me at six months pregnant as German. He ignored my requests for special consideration, like a simple phone conversation that exceeded ten minutes, and I began to hate both him and the baby I carried. I went to dance clubs and lounges with my sorority sisters, but my wedding ring and obtruding stomach steered men clear, and, the ones who still hit on me, I questioned their sanity. There was nothing I could do but desire to hurt Martin badly. I wanted to hurt him to show him how much he was hurting me.

One morning I treated myself to Denny's for breakfast, but when my food was brought out, I couldn't eat it. I sat in the booth alone staring down at my meal until I began to uncontrollably weep. I didn't want to cause a scene, so I left twenty dollars on the table to cover the eight dollar meal and the tip and left. While I was driving to my grandparents' home, Martin called. I was surprised because he didn't normally call me in the middle of the day. I answered the phone, and he could hear I'd been crying. He wanted to know what was wrong, but I didn't want to tell him. He kept probing until I told him honestly that it was him. He was the "what" behind my anguish. I explained my feelings as best I could, but he reversed everything I said and tried to make me out to be some kind of villain. The feeling that swept over me felt familiar. My voice softened as I told him I was ending our conversation. He wouldn't hear of it and demanded me to remain on the phone. I told him again, this time more sternly, that I needed to hang up, but he kept on yelling. I turned into my grandparents' subdivision and caught sight of a solitary pole in a nearby field. The pole looked like it could bring peace. It was the savior that would put to an end all of my agonies. My speed picked up as I was drawn into its direction. I told Martin while swearing to God that if he didn't stop talking to me I was going to ram my car into that beautiful steel pole in the soft, green meadow. Swearing to God is something I never do, but I did it in that moment of seriousness. If Martin wasn't near enough for me to inflict bodily harm onto him, then the impact from my car's union with the pole would have to suffice, for this fury was too strong to be contained; it necessitated release. After hearing the serenity in my sworn statement, Martin hung up, and tranquility fell upon me without any assistance from the steel rod. I entered my grandparents' home without speaking to anyone and headed upstairs to my room where I peacefully slept. About an hour later, my telephone rang and awakened me. Martin was on the other line. This time, it sounded as if he had been the one who was crying. Through his sniffles, he said he was genuinely concerned for me and asked me to write down a number to call to talk with someone. The number was to Military One Source. They gave me thirty free hours of therapy to take advantage of immediately.

The licensed practicing counselor I was referred to was a godsend. He was great because he listened to me. He didn't try to tell me what or how I should feel like my mother, and he also didn't manipulate my words and make my issues about him, like Martin. He just listened. I promise that the more I saw that man the more fond of him I grew. His gray hair or wrinkled pinkish skin was unimportant. The more I spoke to him the more I was able to hear myself and resolve my own problems. He helped me to realize that everything I felt and how I internalize things are direct results of my childhood. The reason I was so angry at my mother was because of the things she allowed to happen to me in my youth. I was even angry at her for allowing my father to beat her. This was all amazing to me and truly insightful. He said that Martin was presently incapable of being a husband because he has yet to mature into his life role and that could also be a result of his rearing. The counselor was able to sift through the scattered pieces of my life until I was able to see glimpses of a completed puzzle. Even though I was aware of many of my positive attributes, his acknowledgement of them gave them substance. I didn't want my sessions with him to come to an end. My mother and grandmother didn't approve of me seeking professional help, for this is not a prevalent practice in the African American community. We are taught to turn to our faith or encouraged to forget about the problems that plague us—that's what my mother did, and that's what her mother did, and her mother's mother, etc. But, talking about my feelings with an objective listener began my first steps towards healing. The answers I was in search of in college came to me. Each time we talked, layers of emotional damage peeled away. I was exposed. I revealed my true self to someone and was finally understood. Perhaps he understood me all too well because, at the end of my final session, he asked me if I was interested in being medicated and diagnosed me as having a mild personality/anxiety disorder. Even without a prescription, that was a hard pill to swallow.

*"People are like stained-glass windows. They sparkle and shine when the sun is out, but when the darkness sets in, their true beauty is revealed only if there is a light from within."*

—Elisabeth Kubler-Ross

# CHAPTER THIRTY FOUR
## *COLD WAR*

Martin completed his basic and technical training for the United States Armed Services and moved our family to a small West Texas town where he was stationed. We were eager to move despite neither of us not knowing anything about The Lone Star State and even less about the desert-like city which we were relocating to. Our westward migration was the fifth major life change we experienced in our two-year relationship—moving into together after college, marriage, first baby, homeownership, and now having to adjust to military life. A thousand miles away from the influences of family, we were forced to be each other's ally, here in the desert where tumbleweeds blow and cactus grow. Here where it took us weeks to see another face of similar complexion outside of the gates of the military installation, we were at a place of no retreat. If a problem arose, facing it was our only recourse. I was due to deliver our second child in less than two months— our sixth major life change. We decided I wouldn't return to work after delivering the baby. Martin was willing to bring my desire of being a housewife into fruition. For the first time, he would be the sole provider for our family. Martin shared with me that he relished in knowing I had to depend on him financially. He enjoyed having all of the bills for our new Texas residence solely in his name and being the final decision maker for our household. However, it was not easy for me to totally relinquish my financial independence. In fact, nothing about our move was easy.

Base housing was unavailable to us, so we needed to find a place that could be covered by Martin's housing allowance, and I was assigned this arduous task. He wanted to live as close to the base as possible and said that we could not afford for our rent to exceed seven hundred dollars. What luxurious apartment could I find for such an amount? The place I found on the internet was listed as Spacious Luxury Apartments. It sounded perfect and turned out to be everything but. Fitting over 2,700 square feet worth of furniture in a 1,100 square feet apartment whose only luxurious features were its cheaply updated fixtures is no easy task. Much of our furniture was damaged in transport and some items were accidentally left behind in our house in Georgia.

Now that Martin was our family's breadwinner, he became fiscally conservative when it came to things I desired. I wanted to get my hair done, and he told me I could do it myself. I wanted a special cable program, and he told me I didn't need it. Despite our tight budget, Martin managed to acquire things for himself at his leisure, such as new rap CDs on Tuesdays and sneakers. For our first few months in Texas, I received disability pay for my pregnancy. This check helped to limit my dependency on Martin, but, when those short-term disability checks stopped, and my bank account was depleted once again for having to pay mortgage on our vacant Atlanta home, I became discontent with my new role of homemaker.

We had arrived to Texas with only one vehicle, so, while Martin worked, I was stuck at home without transportation. It wasn't too bad while caring for only one child at the time. I sort of got into a routine: wake up and prepare breakfast for Martin; feed, change, and dress the baby; make myself look presentable for when Martin comes home for lunch, prepare Martin's lunch, lay the baby down for a nap, try to take a nap myself, prepare dinner for Martin, clean up after dinner, keep the baby busy so Martin can rest after coming home from work, put the baby to bed, and wake up to do everything all over again the next day. Did I say it wasn't that bad? I lied. It was horrible. Even though Martin tried desperately to please me by proving he could be a husband who financially provided for his family, I needed more. I was on my last trimester of pregnancy, and I physically needed help. My back ached from cleaning and lugging our toddler in and out of her high-chair and in and out of the bathtub. I was exhausted because I couldn't obtain the rest that my body desperately craved. But Martin offered little to no assistance with the household chores and at night didn't render moral support by volunteering to massage away my aches while I lay crying in our bed. I would complain that back hurt, and he'd say that his hurt, too. I asked him once to pass me my purse, and he flung the heavy bag at my stomach. His actions came as a surprise to me considering how he missed most of my pregnancy. Outside of our personal finances, Martin rendered no sympathy toward my physical condition.

Martin noticed my increasing stress and thought money was the root of my concerns. He took out a loan to cover one month of our mortgage and volunteered to work a second job, but having him at home less was the opposite of what I required. The truth is I didn't trust him anymore, and I really didn't want his help. He was the reason why I was even in these situations— pregnant and on my way to the poor house. If he aggressively sought professional employment in Atlanta instead of enlisting into the military when he had a Bachelors degree, I wouldn't have the financial pressure of trying to sell an unsellable house. Hell, if it wasn't for him, I wouldn't have even picked that damn house which needed modern modifications. If he was more attentive to his pregnant wife, maybe I wouldn't have missed the opportunity of enjoying both my current and past pregnancy. He robbed me of joy and stability. It was all of his fault. Everything was his fault. Join the military for financial security. Hah! I made more money as a first-year teacher in Atlanta. I didn't trust him with my heart, with our finances, or with our family. Screw his strides.

We had left Atlanta in hopes of our developing family getting a fresh start, but the core of our souls carried all of our problems with us. A thousand miles away, yet we still could not escape our pasts. The things I didn't say before, the questions I never asked emerged. Martin came home from work on time and didn't go out anywhere to socialize, yet I still did not trust him. Constantly, I questioned him about his activity in technical school. If he wasn't giving me his attention at that time who was he giving it to? I was carrying the son he longed for, and he acted as if he didn't care, why? I convinced myself he cheated on me, and there was nothing he could say or do to make me believe otherwise. His heart was elsewhere— I just needed to prove it. Each time I accused him, he denied the accusations. I checked our telephone records, his voicemail, his call log every chance I could just to produce evidence of his lies. I found nothing but was still unconvinced. The contents in my mind rotated, shifted, and changed courses more rapidly than a Tilt-A-Whirl. My anxiety over Martin's fidelity and our finances disturbed my sleep. Unable to bring pause to the thoughts that flooded my psyche, it didn't take long for me to require another referral for professional counseling. And the avenue for marriage counseling also needed to be explored.

The downward spiral of which my life alighted manifested in the form of post-partum depression after the birth of my second child. When I first held the male babe in my arms to nurse, there was no joy, only disappointment. The eve of his birth he laid in his clear molded acrylic pediatric basket weeping. For what, I cared not. I called for a nurse to remove him from my room immediately. She implored for me to hold him, to swaddle him, to show this baby who just entered into a cold, foreign world that he is loved. I yelled at her in refusal and demanded that she take him out at once. He was my child, my son, but I couldn't feel any initial love for him. Teary-eyed, I admitted the sad fact to my husband as I nursed our newborn in our home. There was nothing he could say to bring me solace, especially after I caught him watching women gyrate their naked bodies from his computer screen one day after I came home from giving birth. Now, I felt like a failure as a mother on top of being a failure for a wife. But my dear son refused to live life unloved. He reached for me, cried for me, and nestled with me to show that no matter how I felt about him, he loved me. And, over the weeks my heart was forced to melt into seas of love. Like Christ, to gain my affection, my babe first showed me love.

Getting my children on the same schedule proved to be next to impossible. They pooped at the same time, cried at the same time, were hungry at the same time, but refused to sleep at the same time. It didn't take long for me to realize that staying at home full-time with the children was not in my or their best interest. Martin left work a few times early because he was concerned about the fragility of my mental state and their welfare. Even though he liked the masculine sentiment of being able to afford his wife the coveted luxury of staying at home, he agreed to me placing our children in childcare while I sought out employment. The area schools weren't hiring secondary English teachers, so I snatched up the first job I could find—a cashier at a supermarket. I didn't care where I worked as long as I could work to get out of the house, away from Martin and the children, and make a few extra dollars to assist with my thirteen hundred dollar a month mortgage payment and two-hundred-and-fifty dollar car note.

I wasn't at the high-end grocery store for a full week when I had to request un-paid family leave. Both of my children contracted the respiratory virus RSV, but in my six-week old son, the virus was life-threatening. I noticed decreased activity and a sudden lack of appetite in my newborn who was growing faster than a weed. The abnormal changes concerned me to the point that I suggested that Martin and I take him to see his pediatrician. Upon looking at him, the doctor ordered that he be immediately admitted into the local children's hospital. At admittance, my son's oxygen level was at thirty percent. I watched nurses repeatedly prod his flesh with needles in search of his tiny veins. I saw the baby who I once had difficulties loving hooked up to an oxygen machine and a heart monitor. He remained in that hospital for a week, and there was no one there but Martin and me. I wailed uncontrollably for my precious son and felt ashamed and regretful for how I treated him moments after his birth. Martin lovingly put his arms around me for consolation, but I pushed him away. I needed to feel this grief: I deserved it, but my innocent child did not. Martin didn't take my rejection of him well at all and started hardening his heart towards me and our son. One day I fell asleep in the hospital chair and Martin was awake talking on the phone to "his sister." The cries of our son disrupted my rest, and I asked Martin if he was going to get up to tend to our hospitalized baby. His reply was "I'm on the phone."

My mother flew in to assist with the babies once our son returned home from the hospital. Her help was much needed and appreciated, but her two-month stay was bound to stir up feelings from the summer that were never put to rest. Martin suggested that I talk to her tenderly and tell her how I felt, explain to her gently how she hurt me. I took his advice. I knocked on our guest bedroom door and asked permission to enter. I asked if I could discuss something with her, and she agreed. I started out the conversation by telling her how much I loved her and appreciated her before transitioning to my main point of discussion. She cut me off as soon as I got to the meat of our talk only to begin singing her own praises. I sat quietly and listened to her lecture me on what a great mother she was as if I had never lived with her. She said she did the best she could do as a single parent before mentioning how she never asked to be a single parent, and how she sacrificed dating for me and my brother, and how she experienced everything she ever went through in order to break the generational curse of our family. She told me that my grandmother, not her, played favoritism with her children and if

I should be angry with anyone, it should be with my father, not her. When she was done with her tangent, I tried to resume from where she cut me off, but my mother stood up to walk out of the bedroom while I was in midsentence.

As she prepared to exit she told me coldly, "Get over it. I refuse to live in the past," right before she quoted a scripture. She walked throughout our second floor apartment shouting out prayers and speaking in the recycled tongue that I always hear her use whenever she tries to pray in the spirit. All the while I was left sitting alone on the bed in my guest bedroom feeling like a child stranger in my own home, once again like that ignored little girl who hungered for her mother's attention. I decoded her indifference to my vulnerability as disrespectful, selfish, and unloving. For once in my life, she was unable to place my concerns before her own. If she was unwilling to see and acknowledge how her personal choices impacted her children, I wanted nothing to do with her. I didn't ask her for an apology. All I wanted was acknowledgement. It saddened me to see a woman in her mid-forties avoid taking responsibility. I didn't hate my mother. I pitied her along with the man who victimized her. Her presence added to the building tensions between me and Martin and when she departed from her two-month stay, all out war waged between us.

Martin left for temporary duty at another location just two days before my mother's departure and one day before our daughter's second birthday. I was alone with my children for the first time since my son's hospitalization. The blessing was that we now had two vehicles. I bought Martin a new car just before he left on TDY. We needed it although we honestly couldn't afford it. Both of our families knew we had two children and only one vehicle. Both of them knew about our son's recent hospitalization, and even though some of our relatives had vehicles and/or money to spare, no one offered their help. I bit the bullet and financed another vehicle for Martin's personal use. He was excited about it. He said it made him realize that he had no one else to depend on but me. I was glad to see that he was finally getting the point. In a marriage, people want to offer up their advice and act like they know best for your family, but when tough times hit and you look to those same advisors who have your best interest in mind for help, you learn quickly who your true partner in life is. While Martin was gone, I went to use his computer and noticed he still had an application running. I didn't want to exit off in case it was something important, so I enlarged the icon to detect its importance. It was nothing. It seemed that Martin was just downloading songs to upload onto his iPod. But, then I noticed that all of the things listed in the play list weren't songs. Some of the things listed were videos. I'm not technologically savvy and had no clue one could retrieve videos off the internet without purchasing them, so I was curious to see what movies he found to watch. Before he left, Martin had been spending substantial amounts of time alone in our home office. He said that he was in there reading up on hip hop since the city in which we dwelled lacked access to an exclusively hip hop radio station. It concerned me that he spent so much time filling his mind with such garbage: who has beef with whom, who was dating who in the industry, who switched labels and why, etc. Martin claimed that music was his only outlet and our marriage counselor agreed that his behavior was perfectly healthy and said that every man needed "a man cave." Curiously, I clicked on the first link and a gigantic brown-skinned ass with a red thong wedged between it popped onto the computer screen and jiggled and dropped and spread in front of my eyes. I clicked off of that sucker as fast as I could. Then, I chose another link. This time a video vixen appeared and this wasn't on a music video. The site he downloaded for obtaining music was filled with pornography and the bulk of it was footage of this former video model. I was stunned. I had no idea my husband was into porn. I had knowledge of him knowing the names of models in magazines geared towards black men, but I never knew he watched porn and in such great amounts. I owned pornography that I confiscated from my younger brother when

I was in college. When I asked my husband to watch them with me, he always refused. I figured it wasn't really his cup of tea; maybe it just wasn't his type of porn. When he returned home, I called him over to his computer and showed him my findings. He said it was just a short phase he went through, and it wasn't anything serious. He said that day I walked in and caught him watching the shaky butts on his computer was the first time he watched something like that. In fact, he was on a hip hop site at first and the girl with the shaky booty just popped up.

"Just popped up, huh," I probed.

"Yeah. It just popped up."

"After it 'popped up' you didn't click it off I see."

"Naw. You right. I didn't."

I took him at his word and didn't make a big deal out of it.

Two months later, he went on another TDY around the time of my birthday. While he was gone, I emailed him something. I went into his email account to see if he received it since he wasn't answering my phone calls or calling me regularly. While signed into his account, I noticed an email from an adult site that he joined while he was away the last time on temporary duty. I opened the email and played around with various sequences until I discovered the correct pass code. Apparently, he was trying to find local women to become romantic with while he was away on TDY. He wasn't seeking out women he knew; he was seeking out total strangers. My heart stopped as I thought about potential health risks. This was stuff one heard about on television; I didn't think real people were actually into it. I was disgusted and then embarrassed. He didn't ever TDY alone. So, did his co-workers know about his behavior? Was I the last to know that I was getting played? He missed our daughter's birthday and left me alone for two weeks with two small children after I just purchased him a vehicle so he could solicit sex online. My husband is a handsome man and this type of risky, perverted activity was beneath him. I started searching through more of his emails and discovered one he sent over a year ago to a girl from college, right before he left

Delaware to meet me in Atlanta. He knew she liked him. He told me how she boldly confessed in college that she didn't care if he had a girlfriend, she wanted him. Knowing this, my husband, then fiancé, while in his right mind, offered to stop by and visit her at her home in Virginia while he was on his way to join me in Atlanta.

I was hurt. Two children and a mortgage payment later, I was just beginning to really know the man who I married. During my search I also found social networking sites he joined after our nuptials and while he was unemployed. In his profile on these sites he registered himself as single. And there was yet another site that he recently joined and used our son's name as his password. I checked the history of his internet searches and found one adult site after another geared towards black women with fat asses. *So this is what happens when I give him his requested space,* I thought. *Hip Hop my ass.* The poem he read to me on our wedding day I removed from my bedside. Pictures we took while we dated I destroyed. He was spending all of his free time looking at other women and searching for other women just days after I gave birth to his child. I sacrificed my body for this ungrateful son of a bitch. I could have easily been in one of his coveted magazines before I bore his children. He slept with a model—me—every night.

Enraged, I called up the car lot where I purchased his vehicle and wanted to know the implications for voluntarily surrendering it. I downloaded applications for school districts in the Atlanta and Delaware areas. I realized that my leaving would probably be the perfect remedy for him. He would be free from all of his marital and parental responsibilities once I left with the children. He would be free to drink, party, and whore around as much as he'd like conspicuously. Meanwhile, my life would be forever changed. I would have to sacrifice dating and going out all because I had the full responsibility of both children. Fuck alimony—his ass wasn't rich—and me living the life of a single parent while he lived as a bachelor wasn't even going to happen. He was going to have to realize he was a grown man with adult responsibilities and that meant more than him just sending support checks and having infrequent visitations because of the geographic distance between us. As much as it was going to pain me, I was willing to yield one child into his custody. They say Karma is a bitch. I guess she was giving me a taste of what I put Side Jawn's girlfriend through during her pregnancy and even after the birth of her child—the anxiety, the insecurity, the questioning.

I couldn't wait for Martin to return from his trip to confront him. I needed to do it over the phone. I told him he was to place the vehicle entirely in his name, or I was going to get rid of it. My intentions to leave him were made Casper-clear along with my desire for a divorce. I revealed to Martin my longing for additional children, but told him that I was unwilling to ever bear another child of his. He needed to know the joys of motherhood he robbed me of. "I hate you," I told him "Happy twenty fifth birthday to me!" I slammed down the phone that didn't ring again for the remainder of the night. All that needed to be said was said.

When his flight brought him back from Maryland to the Big Country, he had to take a cab home because I refused to pick him up. And, when he came home, I had nothing to say to him. Later that evening, I got myself dressed and went to a club alone to celebrate living for a quarter of a century. The music blared, the DJ gave me a birthday shout out, and I sat alone watching people all around me have fun on my special day. The next afternoon Martin and I sat on the floor across from each other inside of our home office and talked. He apologized to me for everything and asked for my forgiveness. More than anything in the world he didn't want me to hate him. Martin always cared about how others felt about him.

"I love you," he said to me, and I replied, "You have no idea what love is."

Martin didn't argue. He wanted to know what he needed to do to prevent me from leaving. He said that our family meant everything to him. From the beginning of our relationship, I made many sacrifices for him, and I wanted to know what he was willing to sacrifice for me. I needed him to make a sacrifice in order for me to stay. He needed to prove that he loved me more than himself. Martin listened to my request, and sat silently. There was nothing he was willing to give up on his own. Martin never knew the requirements of a marriage. His parents only drilled into him the need for financial security. He didn't understand why I was displeased when he was providing for our family. He didn't know of any other way to show his love. When Martin had a problem with me, he didn't communicate it. He kept it to himself. In fact, rarely did Martin communicate his problems with anyone. Instead, he acted out. I knew my husband was impressionable. I knew that since college. It was one of his flaws I overlooked, hoping he'd outgrow it. I thought that once we moved away from the bad influences then he'd be alright and would learn how to be a leader himself. He was the type of man who watched music videos and *MTV Cribs* and said, "Wow, I want that" but had no ambition to obtain it. He would look at men who had a lot of women and envy them as opposed to pitying the predatory womanizer. I believed that my husband continually fed his spirit with filth—the music, the videos, the conversations with perverted acquaintances, the magazines, the internet sites—so I asked him to detoxify himself for one month. Rid himself of these things and substitute them with scripture, with music that edifies, with men who have successful marriages who can teach him how to love his wife and the true meaning of being a man. He agreed, and I agreed to give our marriage another chance.

Martin lacked will power and had to be forced into doing what was in his interest. He allowed to me to go through his CD collection and discard anything with questionable content. Needless to say, the majority of his collection was thrown away. I allowed him to keep Common Sense hoping that some of it would rub off, Nas (after "Oochie Wally"), Lupe Fiasco, and

Outkast. I also allowed R&B that wasn't flooded with vivid sexual images. But Martin agreed to me getting rid of his compact discs because he knew that he had uploaded the majority of them onto his computer and iPod. So, I went into both of them and deleted the albums from them, too. That's when he snapped. He revealed that he really wasn't trying to change at all. I borrowed his car once without him knowing and discovered a rap CD he borrowed from a coworker. It infuriated me that he was still sneaking around and was not giving my request of a personal sacrifice his full effort. Immediately, I called him to inform him of my discovery. He didn't bother to apologize; he only asked that I not destroy the CD because it didn't belong to him. With that said, I broke it into as many tiny pieces as I could. Martin's lack of sincere effort confirmed his lack of love for me, and I began to think "If you can't beat him, join him."

*In marriage, each partner is to be an encourager rather than a critic, a forgiver rather than a collector of hurts, an enabler rather than a reformer.*

*—H. Norman Wright and Gary J. OliverR*

# CHAPTER THIRTY FIVE

# *FOR BETTER, FOR WORSE*

W*ill you love him, comfort him, honor and keep him, in sickness and in health, for richer, for poorer, for better, for worse, forsaking all others, keep yourself only unto him as long as you both shall live?*

When I stood before our family, friends, and God and repeated this very statement, I didn't understand the magnitude of my vows and how quickly they would be tested. What did I publically swear to? Was this it? Was this always going to be it—me giving of myself only not to receive? I deserved better. I was determined to find better. I received my fair share of attention on the military base, but I didn't want to send off the wrong impression. I avoided making eye contact with men because in the past, men incorrectly perceived that I liked them due to a look they felt I gave. I was brief in conversations with those of the opposite sex out of respect for my husband. But, it was obvious that my husband didn't respect me, so why should I continue to respect him? I met this guy outside of the base through an area acquaintance. He and I tried to make plans in the past to double date, but our schedules never worked out. This time when he called after I hadn't spoken to him in months; he was single, and my marriage was in trouble. My cell phone rang at midnight, and I didn't recognize the number. The night before it rang at the same time and it was my cousin who lives on the West Coast. He had forgotten about the two-hour time difference. I thought the same was occurring until the caller identified himself. He apologized for calling so late and said he anticipated getting my voicemail. Normally, he called my house, but he didn't want to call it that late. He said he changed his phone number and wanted me to have his new one. I told him that his call didn't come as an inconvenience. The fact was I was lonely. Martin wouldn't even share the same bed with me. I needed a little late night conversation in my life. The gentleman was prior military and was studying theology. Much of our conversation was geared towards God. While he and I talked on the phone well into two o'clock in the morning, Martin entered our bedroom to grab something and never bothered to inquire about who I was talking to at such an hour. When it was time to hang up, the former sniper invited me out to lunch later in the day.

I didn't consider our lunch a date because we each paid for our own meals, but it just felt so good to get out of the house and have the company of a man without tension. I wasn't physically attracted to him at all, but he had a sweet personality and was full of compliments. We connected on many levels conversationally, and he made me laugh heartier than I had in months. Later that evening, Martin returned home with the children and put a damper on my day. The silence amongst us was deafening. Just as I began to get back into my funk, my phone chimed indicating I had a text message. It was from the kind sniper. It read that he hoped he wasn't pressing his luck, but he really wanted me to join him for dinner. He was going to cook for me—something Martin didn't do. I accepted his invitation and told Martin to watch the children because I was stepping out for a few hours.

It was next to impossible for me to ever picture myself living in the house that the sniper rented. The outside and inside alike was tore up from the floor up. I tried not to be too judgmental, but I just couldn't help myself. It looked worse than a house rented by a bunch of frat boys. I regretted wearing a skirt while I was seated on his couch, and my eyes kept exploring every crevice looking for vermin. But once he served me my meal, I began to loosen up. The man had serious culinary skills. His food was so delectable, it was intimidating. I didn't think I could ever reciprocate the favor. We watched two movies together, or should I say the movies watched us because we just talked and talked like it was nobody's business. We talked about our childhoods, our Greek affiliations, our past relationships, and the state of my present. After one date with no physical contact, this man wanted me to leave my husband to be his lady. He said I was the type of woman he had been searching for. The only problem was he wasn't my type of man. See, I've already seen what looking only at a person's heart can get you, and, by the looks of his house, his heart was the only thing he could offer me. I was no longer a love-smitten teenager or undergraduate student who could look past material possessions all in the name of love. I was now a mother who had accomplished a great deal in her life and already knew all she had to offer a man. Now, I was asking the question, *what does this man have to offer me?* During our candid conversation, he shared with me that he once had a car repossessed. That explained why he was driving a clunker and lived in this poor excuse for a house because he had bad credit. A man with bad credit is equivalent to a man with a STD in my book. I already struggled with a man in a relationship, and I didn't want to travel down that road again. It was time for momma to start prospering. And, if he was any indication of the options left open to me as a divorced mother of two, then it was definitely in my best interest to remain married. At least my husband was getting his credit together. My evening with that man made me fully appreciate what I had at home. It showed me an example of someone who only had sweet nothings to offer. I drove home close to around three o'clock in the morning fully convinced that I loved my husband. Eagerly, I put my key in the door, turned the knob, and Martin's eyes instantly met mine as I walked into our dark apartment where the only light came from small television screen. His lips parted not to ask me where I'd been or why I neglected to call. My enthusiasm about our marriage faded as quickly as it arose.

Martin's inattentiveness ate away at me, and the constant phone calls and text messages from the sniper made matters even worse. I didn't want to become one of those women who stepped outside of her marriage to get fulfilled. The dinner that guy voluntarily cooked for me, I wanted my husband to do that. The way he texted me and called to check up on me, I desired that only from Martin. When Martin came home from work, I decided to come clean with everything. If I expected honesty from him, my actions also must have integrity.

We occupied the children in their room to play, while he and I had a heart to heart. Our decaying marriage was no secret to us, but the degree that it was affecting me was unknown to my maturing spouse. I didn't evade the truth when I confessed to Martin that I had been out on a date with another man. I told him he would have seen the signs had he only been paying attention. Now, my spouse was asking the questions of a concerned husband. Now, he acted as if he cared about the details. I wanted him to see that while he was paying attention to other women, other men were paying close attention to his wife. But Martin saw it. He knew it. He just didn't expect for me to give them my consideration. Over the next few weeks, night came to a close as dawn peeked through, shining on Martin as he began to ripen into his role of husband.

****

Moving out of the cramped apartment into a newly built spacious four-bedroom home with ample yard space for our children to play was just another one of God's blessings overshadowed by adversity. In this home, Martin made strides to become my partner. He cooked occasionally while also sharing in the chores and in the care of our children. He showed more concern for my needs as well as my wants. But I was unable to shift my mind from our past. One day when I was dropping our children off to childcare, I came into contact with a woman whom I met only twice before. Elaine is her name. I didn't remember it then, but I never forgot her name afterwards. It had been a while since I last saw her and she asked how I was. I smiled and told her well. I started ranting about all of the things I had been busy with: teaching at the local high school, preparing to begin graduate coursework , my tutoring business, my children, etc. She smiled warmly at me as I shared the general details of my life.

When I finished running off my list, her voice suddenly changed. It became firm and less sweet as she said, "I have a word from God for you. He wants you to know that He loves you, and he hasn't forgotten about you. He's going to help you through your depression, and your marriage is going to be alright. He has blessings in store for you, and financial blessings are coming to you soon."

The hairs on my arms stood as the cool waves made their way up and down my spine. How did she know? I didn't share with anyone in Texas what my husband and I were going through. I didn't even know this woman's name. I grabbed her and hugged her tight and wept in her arms in that parking lot. We exchanged phone numbers, and it was difficult for me to remain still while I entered her information in to my mobile phone. I wanted to run. I wanted to shout *Hallelujah!* I wanted to wave my arms and jump in praise. But, all I could do was to speak and allow the Holy Spirit to interpret to God the concerns of my heart. He remembered me. God saw all that I endured. Elaine didn't know that the weekend prior to my meeting her, I shared with my husband my desire to commit suicide. Everything had become too much for me to handle. I contemplated how I could do it without my children growing up and blaming themselves or feeling like I didn't love them enough. I thought about joining the military. I submitted an application to them in fact. My plan was to voluntarily deploy and place myself in harm's way so that I could die with honor and my children would be financially taken care of for life. After I was dead, everyone would regret how they treated me. I accused my husband of not loving me when all the while I didn't love myself. I felt like a fool expecting this man whom I only knew for four years to love me when my own father didn't love me and repeatedly rejected me. I told Martin that I wasn't meant to be loved. No man could ever really love me, not him, not my father, not Frat-boy, not Champ—no one. My husband hugged me stronger than he ever had and told me that the love I was searching for, only God can provide. He told me not to place all of my faith in imperfect men because they will always fail me. He apologized to me for the hurt he contributed to my life and for the first time made me a promise that was un-coerced by me or a minister. He promised to spend the rest of his life trying to make me happy. Tears poured from my heart as I told my husband that I forgive him. I spoke those words over and over again until I could feel peace forcing its way into my soul. I heard of people being prophesized to, but I always remained a skeptic until I met Elaine. That one conversation with her changed my life, changed my perspective, and confirmed my belief in the one true and living God, my Lord and Savior Jesus Christ.

*Love is patient, love is kind. It does not envy, it does not boast, it is not proud. It is not rude, it is not self-seeking, it is not easily angered, it keeps no record of wrongs. Love does not delight in evil but rejoices with the truth. It always protects, always trusts, always hopes, always perseveres. Love never fails.*

*—1 Corinthians 13:4-8 (NIV)*

# CHAPTER THIRTY SIX
## *TRUE LOVE*

Martin and I became more than a couple—we became a team—once I opened my heart back up to the Lord and no longer made Martin the god of my life. I picked up the series of books by Stormie Omartian and read *The Power of a Praying Wife*. She helped me to realize that I needed to stop asking God to change my husband and ask Him to change me. It was easy for me to identify my husband's shortcomings while overlooking my own, and every chance I got I made it my business to remind him of what a lousy husband, man, and father he was. I pointed out his perversion, his cowardice, his immaturity, and his stupidity just to demonstrate how low, in my mind, he was. Instead of getting physical with Martin, I used my words to combat him. Each time I spoke daggers to him, I felt a warped sense of relief. Before our dialogue began, there were times when I made Martin feel absolutely worthless, and when he lived up to my expectations, I objected. Reader, don't think for a minute I am taking fault away from my husband. What I am merely doing is sharing it—recognizing my part as his partner. You see, I was so busy proving how much better I was than him that I forgot to love him in the way God intended for us to love one another. How was he to grow when I was forever reminding him of all of his past iniquities? Imagine if God was to do that to us. Everything I did for him and for our family I made it clear that I was the one to do it—"this is my house" "I pay the bills" "You only have this because of me"—I omitted him and excluded God. During the early stages of our marriage, I neglected to concern myself with my husband's feelings. I didn't think about how he felt about being supported by his wife. I didn't consider his feelings when our son took ill and I rejected his embrace; he could have needed that hug more than me, for it was as much his son as mine that was hospitalized. But, while I was living selfishly, Martin didn't bother to call me out on it. Never once has he brought up the fact that I went on a date with another man—not even once. Sometimes as women we become so independent that we forget how to be interdependent. A person likes to feel useful and appreciated, not constantly emasculated.

Martin is a great man, but he came into my life with one strike against him—he wasn't Frat-boy. And, each time he messed up I became quickly angered because I thought about how my life would have been different had he been Frat-boy. Often times, the baggage from our past relationships carries into our new ones, leaving our mates at an unfair disadvantage. Baggage from past relationships can even extend to including our family and friends, as well as boyfriends and girlfriends. We need to recognize the true source of our anger and frustrations and seek help with appropriately dealing with it.

I had unrealistic expectations when I entered into my marriage. I thought that it was going to be like a fairy tale and we were going to live happily ever after. Notice the biblical definition of love never mentions the word "happy." That's not by chance. The beginning stages of my marriage turned out to be everything but that. What I should have expected is exactly what I got. How dare I think that God was going to allow the road to be smooth when I consciously went against His will and lived in sin? And then I cried and asked Him to fix the mess that I created. Like a good parent, my Father had to let me learn and grow the hard way because I sought my permissive will as opposed to His perfect. I thank Him that He did not respond to me the way I responded to Martin each and every time he wronged me. I rejoice in our struggles for they have only brought us closer.

My experience with entering my sorority prepared me for marriage. My church taught me all of the things a good wife does, but my sorority taught me about persistence and perseverance. I had to work to change my perception. I had to try to show women who didn't know me but had heard negative things about me my true self. I had to fight in order to earn their respect, and in that fight, I was forced to see my own weaknesses. I had to undergo these same exact practices in order to save my marriage.

Once Martin and I began to open up to one another, there'd be evenings when we'd spend hours talking and crying as we struggled to look past ourselves to see the needs of the other individual. Through our talks I realized my husband was not my enemy. My family, inherently and through marriage, is not my enemy. My sorority sisters are not my enemies. The defense mechanism of withdrawing myself that I used throughout the years to cope with my mother's abuse and our family's instability was beginning to cost me the people I loved. When I asked my husband what I could do to become a better wife for him, and he said to become more like my mother, I was taken aback. For years I tried to become everything that she was not. I saw her as weak for letting my father abuse her, and for standing there and taking lashings from my grandmother and aunt, and other people in our family as well as the church. But, where I saw weakness, my husband saw love. When he called her to apologize for the things he'd done to me, she never condemned him. She recognized that he was not his sin. She was even woman enough to apologize to him for her actions after I delivered our daughter. He admired how she didn't have much monetarily to offer, but she offered up herself freely—for every birth or illness of our children, for every time we called. There was no doubt to him that her family was the most importantly thing to her, coming second only to God.

"How can you say this to me," I asked, "after everything that she's done to me. How can you say this when you know how I feel about her?"

Martin spoke firmly in defense of my mother, "Flora, you know better than anybody else all that your mother has been through. She's messed up. After all of these years, she's still messed up. What makes you think that she's ready to hear all that she's done wrong? Don't you think she knows it? Don't you think she recognizes it?" I unsuccessfully struggled to fight off my tears as Martin continued: "We, as children, have to believe that our parents did the best that they knew how to do. There're no rules that come with parenting. Even with our own children, we're going to do things that they won't like—it's inevitable."

"—But, when they come to us with their grievances we can at least listen," I interjected.

"Yes. I agree." He said. "But, as for our parents we just have to accept them as they are. There're plenty of things I feel could have been done differently in my rearing, but there's no need of telling my parents about it now because I know them, and they're not going to be willing to listen. What's done is done. I'm a grown man, and only I am responsible for how I turn out." I shook my head acquiescently. "But, what we can do," he said, "is pour into our children everything our parents didn't pour into us. We have the power as parents to do things differently with our children."

Through his humility, wisdom, and love, my husband earned my respect. The longer I looked at my husband, the more I began seeing myself. And, the truth is, I didn't like what I saw. There is a reason why people share an attraction, and I often pondered Martin and mine because, externally, we appear to be opposites. Martin is reserved. He isn't flashy like me. He's afraid of failure where I am ready to plunge head first to sink or to swim. He's understanding and forgiving when I am ready to condemn.

Martin concerns himself with people's feelings first, and I'll tell them what I think they need to hear with no regard to how they'll feel afterward. But what people do not get a chance to observe is how we connect spiritually. Both Martin and I suffer from low self-esteem. Both of us struggle with feelings of inadequacy. We are both selfish. And, we both push away those who genuinely love us. I've spent wasteful hours identifying my husband's flaws when I am no better than him. Martin battles with watching pornography, while I have a pornographic mind that extends back well into my childhood. I fantasize about things that I am too ashamed to speak about. Martin made the first move in contacting his ex as I thought about mine constantly. No man or woman is perfect. While Martin was first to act on many things, sin is first conceived in the mind. I've shared all of these things with Martin, yet he accepts me for me, and has always accepted me for me while I was always looking to change him.

Our relationship, like us, is a work ever in progress that survives the seasons. We bask in our summer days and cry tears of joy in our spring. We feel the brewing tension that autumn brings and allow the shade of winter to eclipse the smiles from our summers past. This is human nature. But Martin and I have come to the point where it's not unto death; therefore, we have the power to shorten our winters in order to watch for the fall while we rejoice the springs and summers that each new day brings—life.

When this book was conceived in my mind, it was not my intention for it to be labeled a Christian book. I cuss throughout as I depict the thoughts and dialogue from my past, and it would be untrue of me to say that I do not still use profanity today, for this is just one of my many challenges. But I would not be fulfilling my life's purpose if I did not acknowledge the major role that God has and still does play in my life and in my marriage. Martin and I believe that the things we've endured have not been solely for the benefit of our union, but also to encourage other young couples. When people marry young, they should expect to experience growing pains. Fusing two individuals, who have been individuals for a certain number of years, together to make them live, think, and act as one takes a great deal of time, effort, maturation, and sacrifice on the part of each spouse. Despite it all, we are strong advocates for the institution of marriage and know that because of our trials we have the potential of surviving anything together.

Knowing my children have a loving relationship with their father blesses me beyond all measure. Every now and again, I sit back to watch my daughter play with my husband, listening to him call her by name. She laughs as she turns her head away, pretending to ignore his calls. He then tells her, "Come give daddy a hug." My eyes zero in on both of them as my mind plays a scene of the most vividly tragic experience from my childhood. Although my body cringes, I manage to quietly, yet intently, observe his mannerisms as our daughter smiles and retort back in between her giggles, "No daddy!" I watch my husband grab our little girl, who happens to be the same age I was when I played this very game with my father, and swiftly pull her into his embrace while he kisses her innocent, brown face. Her laughter fills the room as well as my heart. I look first at her, then at him with the reassurance that my little girl will be o.kay. I get up from my seat and join them in their moment of affection, while I delight myself in thanksgiving. Of all my blessings that is my ultimate.

# *Afterword*

Growing up in a two-parent household should represent stability; however, in my life, the union of my parents brought only dysfunction which lead to severe psychological and emotional ramifications, like acute disassociation. Living in the midst of violence was as normal for me as a child as watching Saturday morning cartoons. Unfortunately, my circumstance is not unique. Each year an estimated 3.3 million children are exposed to violence against their mothers or female caretakers by family members.[1] In the media, a lot of recent emphasis has been placed on the direct victims of domestic violence; however, few people engage in serious discourse about the children who live in these situations. These children do not live ordinary lives and often lack confidants, professionals, or empathizers with whom they can comfortably vocalize their experiences; or a place to channel their anger. Children who are indirect victims of abuse internalize their feelings and ultimately externalize them through self or community destructive behaviors. Unfortunately, statistics have proven that many of these young people grow up repeating the vicious cycle that their parents morphed into a disparaging example either by inflicting sadistic pain upon others or subjecting themselves to being the recipient of physical violence or emotional abuse. Very few children who are the products of domestic violence beat the odds against them. It is undoubtedly because of my Lord and Savior, Jesus Christ, that I was one of the chosen few.

---

1    American Psychological Association. (1996). *Violence and the Family: Report of the APA Presidential Task Force on Violence and the Family.*

As important as it is for the victim to remove her or himself from the circumstances and seek moral and other support, it is equally important for the children of victims to receive mental help. After all the abuse my mother suffered at the hands of my father—rape, beatings, a gun placed in her mouth while the trigger was pulled in an involuntary game of Russian Roulette— she never sought professional help, and as her child, it was presumed that I would just grow up to forget the heinous acts I witnessed as a young child. Many of the effects of a child living in domestic violence will not manifest until the children are no longer adolescents—that time could be too late. Children witnessing abuse are just as traumatized as those who had to physically endure the suffering. Seeing violent occurrences and living in the aftermath caused me to have problems with social adaptation that persisted well into my late twenties. I earnestly implore readers to not make the mistake of thinking that children will not remember events that took place in their childhood, for the unconscious mind is a wondrous place.